Health Technology Assessment in Japan

Isao Kamae

Health Technology Assessment in Japan

Policy, Pharmacoeconomic Methods and Guidelines, Value, and Beyond

Isao Kamae
Graduate School of Public Policy
The University of Tokyo
Tokyo
Japan

ISBN 978-981-13-5792-3   ISBN 978-981-13-5793-0   (eBook)
https://doi.org/10.1007/978-981-13-5793-0

Translation from the Japanese language edition: *Iryougijyutuhyouka Waakubukku: Rinsyo Seisaku Bijinesu eno Ouyou* by Isao Kamae, © 2016. Published by Jiho. All Rights Reserved.

This Adis imprint is published by the registered company Springer Nature Singapore Pte Ltd.
The registered company address is: 152 Beach Road, #21-01/04 Gateway East, Singapore 189721, Singapore

Recommendation in the Japanese Version

A long-awaited standard text book of health technology assessment (HTA) is published and authored by a leading Japanese HTA expert Professor Isao Kamae. Due to advances in health technology and the financial constraints, fundamental and practical knowledge on HTA is a powerful tool in achieving the best value of healthcare for patients. Countries such as Canada, Australia, the UK, and South Korea that provide universal health coverage already have "institutionalized" HTA within their respective healthcare systems.

HTA integration is as important in Japan, not only in clinical practice but also for the export of health technologies overseas as a growth strategy. However, few textbooks have been written in Japanese in this field, and most were published more than a decade ago, as the country lagged behind the global trends toward the "institutionalization" of HTA.

This book by Professor Kamae offers a comprehensive picture of new challenges for HTA in Japan, in which it pays close attention to the three essential pillars in institutionalizing HTA: namely, (1) systems and policy, (2) guidelines, and (3) the role of the assessment body, in addition to essential knowledge on HTA. It provides a very useful "workbook," with accompanying easy-to-follow exercises and examples for readers to deepen their learning.

I highly recommend this book to all those who seek to address this great challenge.

Yasuki Kobayashi
Graduate School of Medicine
The University of Tokyo,
Tokyo, Japan

Preface for English Version

This book is the English version translated with some modifications and updates of the Japanese version to comply with the pharmacoeconomic government guidelines Ver. 2.0 in 2019. The original Japanese book was published in June 2016 by the Japanese publisher, Jiho, Tokyo Japan. The primary purpose of the original publication was to introduce the official guidelines for cost-effectiveness evaluation implemented by the Japanese Government in 2016. However, as the Japanese version included a wide range of topics and methods of pharmacoeconomics and health technology assessment (HTA) in addition to the Japanese guideline, it was anticipated that an English version might extend the value of the original one, conveying its unique and valuable contents to global readers, beginners or advanced professionals.

The publication of the original book played a timely role in Japan, responding to the new HTA policy in April 2016, which the Ministry of Health, Labour and Welfare (MHLW) Japan introduced as a provisional reform of drug/device pricing systems officially considering cost-effectiveness evaluations. Therefore, to address the public needs for building capacity of HTA, the University of Tokyo Graduate School of Public Policy created an extension HTA certificate program for the industry in which the Japanese version has been utilized as a standard textbook.

The translation was much more difficult than expected due to the need for extensive revision to comply with the MHLW Guidelines Ver. 2.0, disseminated in April 2019, which was considerably revised from the original one.

The author would like to extend sincere appreciation to Mr. Michael LoPresti, director, Intage Healthcare Inc.; Dr. Sven Demiya, RWE and HEOR principal, IQVIA, Japan; and Dr. Elizabeth J. Cobbs, CORE Regional Teams lead, CORE, Merck, USA, for their support and advice in the English translation as pharmacoeconomic and HTA experts, based on their excellent bilingual capability of English and Japanese.

I am also much obliged to Mr. Prasad Gurunadham, editing manager, Mrs. Jeyashree Ramamoorthy, Project manager and the Springer team who patiently supported me despite my slow work throughout all the processes of editing this book in English.

I would also like to thank you my old friend and colleague Lou Garrison, Professor Emeritus, University of Washington, for reading the manuscript and for offering helpful suggestions.

Seattle, USA   Isao Kamae
April 30, 2019

Preface in the Japanese Version

In May 2016, more than 800s of professionals from all around the world gathered in Tokyo at the annual meeting of Health Technology Assessment international to engage in constructive discussions on creating value in healthcare through "health technology assessment" (HTA). Behind this is the new concept of HTA, currently marking a sea change in the world in all aspects of clinical practice, public administration, and business.

HTA refers to "an interdisciplinary field of research to evaluate the clinical impacts and value of health technology in different terms including cost-effectiveness, and the process of applying its outcomes to clinical practice and informing health policy decision making." The worldwide waves of change triggered by HTA have now reached our country, Japan, as well. In April 2016, the Ministry of Health, Labour and Welfare (MHLW) introduced a "new" HTA to the country's healthcare system, launching cost-effectiveness evaluations for pharmaceutical pricing decisions on a trial basis. This is the first step of Japan toward a new era of "value-based decision making" in healthcare, which has become the global trend. The development of the Japanese case will draw international attention to the near future.

This is a workbook for those who pursue their interest in this global healthcare shift and seek to gain expertise in addressing such trends. It is intended for a wide range of audiences, including undergraduate and graduate students, health practitioners, policymakers, and industry, or anyone interested or engaged in healthcare. It takes a unique approach including topics and methods under study and, therefore, some of its contents have never been referred in the other textbooks. Thus, the aim of this book is, in a plain language as much as possible, to offer a broad and deep understanding of the basic concepts of HTA and background knowledge in related areas such as medical statistics, epidemiology, public health and the advanced methods applied for HTA.

The features of this book include:

- The minimum essence of specialized expertise required for learning and practicing HTA.
- Reference to the MHLW's official guideline, "Guideline for Preparing Cost-Effectiveness Evaluation to the Central Social Insurance Medical Council" (the first version in January 2016), with explanations and comments on the main

points of the new HTA system alongside the full guideline statements (Chaps. 2–4).

- Easy-to-follow exercises for beginners to develop practical expertise (Chap. 5).
- Clarification of the points to learn as summary: the "Key Points" frame summarizes the key concepts upfront in each section, and a set of questions noted as "Self-Check" explores the learner's level of understanding at the end of each section.
- A brief discussion of methods involved in HTA for intermediate learners (Chap. 6) and topics addressed in recent studies to meet the needs of advanced readers.

I hope this book serves readers as an HTA workbook presented in an entirely new style, emphasizing both scientific methodology and practice, thereby contributing to the future development of HTA in the academic field in Japan.

The publication of this book owes to the outcomes of the Health Technology Assessment and Public Policy Project, launched in 2012 at the University of Tokyo Graduate School of Public Policy. I would like to extend my deepest appreciation to Professor Hideaki Shiroyama of the University of Tokyo, Director Ryozo Hayashi of the Meiji Institute for Global Affairs, and President Toshihiko Fukui of the Canon Institute for Global Studies for their continued understanding and their research and education support in the field of HTA since the project launch. I am also grateful to Professor Yasuki Kobayashi of Public Health at the University of Tokyo Graduate School of Medicine for his recommendation of this book.

I am much obliged to Mr. Takashi Sugimoto, Project Researcher, and Mr. Kaoru Yamabe, Visiting Researcher, for writing the examples of critical appraisal presented in this book, Ms. Junko Okuhara for her assistance as a project academic support specialist at the Graduate School of Public Policy, and Ms. Yumiko Minami and the press team at Jiho, Inc. who patiently supported me throughout the planning and editing of this book, despite my being a slow writer.

Finally, I would like to thank my wife who has been at once my strongest supporter as well as faithful critic for more than 40 years.

On my flight home from the ISPOR annual meeting in the USA, May 26, 2016

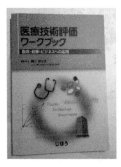

Photo: Japanese version
Tokyo, Japan

published by Jiho, Tokyo, June 2016
Isao Kamae

Contents

Basics to Know

1

1.1 What Is Health Technology Assessment (HTA)?

1.1.1 Key Points

- HTA continues to grow internationally.
- There is a global movement toward "value-based medicine."
- Industry-government-academia HTA initiatives have gained traction in Asia.
- Economic evaluation became mandatory in pharmaceutical reimbursement decision-making in Canada and Australia in the early 1990s.
- Introduction of HTA accelerated in European nations following the establishment of NICE in the UK in 1999.
- The British approach to HTA influenced nations in Asia and Latin America.
- The USA seeks its own approach without establishing a federal HTA agency.
- A European-style HTA agency has not yet been established in Japan, but HTA was introduced on a trial basis in 2016 and with a full scale in 2019.

1.1.2 Essential Knowledge

1.1.2.1 Brief Overview of Health Technology Assessment

Health technology assessment (HTA) refers to a multidisciplinary process to scientifically analyze, summarize, and understand information about medical, social, economic, and ethical issues related to the application of a health technology. From a scientific point of view, the method of assessment must be systematic, transparent, and statistically unbiased.

The aim of HTA is to inform the formulation of safe and effective health policies that are patient-focused and seek to achieve the best value of healthcare. Accordingly, HTA is a broad concept and term, generally used to refer to the designing of government policies and the HTA system rather than an academic discipline.

© Springer Nature Singapore Pte Ltd. 2019
I. Kamae, *Health Technology Assessment in Japan*,
https://doi.org/10.1007/978-981-13-5793-0_1

Underlying the emergence of HTA are the acceleration of demographic aging, rising national health expenditure (in Japan, particularly the increasing expenditure on high-cost medical care over the past decade), and advances in health technology (including individualized medicine, molecular targeted agents, regenerative medicine, and information and communication technology) worldwide. Consequently, fears of a healthcare market collapse and concerns over sustainable universal healthcare have been growing, making the promotion of efficient resource allocation an urgent task shared by nations worldwide.

HTA tends to focus primarily on innovative health technologies, and particularly on pharmaceuticals and medical devices in a narrow definition but can broadly include any products or processes in health systems. While definitions and views on HTA are largely consistent among different international HTA agencies, such as the International Network of Agencies for Health Technology Assessment (INAHTA) and Health Technology Assessment international (HTAi) [1, 2], Towse et al. identify the application of HTA at two levels to two types of health technologies, micro and macro, as follows [3]:

1. Micro-technologies: new drugs, devices, and surgical procedures seen as incremental to the healthcare system; clinical practice guidelines are also included.
2. Macro-technologies: elements of the architecture or framework of the healthcare system (including number and types of hospitals and physicians).

The above international agencies and Towse et al. equally recognize HTA as an issue of public policy.

In 2005, the European Federation of Pharmaceutical Industries and Associations (EFPIA) also endorsed a set of key principles to guide the conduct of HTA.

In terms of decision-making, HTA is central to determining coverage for pharmaceuticals when considering HTA as posing barriers to the licensing of new technologies by the government. With the establishment of the National Institute for Health and Care Excellence (NICE) and through its activities, HTA has become a core concept in the evaluation of medical innovation, having internationally profound impacts [4, 5].

One of the features of NICE is its transparency in providing information. HTA issues guidance for a range of areas, from clinical practice to public health, in addition to methods of HTA including cost-effective analysis, most of which can be viewed online (Fig. 1.1). NICE has adopted a threshold range of 20,000–30,000 GBP/quality-adjusted life-years (QALYs) gained for the quantitative assessment of cost-effectiveness. However, under the new scheme of "value-based assessment," introduced in 2014, it now uses a new threshold range from 20,000 to 50,000 GBP/QALY gained, taking into account the burden of disease and the wider societal impact of threshold modifiers, in addition to the previously considered certainty of incremental cost-effectiveness ratio (ICER), health-related quality of life (HRQOL) inadequately captured, innovative nature of technology, and non-health objectives of the National Health Service (NHS), the UK's public health services (Fig. 1.2).

The successful implementation of HTA as a public policy is based on three pillars, namely, systems and policy, guidelines, and HTA assessment bodies, and on the foundation of pharmacoeconomics as an academic discipline (Fig. 1.3).

- Technology appraisal
- Clinical
- Public health

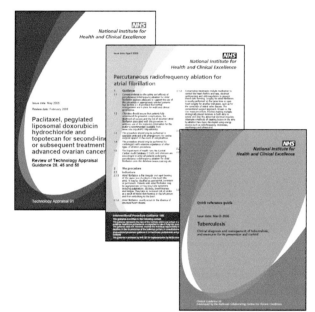

Fig. 1.1   NICE guidance

Fig. 1.2   NICE's decision-making: new approach

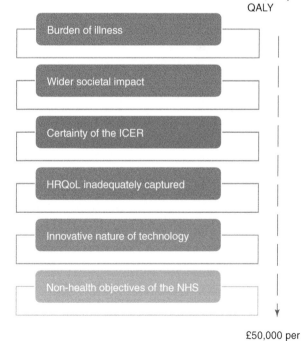

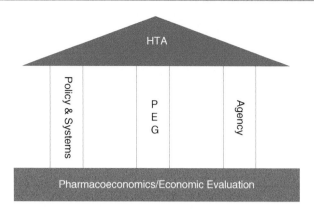

Fig. 1.3 Three pillars of Health Technology Assessment

1.1.2.2 International Overview of HTA Agencies

Pharmacoeconomics is a discipline for the quantitative evaluation of clinical effectiveness relative to cost. It has seen a dramatic improvement in its scientific methodology and practical applications. This lead to the establishment of NICE in the UK, in 1999, which strongly influenced other European nations to set up HTA agencies as well [4, 5].

HTA development began with the decisions by the governments of Canada and Australia in the early 1990s to require economic evaluation in their respective pharmaceutical reimbursement schemes. At that time, the introduction of HTA by these two nations made a strong impact on the pharmaceutical policy making of governments in Europe and the USA, triggering arguments for and against HTA. Although strong opposition by industry interrupted national HTA efforts, the establishment of NICE in the UK accelerated its subsequent introduction in Europe, eventually leading to the establishment of similar agencies. The adoption of HTA in Europe was marked particularly by the establishment of HTA agencies Institute for Quality and Efficiency in Healthcare (IQWiG) and French National Authority for Health (HAS) in 2004 by two influential nations, Germany and France, respectively. While the methods for HTA adopted by IQWiG and HAS differ from NICE, they all share the concept of using evidence for cost-effectiveness to inform coverage and reimbursement policies. Such trends in Europe have spread to countries in Asia, resulting in the establishment of national HTA agencies such as Health Insurance Review and Assessment Service (HIRA) and National Evidence-based Healthcare Collaborating Agency (NECA) in South Korea, the Division of HTA and National Institute of Health Technology Assessment (NIHTA) in Taiwan, and Health Intervention and Technology Assessment Program (HITAP) in Thailand (Table 1.1).

Latin American nations have also been influenced by trends to implement HTA policies, leading to the establishment of national HTA agencies, such as Institute for Clinical Effectiveness and Health Policy (IECS) in Argentina, Department of

Table 1.1 Health Technology Assessment agencies in the world

- Canada: CADTH 2006 (the former CCOHTA 1990)
- Australia: PBAC 1992
- United Kingdom: NICE 1999
- Germany: IQWiG 2004
- France: HAS 2004
- United States: PCORI 2010
- South Korea: HIRA 2008, NECA 2009
- Taiwan: HTA team/NIHTA 2007
- Thailand: HITAP 2006

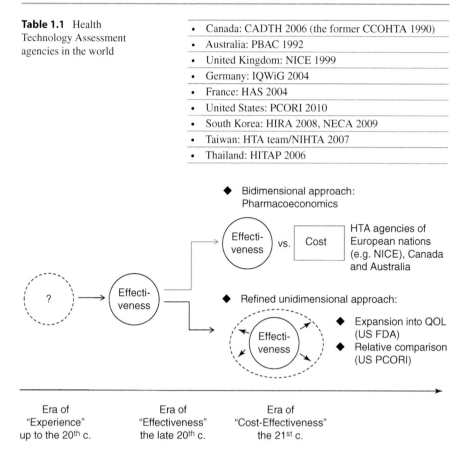

Fig. 1.4 Differential approaches to effectiveness and cost

Science and Technology (DECIT) in Brazil, the Ministry of Health (MoH) in Chile, and National Center for Health Technology Excellence (CENETEC) in Mexico.

The growth and expansion of HTA indicates the significant role the UK has played, like the historical role it played in the Industrial Revolution, which brought about major changes in technology, industry, and social structure. At any rate, the establishment of national HTA agencies in Europe also triggered the development of international societies such as International Society for Pharmacoeconomics and Outcomes Research (ISPOR) and HTAi, as well as networks such as European Network for Health Technology Assessment (EUnetHTA) and International Network of Agencies for Health Technology Assessment (INAHTA).

Figure 1.4 proposes a way to visualize such historical transitions in the institutionalization of HTA, of nations' approach to cost-effectiveness evaluation in terms of data emphasis. Following the era of "experience" up to the twentieth century and "effectiveness" up to the late twentieth century, this is currently the area in which cost-effectiveness is evaluated in two dimensions, an approach employed primarily by nations in Europe.

In contrast, the Patient-Centered Outcomes Research Institute (PCORI), established in the USA under the Obama administration, does not utilize cost-effectiveness evaluation in carrying out its vision of comparative effectiveness research and has prohibited from using the ICER threshold in policy making, as is done in the UK. On the other hand, the US Food and Drug Administration accepts the use of patient quality of life as a measure of clinical outcomes in new drug application and has issued the first worldwide guidance on "Patient-Reported Outcome Measures." Thus, the approach taken by the USA is unique and contrasts that taken in Europe, in that it focuses on the refinement of effectiveness research as a one-dimensional evaluation of effectiveness.

The HTA approach in Asia is essentially like that of UK NICE. Compared to nations like South Korea, Taiwan, and Thailand, who has already implemented HTA into their systems, Malaysia, Singapore, Philippines, China, and Japan are making some progress. Although systems in other nations are still developing, the trend toward HTA has undeniably reached Asia.

A Japanese system for HTA to evaluate cost-effectiveness such as in Europe and the USA did not existed until 2011 as the discussion on the implementation of cost-effectiveness evaluation. It finally started within the Central Social Insurance Medical Council (known as Chuikyo) in 2012. Underlying this was the government's announcement of May 2011 to "consider the adoption of medical economic methods in the assessment of medical innovation" in the reform of social security pursued by the Democratic Party of Japan, which led to the launch of the first meeting of the Special Committee on Cost-Effectiveness at Chuikyo within the Ministry of Health, Labour and Welfare (MHLW) in May 2012. Cost-effectiveness evaluation was also made a part of the Japan Revitalization Strategy revised in 2014, issued in June 2014. After the discussion at the Chuikyo working group, the implementation of HTA was made a national goal [6], leading to its introduction on a trial basis in April 2016 [7].

Although Japan's HTA initiative fell behind three nations in Asia, namely, South Korea, Taiwan, and Thailand, it is, at the same time, an opportunity to develop an HTA system unique to Japan that may serve as a model for other nations in Asia by being different from the systems in the above nations, designed based on the approach of UK NICE. Eventually, a new HTA system was officially institutionalized in April 2019.

1.1.3 Self-Check!

1. What does HTA stand for?
2. What are the two levels of HTA?
3. What is the name of the agency in the UK that contributed to the establishment of HTA across the world?
4. What are the three pillars of HTA?
5. When was a system for HTA first introduced in Japan?
6. What is INAHTA?
7. Does PCORI promote cost-effectiveness research?
8. Does FDA accept quality of life as outcome measure?

9. Which countries in Asia pioneered HTA implementation?
10. What is the name of the Chuikyo working group for HTA launched in Japan in 2012?

1.2 Value-Based Medicine and Economic Evaluation

1.2.1 Key Points

- A paradigm shift in the twenty-first century toward "value-based medicine."
- The concept of value-based policy making and pricing/reimbursement decisions is established in Europe.
- Pharmacoeconomics is the basis of the economic evaluation of medicines.
- Economic evaluation compares cost with effectiveness as a measure of outcome.

1.2.2 Essential Knowledge

The rise of scientism in medicine brought a paradigm shift in Europe and the USA in terms of what factors the practice of medicine should be based on (Fig. 1.5). That is, experience-based medicine, which has been dominating since the times of ancient Greek medicine, was replaced in the late 1990s by evidence-based medicine (EBM), which emphasizes the use of scientific evidence from clinical research, thus becoming an international standard.

EBM was first proposed by Sackett et al. at McMaster University, Canada [8]. This new school of medicine under EBM emphasized the importance of selecting

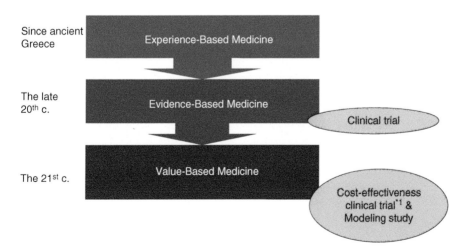

Fig. 1.5 Paradigm shifts in medicine. *1 It originally began in late 1980s or early 1990s

diagnosis and treatment methods based on empirical data and was committed to systematizing its scientific methods and practical approaches in education. Empirical data refer to data that have demonstrated efficacy in randomized clinical trials, and the introduction of EBM was closely linked to clinical trials. Sackett also advocated the promotion of EBM by clinicians, and this made EBM the symbol of new scientism in clinical practice.

In the twenty-first century, the "value" of health technology, a concept even broader than the evidence from clinical trials, was increasingly emphasized, leading to the establishment of a new concept: value-based medicine (VBM). VBM emphasizes that, although medical evidence may be a priority in decision-making for physicians, decision-making for the patients or society requires the evaluation of other factors that influence value in addition to evidence. Accordingly, in place of the limited concept of EBM for clinicians, the broader concept of VBM began to spread worldwide.

Value in VBM is generally defined in the USA as effectiveness (e.g., years of life gained by treatment), which is clinically a broader concept compared to the efficacy demonstrated in clinical trials as evidence in EBM [9]. However, the term "value" may encompass an even broader range of factors, such as patient quality of life and ethical and economic factors, which are recently considered in the practice of HTA in Europe.

Nations worldwide have traditionally faced the dilemma of balancing free market and government intervention, two conflicting elements of public healthcare policies. However, with the establishment of VBM, the implementation of HTA within health systems has become critical. In Europe, this led to the establishment of policy making and pricing/reimbursement decision-making processes based on the value of health technologies.

Such economic evaluation in HTA utilizes concepts and methods from pharmacoeconomics [10, 11]. Pharmacoeconomics is the discipline of evaluating the impact of health technologies (including pharmaceuticals and medical devices) on patient outcomes relative to the required cost, by involving methodology and application research. The objective of pharmacoeconomics is to obtain evidence in economic evaluation by scientific analysis.

Fig. 1.6 Five layers of health economics. Pharmacoeconomics is a subclass of "Economic Evaluation" of healthcare

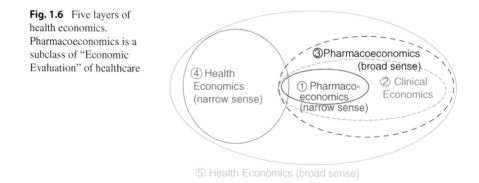

Fig. 1.7 An evaluation model in pharmacoeconomics

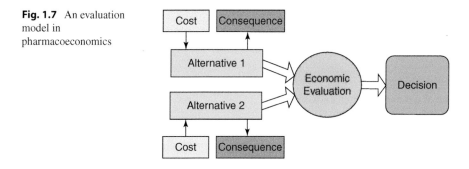

Pharmacoeconomics is often confused with health economics. Health economics can be viewed as consisting of five subdisciplines (Fig. 1.6). Three of the five subdisciplines involve economic evaluation, namely, (1) pharmacoeconomics (narrow sense) (assessment of pharmaceuticals), (2) clinical economics (assessment of a wide range of health technologies, including examinations and procedures in addition to pharmaceuticals), and (3) pharmacoeconomics (broad sense) (assessment of technology for prevention and community healthcare in addition to clinical practice), among which pharmacoeconomics covers the largest scope in terms of economic evaluation. The subdiscipline of (4) traditional health economics, in a narrow sense, has little common ground with pharmacoeconomics, as it mainly focuses on the economic analysis of systems and financing of healthcare.

Pharmacoeconomic evaluation involves the comparison of one intervention group to another. As shown in Fig. 1.7, the value of new and old interventions is evaluated by comparing an intervention of interest (new intervention) to a control intervention (traditional or standard intervention) in terms of the balance between cost and effectiveness as an outcome measure. The results of evaluation are subsequently used to inform decision-making. The primary method of evaluation is cost-effectiveness analysis. For example, assuming the cost and effectiveness (expected years of life) of a new drug and a control drug are found to be USD 80,000 and 2.5 years and USD 60,000 and 2 years, respectively, then the incremental cost and effectiveness of the new drug compared to the control are estimated with USD 20,000 and 0.5 years. The incremental cost-effectiveness ratio (ICER) is thus calculated as USD 20,000 ÷ 0.5 years = USD 40,000/year, which represents the additional cost of the new drug associated with one additional year of life. ICER is always calculated in a cost-effective analysis as a measure of value for money.

1.2.3   Self-Check!

1. What does VBM stand for?
2. What is the name of discipline involving the economic evaluation of healthcare?
3. What is the primary measure of the value for money?

1.3   Introduction to Cost-Effectiveness Analysis

1.3.1   Key Points

- Decision analysis is the most fundamental approach in cost-effectiveness analysis.
- Decision analysis calculates the expected benefits of available alternatives and identifies the alternative with the maximum value.
- The results of cost-effectiveness analysis are presented in a standard cost-effectiveness table with incremental cost-effectiveness ratio (ICER) as the summary measured.

1.3.2   Essential Knowledge

Decision analysis is the most fundamental approach to cost-effectiveness analysis, being used to calculate the expected value of benefits and costs associated with each available alternative to identify the alternative with the maximum expected value.

An example of decision analysis is presented in Fig. 1.8. In this hypothetical case, a 50-year-old male patient is to decide whether to receive a laparoscopic

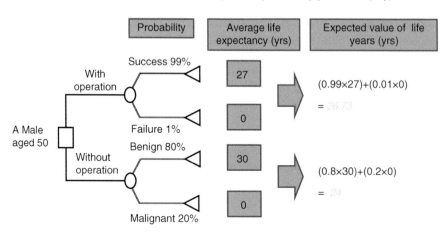

Fig. 1.8 Calculation of expected effectiveness

cholecystectomy (gallbladder removal surgery) for gallbladder polyps found during medical examination. Typically, decision analysis proceeds through the following steps:

1. Identification of alternatives to be considered: Whether to receive laparoscopic cholecystectomy.
2. Structuring of the problem: A decision tree is constructed to model the decision process. A decision tree consists of decision nodes (squares), chance nodes (circles), terminal nodes (triangles), and branches that connect these nodes and represent the possible outcomes of each chosen alternative. In the simplest case, the following outcomes are expected: if surgery is chosen, it can be either successful or not; and if surgery is not chosen, no actions are taken and the possibilities are that polyps are either benign or malignant.
3. Assigning values: Probability estimates are assigned to branches emanating from chance nodes, and payoffs (resulting benefits) are assigned to terminal nodes. In this example, payoffs are assigned in terms of average life expectancy for each terminal node.
4. Calculation of expected value: The expected value for each chance node is calculated as the sum of all expected values, each calculated as the payoff multiplied by its probability.
5. Identification of the alternative with the maximum value: Since life expectancy is 26.73 years for surgery and 24 years for no surgery, the alternative to receive surgery is identified as the best option.
6. Sensitivity analysis: It determines, for instance, how the expected value changes if the probability of polyps being malignant becomes 80%.

Figure 1.9 presents another example, where the expected cost is calculated in the same manner. The cost for each terminal node represents the cumulative cost incurred from the decision to the terminal node. By substituting the payoff for each terminal node in Fig. 1.8 with the cost, the expected cost for each chance node can be calculated using the same formula. In this case, the expected cost is JPY 3.03 million for surgery and JPY 1 million for no surgery.

Figures 1.8 and 1.9 indicate that, while surgery offers a longer life expectancy, the incurred cost is also higher. Therefore, the results of the cost-effectiveness analysis are summarized in a cost-effectiveness table (Table 1.2), in terms of intervention, cost, effectiveness, average cost-effectiveness ratio, difference in cost (incremental cost), difference in effectiveness (incremental effectiveness), and ICER. The table presents ICER as an index that summarizes the cost-effectiveness of the intervention.

The advantages of a decision analysis include presenting alternatives in a relatively simple way, clearly modeling the decision process, identifying missing data, and using it as a tool for more rational decision-making. At the same time, its limitations include requiring the training of analysts and additional intellectual labor, reliable data not always being available, no standard way of modeling, not reflecting the complexity of reality, and not allowing for multifactorial decision-making.

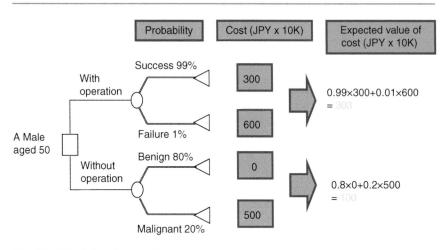

Fig. 1.9 Calculation of expected cost

Table 1.2 The result of the analysis: cost-effectiveness table

Intervention	Cost (JPY × 10K)	Effectiveness (life years)	Average cost-effective ratio (JPY × 10K/ years)	Incremental cost	Incremental effectiveness	Incremental cost-effectiveness ratio [ICER] (JPY × 10K/ years)
With operation	303	26.73	11.3	203	2.73	74.36
Without operation	100	24	4.16	–	–	–

1.3.3 Self-Check!

1. ICER is JPY 74.36 × 10k/year in Table 1.2. Explain how it was calculated.
2. Briefly explain what an ICER of JPY 74.36 × 10k yen/year means in the example presented in Table 1.2.
3. For the decision tree presented in Fig. 1.8, determine how the analysis results change if the possibility of polyps being malignant changes to 80%.

1.4 Assessing Cost-Effectiveness

1.4.1 Key Points

- Cost-effectiveness analysis determines the balance with a ratio of incremental cost to incremental effectiveness as a measure of cost-effectiveness.
- The incremental cost-effectiveness ratio (ICER) is defined as the ratio of incremental cost to incremental effectiveness.
- A new technology is considered cost-effective if it lies below the threshold line of the cost-effectiveness plane.
- While no absolute standard of threshold exists, the UK NICE uses a threshold of GBP20K–30K/QALY.

1.4.2 Essential knowledge

In an economic evaluation, the simplest way of comparing a new technology with the standard one (e.g., new and standard drugs) is to compare the average cost per effectiveness. For example, as shown in Fig. 1.10, if the cost and effectiveness are JPY 6.2 million and 0.72 quality-adjusted life-years (QALYs) for a new drug and JPY 5.4 million and 0.52 QALYs for the standard drug, respectively, the average cost per 1 QALY for the new and standard drugs are calculated as 8.61 (= 6.2/0.72) million JPY/QALY and 10.38 (= 5.4/0.52) million JPY/QALY, respectively. Accordingly, the average cost associated with the new drug is lower than that of the standard drug, suggesting the new drug is superior.

However, the total cost incurred for the new drug is higher and, thus, it is not always appropriate to choose one technology over another based solely on average costs. The

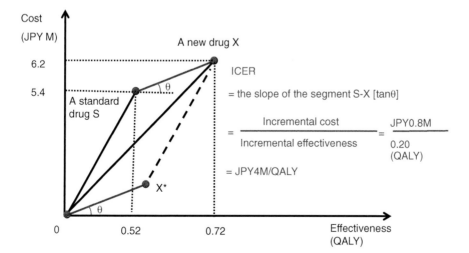

The segment 0-X* is a parallel translation of the segment S-X to the origin.

Fig. 1.10 Incremental Cost-Effectiveness Ratio

key information for consumers in making such decisions is whether the transition from the standard to a new drug offers an increase in effectiveness worth the increase in cost, which is also critical for budget decisions in public policy (see Sect. 7.3).

The technique used to determine the ratio of cost increase to effectiveness increase as a measure of cost-effectiveness is referred to as incremental analysis. The concept of incremental analysis is frequently used in daily life. For instance, if a passenger traveling on the Euro Star train) finds the price for the first-class car is out of his/her price range, the passenger has no choice but to take coach class. On the other hand, if the price is within the budget, a rational passenger would consider whether the first-class car can make the added benefit (such as seats being more comfortable) worth, considering the difference in price between the two classes of cars.

Returning to the example in Fig. 1.10, the ratio of cost increase to effectiveness increase is represented by the slope of segment SX (the line through points S and X, representing a standard drug S and a new drug X, respectively). This slope is referred to as ICER and defined as follows:

$$ICER = \text{Incremental cost} / \text{Incremental effectiveness}$$

$$= \frac{\left(\text{The cost of new drug X} - \text{the cost of standard drug S}\right)}{\left(\text{The effectiveness of new drug X} - \text{the effectivness of standard drug S}\right)}$$

For the example, in Fig. 1.10, given that the incremental cost of new drug X relative to standard drug S is JPY 0.8 (= 6.2–5.4) million and the incremental effectiveness between the two drugs is 0.2 (= 0.72–0.52) QALY, ICER is calculated as 4 (= 8/0.2) million JPY/QALY.

When the standard drug is plotted at the origin, which translates segment SX, ICER is represented by the slope (tan θ in Fig. 1.10) of the new segment OX*,

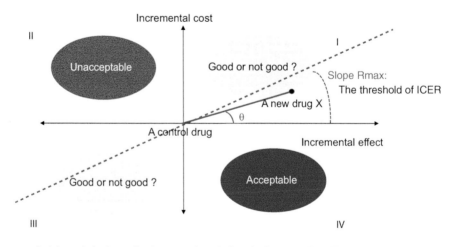

Judging rule in Cost-effectiveness: Area below the line at a slope Rmax is good, otherwise not good.

Fig. 1.11 (Incremental) Cost-Effectiveness Plane

which passes through the origin. This is the basis of the cost-effectiveness plane used in evaluating cost-effectiveness (Fig. 1.11).

In accordance with the xy-plane, formed by the x and y axes, the cost-effectiveness plane can be called the effectiveness-cost plane. At the same time, it can also be referred to as the incremental effectiveness-cost plane, as it represents the incremental effectiveness and the incremental cost of new drug compared to the control drug located at the origin. Therefore, it should technically be called the incremental effectiveness-incremental cost plane, although it may be simply called the cost-effectiveness plane as long as its meaning is clearly understood.

The cost-effectiveness plane, as shown in Fig. 1.11, consists of four quadrants. If the ICER lies in the fourth quadrant (more effective and less costly and referred to as simple or strong dominance), the new drug is cost-effective. Similarly, if the ICER lies in the second quadrant (costlier and less effective), the new drug is not cost-effective (being dominated). On the other hand, in the first and third quadrants, ICER can take any value from 0 to infinity and thus requires a standard (referred to as a threshold and represented as Rmax in Fig. 1.11), to which ICER is compared for evaluating the cost-effectiveness of the new drug. Once the threshold Rmax is defined, the line through the origin with the slope Rmax can be used as threshold. That is, the drug is evaluated as being cost-effective if ICER falls below the threshold line, and not cost-effective if ICER lies above the line. In Fig. 1.11, new drug X lies below the threshold line (that is, $\tan \theta <$ Rmax) and is thus evaluated as being cost-effective.

An absolute standard for the threshold does not exist, being determined by the society's willingness to pay depending on the economy of each nation. National Institute for Health and Care Excellence (NICE) in the UK has adopted a threshold of 20,000–30,000 GBP/QALY. World Health Organization (WHO) has recently endorsed a threshold of 1–3 times per capita GDP, although it lacks a theoretical basis and was likely recommended for convenience.

"Cost-effective" does not necessarily mean "cost reduction." For instance, if ICER lies in the first quadrant, the cost will increase even below the threshold line. A "cost reduction" may be thus achieved in rare cases, where ICER lies in either the fourth (simple dominance) or third quadrant, below the threshold line, although new technologies almost always fall into the first quadrant. Also, the value of ICER varies depending on a selection of comparator, which requires further discussion on its selection (see Sect. 7.4).

1.4.3 Self-Check!

1. The cost-effectiveness of a new drug was reported to be 2 million JPY/QALY. Explain why this statement is insufficient.
2. The ICER of a new drug X relative to the standard drug was calculated to be 6 million JPY/QALY. Evaluate the cost-effectiveness of the new drug using a threshold of one time the nominal GDP per capita in Japan. Additionally, consider a threshold of twice the nominal GDP per capita.
3. The cost and effectiveness of a standard drug are 3.5 million JPY and 1.25 QALYs, respectively, while the effectiveness of a new drug is found to be 1.37 QALYs. What is the maximum allowable cost for the new drug for it to be evaluated as being cost-effective using a threshold of 6 million JPY/QALY?

1.5   Cost-Effectiveness League Table

1.5.1   Key Points

- Cost-effectiveness league tables are used to rank different health technologies by their relative cost-effectiveness.
- League tables from global clinical trial collaborations that list the cost-effectiveness of interventions by country may provide valuable information.
- The argument that "preventive care is more cost-effective than curative care" is not always true.

1.5.2   Essential Knowledge

If the cost-effectiveness of different health technologies is quantified using a common unit of measurement (e.g., cost/QALY), technologies can be ranked in terms of their relative cost-effectiveness. Table 1.3 shows a typical example of such ranking. In this league table, the ICER of an intensive tobacco-use prevention program for students in the seventh and eighth grades is calculated as 23,000 USD/QALY, suggesting the intervention is cost-effective. On the other hand, the ICER of screening all 65-year-olds for diabetes compared to screening the 65-year-olds with hypertension for diabetes is calculated to be as high as 590,000 USD/QALY. This suggests that the intervention ICER varies significantly with design and comparators even for preventive measures, and preventive care is not always cost-effective.

While league tables can be created relatively easily given ICER values, one needs to be careful about the comparability of different interventions. Particularly, attention needs to be paid to the comparability of monetary units (converted to 2006 USD in Table 1.3), and the choice of comparator based on which ICER is determined (indicated as intervention A compared with intervention B in Table 1.3). Furthermore, many league tables have theoretical limitations as they present indirect comparisons of interventions. The comparison of different types of health technologies without careful consideration is thus not encouraged.

In global clinical trial collaborations, the cost-effectiveness of an intervention may be listed in a league table by country. Table 1.4 shows a comparison of the cost-effectiveness of pneumococcal vaccination in ten Western European countries, reported by Evers et al. The table presents variations in ICER among different age groups, in addition to variations among countries. When a threshold of 40,000 EUR/

Table 1.3 Cost-effectiveness league table

A powerful anti-smoking prevention program for junior high school first and second grade vs. No program	23,000/ QALY
Screening for all the 65-year-old diabetic patients vs. Screening for 65-year-old diabetic patients with hypertension	590,000/ QALY

USD in 2006

Cohen JT, Neumann PJ, Weinstein MC: Does Preventive Care Save Money? Health economics and the presidential candidates. N Engl Med, 358(7): 661–663, 2008

Table 1.4 Cost-effectiveness analysis in pneumococcal vaccination: comparison among ten European nations

Cost-effectiveness ratio per QALY in pneumococcal vaccination € (1999)				
	Age group			
County	65–74	75–84	≥85	≥65
Belgium	19,324	25,194	**57,219**	**22,847**
Denmark	8056	8753	23,786	**9239**
England and Wales	13,820	19,539	**41,664**	**17,228**
France	14,023	24,073	23,743	**17,444**
Germany	–	–	–	**17,093**
Italy	–	–	–	**16,544**
Netherlands	10,784	17,456	**55,790**	**13,740**
Scotland	12,437	14,319	25,569	**13,920**
Spain	12,720	8878	**46,000**	**12,027**
Sweden	20,385	23,490	**48,108**	**23,657**

Evers SM, et al.: Cost-effectiveness pneumococcal vaccination for prevention of invasive pneumococcal disease in the elderly: an update for 10 Western European countries. Eur J Clin Microbiol Infect Dis, 26(8): 535, 2007

QALY is used, the vaccine is evaluated as being cost-effective in countries for all persons 65 years or older as a single group (ICER for the age group ≥65). However, when ICER is compared among 10-year intervals, values above the threshold are obtained in countries other than Denmark, France, and Scotland for persons at 85 or older (values in bold in the age group ≥85), suggesting that the cost-effectiveness of the vaccine decreases with age.

From a different perspective, another stream of research examined the distribution of ICERs for a wide range of health technologies, according to the ICER level. Greenberg et al. have determined the distribution of ICERs for cancer therapies that have been published and accumulated in a database and reported, as per Fig. 1.12, that many of the therapies are cost-effective. Additionally, in 2008, while the US presidential candidates were chorusing the need for cost-effective preventive care, a report by Cohen et al. published in the *New England Journal of Medicine*, which studied a database and concluded that the distribution of ICERs is not much different between preventive and curative care, attracted attention [12]. Therefore, arguments that preventive care is more cost-effective compared to curative care, which is also common in Japan, are not necessarily true. Any claim that a preventive care is cost-effective must be validated by economic evaluation.

1.5.3   Self-Check!

Referring to Table 1.4,

1. What is the value of ICER for the age group 75–84 in Scotland?
2. Does the above ICER suggest the intervention is cost-effective?
3. Does the value of ICER for the age group ≥85 in Belgium suggest the intervention is cost-effective?

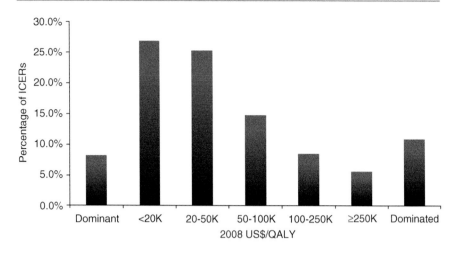

Fig. 1.12 Cost-effectiveness of cancer treatment. (Greenberg D, Earle C, Fan CH, et al.: When is cancer care cost-effective? A systematic overview of cose-utility analyses in oncology. J Natl Cancer Inst, 102(2): 86, 2010)

4. Should pneumococcal vaccination be recommended as a cost-effective intervention for the age group ≥65?
5. What is the main problem with the presented ICER values?

1.6   Common Misconceptions[1]

1.6.1   Key Points

- Coverage decisions consider "cost-effectiveness" in addition to the current "effectiveness."
- Cost-effectiveness analysis is not equivalent to the valuation of human life in monetary terms.
- The primary objective of introducing economic analysis is to measure the value of health technology and not reduce health spending.
- While the QALY has its advantages as a measure of clinical outcomes, its limitations must also be noted.

1.6.2   Essential Knowledge

To correctly understand the evaluation of cost-effectiveness of health technology, basic knowledge in pharmacoeconomics needs to be shared. For this purpose, the Guidelines of the Ministry of Health, Labour and Welfare provide definitions for

---

[1] This section is a revised version of the following original article: *Kamae I. Perspective on pharmacoeconomic approaches to health technology assessment (4): a key to proper interpretation of the QALY and the ICER.* Pharmaceutical and Medical Device Regulatory Science 2012; 43(8):686–692.

basic terms (see Glossary), of which quality-adjusted life-year (QALY) and incremental cost-effectiveness ratio (ICER) are of importance.

Despite the definitions already being provided, differences still exist in the understanding of "cost-effectiveness" in everyday Japanese and in the language of pharmacoeconomics. Such differences are sources of confusion as discussed below.

1. *Confusion over Cost-Effectiveness Measures*
   In its May 24, 2012 morning edition, the Nihon Keizai Shimbun (the Nikkei, Japan Economics Newspaper) published an article, titled "Strict coverage policy applied to new drugs based on effectiveness," which reported the launch of the Special Committee on Cost-Effectiveness of the Central Social Insurance Medical Council (Chuikyo). The prompt news coverage of the discussion at Chuikyo toward integrating cost-effectiveness considerations in new drug coverage decisions was evaluated as an indication of the Nikkei's superior insight into the importance of an economic approach to healthcare. However, as effectiveness considerations are already applied to coverage decisions within the existing healthcare system, the above heading should rather state "based on *cost-effectiveness*."

   Additionally, the above-cited article referred to a table, titled "Which of the two drugs is recommended?" from handouts at the meeting of the Chuikyo working group, commenting that economic evaluation is about choosing one drug over another based on the average cost incurred per patient. However, this is not entirely accurate. Cost-effectiveness analysis generally uses ICER, not average cost—although the question of whether to use the average cost or ICER requires further analysis (see Sect. 7.3)—thus causing confusion over the difference between average cost and ICER.

2. *Misunderstanding that the Valuation of Human Life in Monetary Terms Is Against the Philosophy of "Humanistic Medicine"*
   No economic evaluation approaches based on pharmacoeconomics can place absolute monetary value on human life or aim to assign a monetary value to a patient's life. Cost-effectiveness analysis calculates the cost incurred per life-year gained, but does not measure the monetary value of human life.

   In cost-benefit analysis, the value of a statistical life (VSL) may be estimated to determine the monetary value of healthcare benefits. However, VSL is often misunderstood as a monetary valuation of human life, but the cost calculated in economic analysis refers to "opportunity cost" in the language of economics, which considers productivity losses for the society. Since the provision of benefits under universal health coverage also aims at equity in redistributing monetary resources, the improvement in the quality of the health insurance system based on cost-effectiveness can, in fact, reinforce the philosophy of humanistic medicine in pursuit of social equity.

3. *Misunderstanding that the Purpose of Introducing Economic Evaluation is to Cut Healthcare Spending*
   The evaluation of ICER forms the basis of economic evaluation. As described in "Assessing cost-effectiveness" (Sect. 1.4), a new drug is generally more effective compared to the existing standard of care, which means that both cost and effectiveness will increase in a situation that allows for innovations in healthcare. In

such a case because of the monopoly power of the innovator, cost reductions cannot be expected, unless the use of the new drug is deemed capable of inducing further cost reductions. Therefore, it is a mistake to assume that the introduction of economic evaluation will lead to reduced healthcare spending.

The use of economic analysis to manage healthcare expenditure requires not only ICER evaluation but also the use of ICER in assigning priorities among pharmaceuticals, as well as budget impact analysis. Although these assessments are related to economic evaluation, they are beyond the scope of standard cost-effectiveness evaluation (see Sect. 7.6). The purpose of introducing economic evaluation is, therefore, to achieve value-based public policy making.

4. *Misconception that QALY Is the Best Measure of Clinical Outcomes*
The fact that the UK's NICE endorsed the use of QALY as primary outcome generated the misconception that QALY is the best measure of clinical outcomes. Indeed, QALY offers two advantages. First, it quantifies the health benefits associated with the use of health technology in terms of life-years (which has traditionally been valued most by physicians) while incorporating the impact on the patient's quality of life. That is, it is a two-dimensional measure of clinical benefits, in terms of both quality and quantity. Second, since life-years and quality of life can be measured for patients with any type of illness, the use of QALY enables the comparison of health benefits across different illnesses. Existing disease-specific measures of clinical outcomes, such as blood glucose in diabetes, do not allow for comparison of a specific condition to other types of illnesses. Therefore, the use of QALY as a primary measure of clinical outcomes is often justified by its second advantage.

On the other hand, there is the risk of excessive reliance on QALY (see Sect. 6.2). For instance, there exists a controversy over whether 1 QALY represents the same value for a 20- and a 70-year-old. Additionally, since life expectancy decreases with age, QALYs gained as a measure of health benefits may compare poorly for elderly patients. Especially where different approaches are used for utility measurement, the results may not accurately reflect the benefit differences.

1.6.3   Self-Check!

1. What is not accurate about news coverage titled "Strict coverage policy applied to new drugs based on effectiveness"?
2. Cost-effectiveness analysis is a profit-based approach to medicine. Is this statement true?
3. The adoption of a cost-effective health technology will lead to reduction in health spending. Provide three reasons why this statement is false.
4. Give two advantages of using QALY.
5. The QALY gained from a new drug was calculated using a different utility measure from the one used in the calculation of the QALY gained from the comparator. Is it correct to compare those two QALY values?

1.7 Confusing HTA-Related Terminology[2]

1.7.1 Key Points

- Terms related to HTA, such as EBM, VBM, and CER, can generate confusion.
- HTA involves multiple approaches to evaluation and is closely linked to policies and systems.
- The USA and Europe have different views on whether CER includes economic evaluation.
- A three-by-three framework matrix for EBM, CER, and HTA is proposed.

1.7.2 Essential Knowledge

The evidence-based medicine (EBM), value-based medicine (VBM), and comparative effectiveness research (CER) used in the USA are terms related to HTA. Here, we reconsider the concept of HTA. Since the primary objective of pharmacoeconomics, which forms the basis of VBM, is the economic evaluation of health technology, "evaluation" links pharmacoeconomics with HTA. That is, by emphasizing the "evaluation" aspect, pharmacoeconomics is often a synonym for HTA. Depending on the context, this view is not entirely incorrect.

However, while pharmacoeconomics and HTA are similar in nature, the former is a discipline focused on the evaluation of cost-effectiveness, whereas the latter involves multiple approaches to evaluation and is closely linked to policies and systems. For instance, the International Network of Agencies for Health Technology Assessment (INAHTA) defines HTA as "the multidisciplinary field of policy analysis that studies medical, economic, social and ethical implications of the development, diffusion, and use of health technology" [1]. Similarly, according to Health Technology Assessment international (HTAi), "HTA is a field of scientific research to inform policy and clinical decision-making on the introduction and use of health technologies" [2].

What adds to the confusion over the terminology associated with HTA is the term CER, which has been in use in the USA. The term appeared in the process of prioritizing health policy under the former Obama administration. According to the Institute of Medicine (IOM), operating on behalf of the administration, "CER is the generation and synthesis of evidence that compares the benefits and harms of alternative methods to prevent, diagnose, treat, and monitor a clinical condition, or to improve the delivery of care. The purpose of CER is to assist consumers, clinicians, purchasers, and policy makers to make informed decisions that will improve healthcare at both the individual and population levels" [13].

---

[2] This section is a revised version of the following original article: *Kamae I. Perspective on pharmacoeconomic approaches to health technology assessment (2): exploring concept on EBM, NBM and HTA.* Pharmaceutical and Medical Device Regulatory Science 2012; 43(4):319–324.

The ambiguity in the IOM definition has led to confusion in the USA: while the term is commonly understood as comparison and synthesis of evidence by means of traditional clinical trials, which do not include evidence on cost-effectiveness, the American College of Physicians argues it should include cost-effectiveness evidence [14]. Conversely, the common interpretation in Europe is that CER considers comparative cost-effectiveness evidence. In fact, Kalipso Chalkidou, former Director of International Programs at the UK NICE, and colleagues have studied and compared HTA agencies in four major European countries, referring to them as CER entities [15].

To illustrate this confusion over terminology, Luce et al. have proposed a framework, using a three-by-three matrix [16], consisting of the following three column factors:

1. Efficacy: whether there is evidence of efficacy ("Can it work?")
2. Effectiveness: whether there is evidence of effectiveness in real-world practice settings ("Does it work?")
3. Value: whether it offers reasonable value of clinical and economic benefits ("Is it worth it?"),

and the following three row factors:
(a) Evidence generation
(b) Evidence synthesis
(c) Decision-making

for the nine cells, in which the notions of EBM, HTA, and CER are depicted.

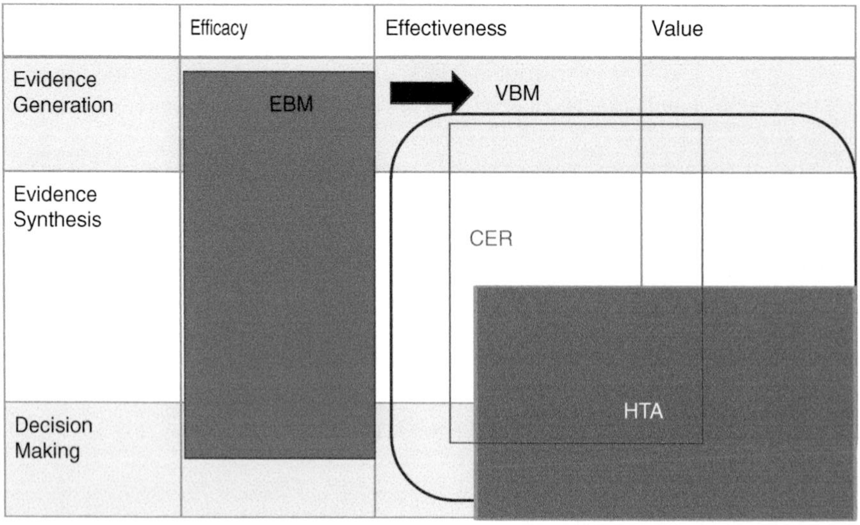

Fig. 1.13 Relationship diagram on paradigm shifts. (Source: Luce BR, Drummond M, Jonsson B, et al: EBM, HTA, and CER: clearing the confusion. Milbank Q. 88(2): 256–276. 2010)

Based on these three-by-three matrix factors, Luce et al. further illustrate the complex interrelationships of these terms, although this lacks consensus among researchers. Associating EBM more closely with efficacy facilitates the understanding of the paradigm shift from EBM to VBM (Fig. 1.13). Here, HTA, which involves value-based policy making, would occupy the bottom right corner.

1.7.3 Definitions by Luce et al [16]

EBM: It is an evidence synthesis and decision process used to assist patients' and/or physicians' decisions. It considers evidence regarding the effectiveness of interventions and patients' values and is mainly concerned with individual patients' decisions, but it is also useful for developing clinical guidelines, as they pertain to individual patients.

CER: It includes both evidence generation and evidence synthesis. It is concerned with the comparative assessment of interventions in routine practice settings. The outputs of CER activities are useful for clinical guideline development, EBM, and the broader social and economic assessment of health technologies (i.e., HTA).

HTA: It is a method of evidence synthesis that considers evidence regarding clinical effectiveness, safety, and cost-effectiveness and, when broadly applied, includes social, ethical, and legal aspects of the use of health technologies. The precise balance of these inputs depends on the purpose of each individual HTA. A major use of HTAs is in informing reimbursement and coverage decisions, in which case HTA should include benefit-harm assessments and economic evaluation.

1.7.4 Self-Check!

1. What is the difference between the USA and Europe in their views on CER?
2. What is the difference between EBM and VBM?

References

1. International Network of Agencies for Health Technology Assessment (2009) HTA Resources. http://www.inahta.org/. Accessed 30 Mar 2016
2. Health Technology Assessment International. What is HTA? http://www.htai.org/. Accessed 30 Mar 2016
3. Towse A, Devlin N, Hawe E, Garrison L (2011) The evolution of HTA in emerging market health care systems: analysis to support a policy response. OHE Consulting Report for PhRMA, Office of Health Economics
4. Pearson SD, Rawlins MD (2005) Quality, innovation, and value for money: NICE and the British National Health Service. JAMA 294(20):2618–2622
5. Rawlins MD (2005) 5 NICE years. Lancet 365(9462):904–908
6. Japan Revitalization Strategy revised in 2014. Introduction of cost-effectiveness analysis in coverage decisions for innovative health technology. p 98. http://www.kantei.go.jp/jp/singi/keizaisaisei/pdt/honbun2JP.pdf. Accessed 30 Mar 2016

7. Central Social Insurance Medical Council Special Committee on Cost-Effectiveness. Proceedings of the 32th meeting. http://www.mhlw.go.jp/stf/shingi2/0000107118.html. Accessed 30 May 2016
8. Sackett DL, Straus SE, Richardson WS et al (2000) Evidence-based medicine: how to practice and teach EBM. Churchill Livingstone, New York
9. Brown MM, Brown GC, Sharma S (2005) Evidence-based to value-based medicine. American Medical Association, Chicago
10. Bootman JL, Townsend RJ, McGhan WF (2004) Principles of pharmacoeconomics, 3rd edn. Harvey Whitney Books, Cincinnati, OH
11. Pharmaceutical and Medical Device Regulatory Science Society of Japan (ed) 2014 Introduction to health technology assessment: toward a comprehensive understanding of cost-effectiveness. Pharmaceutical and Medical Device Regulatory Science Society of Japan, Tokyo
12. Cohen JT, Neumann PJ, Weinstein MC (2008) Does preventive care save money? Health economics and the presidential candidates. N Engl J Med 358(7):661–663
13. Institute of Medicine (2009) Initial national priorities for comparative effectiveness research. National Academies Press, Washington, DC. http://www.nationalacademies.org/hmd/Reports.aspx?searchQuery=CER. Accessed 30 Mar 2016
14. American College of Physicians (2008) Information on cost-effectiveness: an essential product of a national comparative effectiveness program. Ann Intern Med 148(12):956–961
15. Chalkidou K, Tunis S, Lopert R et al (2009) Comparative effectiveness research and evidence-based health policy: experience from four countries. Milbank Q 87(2):339–367
16. Luce BR, Drummond M, Jonsson B et al (2010) EBM, HTA, and CER: clearing the confusion. Milbank Q 88(2):256–276

New HTA Policy in Japan

2

2.1 Past HTA System in Japan

2.1.1 Key Points

- A complex form of HTA already exists for macro-level technologies in Japan.
- HTA for microlevel technologies is also achieved through Japan's unique "Japanese model" of pricing policy.
- Submission of health economic data as part of applications for listing on the National Health Insurance (NHI) list has been recognized in Japan since 1992 although that option has not been fully utilized.
- The Japanese model of HTA is characterized by "quasi-value-based pricing," which involves HTA at the time of pricing for newly listed technologies (Type I) and at the time of repricing (Type II).

2.1.2 Essential Knowledge

Some in Japan and outside Japan have suggested that Japan is a country that has "lagged behind" and that there is no HTA and in particular no value-based pricing (VBP) for pharmaceuticals in Japan because Japan has failed to stay current with the trend toward pharmacoeconomics that originated in Europe and the USA. Although it is true that Japan does not have a system for value-based medicine (VBM) and VBP which evolved from evidence-based medicine and is now prominent in Europe and the USA, a pricing policy which can be referred to as the Japanese model of VBP has been historically developed in Japan. As discussed in Sect. 1.1, the healthcare system in Japan already includes a complex process of HTA applied at the level of macro-technologies, as described by Towse et al., and that process has continued with healthcare reforms started under the Koizumi administration through the administrations of the Democratic Party of Japan and the Abe administration, with a shift in the focus of reforms onto the aging population.

© Springer Nature Singapore Pte Ltd. 2019
I. Kamae, *Health Technology Assessment in Japan*,
https://doi.org/10.1007/978-981-13-5793-0_2

Moreover, a "Japanese model" of HTA has also developed at the level of micro-technologies, as seen in Japan's distinctive pricing policy. As such, the claim that Japan is an "HTA-underdeveloped country" is based on a misguided view stemming from a lack of understanding of the past and present situation of the Japanese health-care system as a whole, and especially its pricing policy.

However, when it comes to the assessment of macro-level technologies in Japan, analyses for which the primary objective is estimation of costs have been largely seen. For instance, during the healthcare reform from fiscal year (FY) 2005 through FY 2007, the Council on Economic and Fiscal Policy recommended containing the growth in healthcare spending within the range of economic growth, but that was a plan with a goal of controlling healthcare spending with the rate of economic growth as the upper limit. The Ministry of Health, Labour and Welfare (MHLW) also announced a policy to cut back growth in social security spending by JPY 220 billion per year for 5 years beginning in FY 2007. Although the spending cut target did have a basis for calculation, the scientific evaluation of the impact of the JPY 220 billion on the cost-effectiveness of healthcare in Japan may not have been sufficient. Additionally, the MHLW has announced placing an annual ceiling on spending on long-term care prevention services for individuals with mild symptoms from FY 2015 and controlling the spending growth within the range of 3–4%, which is equivalent of the growth rate of persons aged 75 years or over. The Ministry estimates a reduction in spending of JPY 200 billion to be achieved by FY 2025.

However, the primary target of HTA evaluations is innovation in healthcare. In a narrow sense, that includes pharmaceuticals and medical devices, and in a broader sense, that includes health systems. The UK's NICE from its inception established a policy of considering the value of innovations in micro-level technologies using cost-effectiveness evaluation. Consequently, even though HTA as a concept is broader than simply economic evaluation, the narrow definition of HTA as the consideration of the cost-effectiveness of healthcare technologies has become the central topic of discussion.

With respect to the assessment of micro-technologies, in August 1992 the Ministry of Health and Welfare in Japan approved the submission of health economic data as part of applications for listing on the National Health Insurance (NHI) price list, as a prompt response to HTA initiatives in Europe and the USA. However, no further development in that system was seen until the introduction of a new policy in 2016, given that there was no written policy from the Central Social Insurance Medical Council (Chuikyo or CMC) on the consideration of pharmacoeconomic studies in pricing decisions. Consequently, speculation among manufacturers that the submission of pharmacoeconomic data would be unlikely to influence pricing decisions became widespread by the end of the 1990s leading to only limited incentives for the industry to submit cost-effectiveness data (see Tables 2.1, 2.2, 2.3, and 2.4).

The "Japanese model" of HTA for the pricing system can be considered a "Japanese quasi-value-based pricing" (quasi-VBP). That is, Japan has established a mechanism for pricing that reflects value for money where prices are reviewed every 2 years with a consideration of market expansion and financial impact, and through experience-based evaluation of effectiveness with a premium added to a baseline price. We thus refer to this scheme as the Japanese model of quasi-VBP,

Table 2.1 Attachment of pharmacoeconomic data for drugs listed between June 1997 and November 2000

	All items	With attachment	Without attachment	Attachment rate (%)
Total	114	37	77	32
Similar efficacy comparison method	103	33	70	32
Cost calculation method	11	4	7	36
With premium for usefulness	20	8	12	40
With premium for marketability	17	3	14	18

Source: Sakamaki H, Hiromori N, Yutani Y, et al.: A Survey of Pharmacoeconomic Data in Applications for NHI New Drug Price Listing in Japan. Jpn J Pharmacoepidemiol, 6(2): 83–100, 2001

Table 2.2 Attachment of pharmacoeconomic data for drugs listed between December 2000 and December 2002

	All items	With attachment	Without attachment	Attachment rate (%)
Total	82	19	63	23
Similar efficacy comparison method	62	11	51	18
Cost calculation method	20	8	12	40
With usefulness premium	13	2	11	15

Source: Ikeda T, Onozuka S: Pharmaceutical price calculation and pharmacoeconomics: A path to application. of drug A Survey of Pharmacoeconomic Data in Applications for NHI New Drug Price Listing in Japan. Office of Pharmaceutical Industry Research's research paper series, 19:25, 2004

Table 2.3 Reasons not to submit pharmacoeconomic assessment evidence

Reasons not to submit	Rate in 70 items without submission (%)
No business benefit in submitting evidence	70
Lack of data for analysis	43
Lack of experts in the company	11
Other	9
No response	7

Source: Ikeda T, Onozuka S: Pharmaceutical price calculation and pharmacoeconomics: A path to application. of drug A Survey of Pharmacoeconomic Data in Applications for NHI New Drug Price Listing in Japan. Office of Pharmaceutical Industry Research's research paper series, 19:25, 2004

which involves a premium at the time of initial pricing for newly listed technologies (Type I) and a premium at the time of repricing (Type II).

Japan can pride itself on this quasi-VBP, which could be hailed as a Japanese brand approach that developed uniquely within its healthcare system. One of its advantages is that the scheme is compatible with pharmacoeconomic methods (see

Table 2.4 Submission of evidence to assess cost-effectiveness for past HTA

	Medicine (2006–2011)	Medical material (2011)	Skills of medical staff (2011)
Cost-effectiveness analysis using QALY	3	1	–
Cost-effectiveness analysis not using QALY	4	1	–
Cost-benefit analysis	–	1	–
The other (Cost analysis, Cost-minimization analysis and etc.)	1	20	125
Total	8	23	125

Special Committee on Cost-Effectiveness, Central Social Insurance Medical Council. July 18, 2012

Sect. 7.7). The incremental cost-effectiveness ratio (ICER), for example, which is an important pharmacoeconomic measure, could be formulated as follows:

1. Price for new drug = price of comparator + (ICER × $\triangle E$) (where $\triangle E$ is the incremental effectiveness),
   while the formula used for pricing in Japan is as follows:
2. Price for new drug = baseline price + premium.

Therefore, assuming that the two equations are equal, "premium" in the second term can be considered equal to the product of ICER and the incremental effectiveness in pharmacoeconomics. Of course, while a compatibility is suggested, there is no fee schedule that exists to convert ICER into a premium under the current pricing system in Japan. Nevertheless, it is useful for future discussions to note that a "premium" under the Japanese pricing system has a pharmacoeconomic basis.

2.1.3   Review of Japanese Quasi-Value-Based-Pricing

Japan has a unique position of its own HTA regarding cost-benefit appreciation in government. Historically, since 1961, Japan has developed nationwide universal health coverage and sophisticated HTA systems which implicitly consider cost and benefit of health technologies and then determine the official price according to the rules devised in the Japanese Ministry of Health, Labour and Welfare (MHLW). Once the price of a new technology is determined by the MHLW, it is automatically approved for inclusion in the National List for reimbursement unless the company of the new technology refuses to sell it in Japan with the official price.

The official price is biennially revised downward. The discount rate in repricing is politically determined by MHLW. Since a constant reimbursement rate of 70% is applied automatically to all drugs and devices after listing on the National Formulary (called the Medical Fee Points Table), there is no room for discussing the issue of reimbursement rates after approval. Hence, in Japan the issues of pricing and

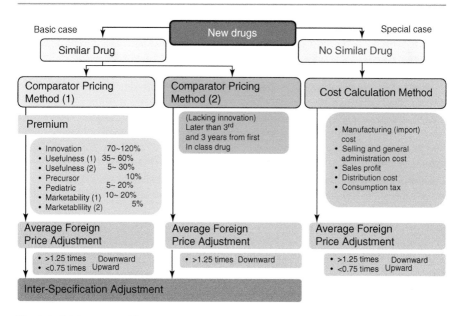

Fig. 2.1 Pricing protocol for new drugs in Japan. Source: Mahlich J, Kamae I, Rossi B, IJTAHC 2017, Ref. [1]

reimbursement have been historically focused on how to improve the government rules to determine the official prices.

The decision flows from approval to pricing is shown in Fig. 2.1 as of March 2018. There are two methods: (1) cost calculation and (2) comparator pricing (or called similar efficacy comparison).

If there is no existing drug from the same category in the market, a new drug is priced based on the cost calculation method. In this method, price is calculated by summing up manufacturing cost, selling and general administration cost, sales profit, distribution cost, and consumption tax. Depending on the extent of innovativeness, efficacy, and safety of the drug, the average sales profit rate, 14.6%, is adjusted in the range from −50% to +100%. In other words, if the drug is an excellent new drug, the sales profit rate of 29.2% may be applied at the best case. On the other hand, if the drug is evaluated to be not as excellent as existing drugs, the sales profit rate of only 7.3% would be applied at the least case.

The comparator pricing method is employed if the existing drugs are available in the market, while the cost calculation method is applied if none is available. In the comparator pricing method, the basic price of a new drug is determined so that the price for a daily dose may be the same as the existing drugs. However, a new drug applied for the comparator pricing method might be rewarded by a premium (i.e., an add-on bonus to the baseline price) if the new drug is superior in terms of its efficacy and/or safety or is more innovative than the existing drugs (four categories of premium: innovation, usefulness (1), usefulness (2), precursor (the world's first registration in Japan)), or if a government policy provides special support for this type of drug (e.g. an orphan drug (marketability premium (1) and (2)) or a pediatric drug (pediatric premium)).

The "premium" for a higher price is a conventional feature of Japanese pricing rules in which a certain proportion of the baseline price is added on top of the baseline price to reflect the additional usefulness of a new drug [2]. That is,

Newprice = Baseline price + (Baseline price × Premium rate).

The pricing mechanism reflects, more or less, a value-for-money assessment based on subjective judgment. It also considers price-volume impact on the national budget over 2 years. Such implicit consideration of cost-benefit for pricing in Japan should be called "quasi value-based pricing" (QVBP). There are two types, Type-I for initial pricing right after approval and Type-II for repricing every 2 years.

A survey of 106 new drugs on the National Health Insurance price listing in 1998–2013 reported that 27 drugs won a premium, but the drugs awarded with a high premium rate are not many [3]. According to the results, the category "Usefulness (2)" was given to 85% of all the drugs which gained the premium rate from 3% to 20%. It is noted that the reason to determine the premium rate was not disclosed for all the cases. The indication criteria for each of premium categories are described without any numerical value. For example, the conditions required for innovation premium are described as follows:

1. The newly entered drug has a clinically useful new mechanism of action.
2. The newly entered drug has been shown objectively to have greater efficacy and safety than existing (comparator) drugs in the same class.
3. The newly entered drug has been shown objectively to improve treatment of the indicated disease or trauma.

The innovation premium is given to a new drug if and only if all three conditions are satisfied, but the statement of each condition is so descriptive that it might be insufficient to give a clear guidance for the indication of innovation premium. Such a definition also does not tell us any scientific rationale for questioning why the premium point rate can be specified in the possible range between upper and lower limits of premium.

Although the MHLW knows that the Japanese official pricing rules are not prescribed in any scientific terms, the MHLW was not so much positive to introduce pharmacoeconomic methodology for reimbursement and pricing decisions until 2011. There were three reasons: (1) The cost-QALY threshold approach for reimbursement decisions such as the UK NICE established, which might violate the principles of equity in the Japanese universal health coverage, would be difficult for Japanese people to accept. (2) Reimbursement and pricing decisions are made almost automatically at the same time within 60 days (at most 90 days) after approval in the Japanese HTA, and so pricing issue cannot be separated from reimbursement. (3) The Japanese-style QVBP rules are quite complex, and it is not easy to integrate the pharmacoeconomic methodology into the current system not to change the rules of QVBP so much. Those conditions impeded making Japan a leading country that drives a modern HTA system, especially in terms of economic evaluations, although Japan has a complex HTA system of its own style in the long run over 50 years.

2.1.4 Self-Check!

1. Is Japan an "HTA-underdeveloped country?"
2. What is the primary target of HTA evaluations?
3. When was the submission of health economic data as part of applications for listing first approved in Japan?
4. What are the trends observed in Tables 2.1 and 2.2?
5. What was the primary reason for companies not submitting health economic data?
6. Which method of evaluation has been used for the majority of health economic data submitted in the past?
7. Has there ever been a Japanese model of HTA?
8. What are the two types of Japanese quasi-VBP?
9. What is a "premium" in the Japanese pricing system equivalent to in theoretical pharmacoeconomics?

2.2 Road to the Implementation of a New HTA Policy in Japan

2.2.1 Key Points

- Cost-effectiveness considerations in the listing decision of outpatient smoking cessation treatment (the Nicotine Dependence Management Fee) in April 2006 was a pioneering case toward the introduction of a new HTA policy in Japan.
- In April 2011, the newly appointed chairman of the Chuikyo, Akira Morita, expressed his commitment to consider the implementation of cost-effectiveness evaluation in Japan.
- In May 2012, the first meeting of the Chuikyo's Special Committee on Cost-Effectiveness was held.
- The revised Japan Revitalization Strategy issued in June 2014 included a plan to implement cost-effectiveness evaluation in coverage and pricing decisions for innovative healthcare technologies.
- A new HTA policy was introduced on a provisional basis starting in April 2016, and lead to a full introduction in April 2019.

2.2.2 Essential Knowledge

The listing of outpatient smoking cessation treatment (the Nicotine Dependence Management Fee) on the NHI price list in April 2006 was preceded by Chuikyo discussions which included some notable points in terms of cost-effectiveness evaluation. Specifically, with the consideration of the Nicotine Dependence Management Fee and the listing of pharmacological agents, verification of their cost-effectiveness was requested by payers. Additionally, they requested that the evidence be based on economic evaluations conducted in Japan. The use of modeling was not accepted by the Chuikyo at the time, but ultimately the listing decision was made with consideration of the ICER presented (see Table 2.5). Although verification of the cost-effectiveness at the time was an incomplete evaluation with no economic evaluation guidelines followed, it was nonetheless a notable pioneering case toward the introduction of a new HTA policy in Japan.

The movement toward the implementation of a new HTA policy for cost-effectiveness evaluation in Japan began around 2011 (see Table 2.6), as the so-called issue of HTA in Japan. As discussed in Sect. 2.1, the MHLW (then the Ministry of Health and Welfare) had first approved the submission of economic evaluation data as part of applications for listing in 1992. However, because no guidelines had been published for conducting economic evaluations, such data was almost never utilized. Finally, in April 2011, the newly appointed chairman of the Chuikyo, Akira Morita, expressed his commitment to initiate discussions on the implementation of cost-effectiveness evaluation in Japan. In May 2011, the government made the announcement to "consider the adoption of health economic methods in the assessment of innovations in healthcare" during the social security reform pursued by the Democratic Party of Japan. Moreover, a road map for the partial implementation of

Table 2.5 The summary of early arguments in Central Social Insurance Medical Council in 2006 (from the angle to utilize economic evaluation)

• The public payer asked to consider cost-effectiveness of medical technologies in coverage decisions for national health insurance.
• Domestic studies are required, not overseas ones.
• A positive value of ICER is accepted even though it does not necessarily provide cost savings.
– However, economic evidence based on modeling study is not acceptable for decision making.

Fukuda T: On policy use of economic evaluation in health care: Covering smoking cessation treatment as an example. Monthly IHEP, 152: 39–43, 2007

Table 2.6 The process toward the introduction of the system

April 2011	Central Social Insurance Medical Council "A new chairman's implication for considering introduction of cost-effectiveness assessment"
May 2011	Democratic Party of Japan's reform of the social security system "Considering application of a health economic method for health innovation assessment"
May 2012	Central Social Insurance Medical Council "Establishment of the Special Committee on Cost-Effectiveness"
June 2014	Abe Cabinet's the revised Japan Revitalization Strategy "Introduction of cost-effectiveness assessment for covering and pricing of innovative health technologies"
December 2015	General assembly of Central Social Insurance Medical Council "approval of a provisional implementation of cost-effectiveness assessment from fiscal 2016"
April 2016	Central Social Insurance Medical Council "Provisional implementation of cost-effectiveness assessment"

a new HTA policy was proposed at the time of the FY 2014 reimbursement policy revisions.

The first meeting of the Chuikyo's Special Committee on Cost-Effectiveness was launched in May 2012, consisting of six members from the payer side, six members on the provider side, four public representative members, four expert members, and three observer members. In June 2014, the Chuikyo's special committee requested that some companies submit preliminary data, based on which the feasibility of analysis and the evaluation system were considered. From May 2012 to January 2016, a total of 33 meetings of the Chuikyo's special committee were held. Within those nearly 4 years of discussion, the previously proposed plan to introduce cost-effectiveness evaluation on a limited scale in FY 2014 was postponed. However, the introduction of a new HTA policy in April 2016 on a provisional basis was approved at the general meeting of the Chuikyo on December 16, 2015, with a future plan for a full implementation of HTA in Japan.

The developments mentioned above are significant as part of the healthcare and medical strategy proposed by the Abe administration. In September 2013, Prime Minister Abe published an article in the international medical journal, *The Lancet*, on Japan's strategy for global health diplomacy, marking the first time that a Japanese prime minster has personally published such an article. The primary objective of the publication was to associate global health with peace-oriented diplomacy, thereby establishing a new global strategy for Japan. The underlying issues included the worldwide acceleration of population aging, rising national healthcare expenditures (particularly rising expenditures due to high-cost medical care over the past decade), and advances in health technology (including personalized medicine/targeted therapy, regenerative medicine, and information and communication technology). Fears of a collapse in healthcare market mechanisms and concerns over sustainability of universal healthcare as consequences of these issues are shared globally. As part of the solution, the Abe administration proposed a set of policies to achieve efficient healthcare resource allocation. In fact, the revised Japan Revitalization Strategy issued on June 24, 2014, proposed a plan to implement cost-effectiveness evaluation in coverage and pricing decisions for innovative healthcare technologies.

Under this policy, the following plans were proposed:

1. To meet the needs of patients for innovative healthcare technologies while at the same time guaranteeing sustainable universal health coverage
2. To introduce cost-effectiveness evaluation in the pricing scheme on a provisional basis starting in FY 2016
3. To explore ways under exceptional rules to enable the listing of healthcare technologies that have been evaluated as not being cost-effective (or too costly to be listed under the current system)

The Chuikyo handout (December 16, 2015) quoted the phrase, suggesting a full implementation of HTA, "The same policy was stated in the 2014 Basic Policies for Economic and Fiscal Management and Reform (referred to as the Large-Boned Policy). Moreover, in the 2015 Basic Policies, a plan was proposed to 'aim to implement cost-effective considerations in coverage and pricing decisions for pharmaceuticals and medical devices first on a provisional basis at the time of the FY 2016 reimbursement policy revisions, quickly followed by a full-scale implementation'."

2.2.3 Self-Check!

1. What was the pioneering case in the Chuikyo's discussion to introduce cost-effectiveness considerations?
2. Is the new HTA policy only one of several institutional reforms of the Ministry of Health, Labour and Welfare?

2.3   Overview of the 2016 Provisional Implementation of HTA in Japan

2.3.1   Key Points

- Cost-effectiveness evaluation was introduced on a provisional basis for the time of repricing for selected pharmaceuticals and medical devices from FY 2016.
- For the appraisal, a qualitative evaluation with products being either "cost-effective" or "not cost-effective" was set.
- Pricing is to be adjusted based on assessment results.

Materials from a meeting of the Chuikyo held on December 16, 2015, at which the provisional implementation of cost-effectiveness evaluation was approved to start in FY 2016, outlined the following guidelines for the repricing of products on the NHI list:

1. Pharmaceuticals and medical devices with a high degree of financial impact, innovativeness, and usefulness will be considered.
2. Products subject to evaluation will be selected and publically announced according to criteria determined by the Chuikyo's Special Committee on Cost-Effectiveness.
3. Companies will be required to submit data for selected products (companies may also choose to submit their data on a voluntary basis, if desired).
4. Companies will conduct and submit their assessments in accordance with the Guideline for Preparing Cost-Effectiveness Evaluation for the Central Social Insurance Medical Council.
5. Data submitted by companies will be reanalyzed by an official, independent body.
6. Results submitted by companies and the reanalysis group will be appraised by the Special Organization for Cost-Effectiveness Evaluation (tentative name) from two viewpoints (i.e., (1) scientific validity and (2) ethical and social impact).

7. If the Special Organization for Cost-Effectiveness Evaluation (tentative name) deems necessary, companies that have submitted their data may present themselves to the Special Organization and express their views.
8. Based on the appraisal results, the data may be reanalyzed if deemed necessary.
9. Products will ultimately be evaluated qualitatively as being either "cost-effective" or "not cost-effective," based on evidence such as their ICER.
10. An ICER figure based on which the cost-effectiveness will be evaluated (known as a threshold) will not be specified at this time of provisional implementation but will be further discussed based on the data accumulated.
11. The results of the appraisal by the Special Organization for Cost-Effectiveness Evaluation (tentative name) will be submitted to the Drug Pricing Organization or the Special Organization for Insured Medical Materials and will be used to adjust the price determined based on the standard pricing (repricing) process used by each of the two organizations. The specific method of price adjustment will be determined at the time of the FY 2018 reimbursement policy revisions.
12. The Special Organization for Cost-Effectiveness Evaluation (tentative name) will consist of a panel of health experts, including healthcare professionals, insurers and patient representatives, and economists, and its discussions will not be publically disclosed.

Pharmaceuticals and medical devices that are to be newly listed will be assessed through the same process as described for repricing of listed products, but it was determined that at the time of the provisional implementation the assessment results will not be used for initial pricing decisions. Figure 2.2 outlines the assessment process (yellow-colored area indicates newly added requirements under the new HTA policy).

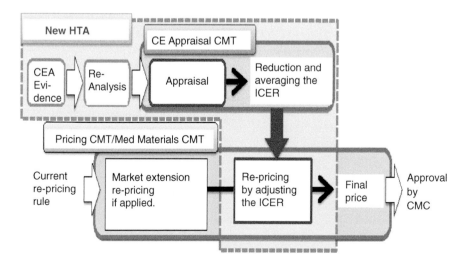

Fig. 2.2 Decision processes for re-pricing adjustment

2.3.2 Outline of Cost-Effectiveness Appraisal in Provisional Implementation

The discussion on the implementation of cost-effectiveness evaluation at the Special Committee on Cost-Effectiveness of the Chuikyo, which started in May 2012, led to the pilot implementation beginning in April 2016 [4]. The initial plan 2016 was to test the feasibility of new policy on cost-effectiveness evaluations at five steps by March 2018: (1) selection of products to be evaluated, (2) submission of the economic evidence resulted from a cost-effectiveness analysis (CEA) conducted by companies, (3) reanalysis (by an independent expert group commissioned by the Chuikyo), (4) appraisal of the results of CEAs by company and/or the reanalysis group, and (5) price adjustment based on the results of the appraisal with a cost-QALY ratio [5–8]. The first to third steps, similar to the assessment steps established by the UK's NICE, generate economic evidence in the form of cost-QALY ratio according to the methodological guideline implemented by the Chuikyo in January 2016 [9, 10].

As target products, seven drugs (for cancer/HCV) and six medical devices existing in the market were selected, considering large budget impact on the national health expenditure, and then the processes up to Step 3 were completed in Summer 2017. Subsequently, a draft of the methods for appraisal and pricing at Steps 4 and 5 was proposed in November 2017, suggesting a three-level assessment of ICER and the algorithmic rules for price adjustment according to the ICER [11–14].

As of March 2018, however, the methods at Step 4 and 5 is projected to require more time to get consensus than what was initially planned since the proposed methods were seriously criticized by the academia and the industry. Consequently, the schedule for the pilot implementation of cost-effectiveness evaluation has been revised so as to reach a decision on full-scale implementation by the end of FY 2018. The Chuikyo stated on November 22, 2017, as follows [12]:

- *The scheme for cost-effectiveness evaluation to be implemented will target pharmaceuticals and medical devices with a large market, including the products priced by the cost accounting method, for which cost-effectiveness will be assessed and the results will be used to inform repricing decisions.*
- *As a step to implementing this scheme and based on the results of pilot examination at this point, price adjustment will begin in April 2018 for 13 products that are subject to evaluation under the pilot implementation, and concurrently, solutions will be discussed to address the technical issues identified in the pilot implementation.*
- *Simultaneously, discussion on the details of full-scale implementation will continue with the aim of reaching a decision by the end of FY2018.*

Based on this statement, it was suggested that the full-scale implementation would begin in FY2019, at the earliest. Although it was not so much clear yet as of March 2018 what the term of "full-scale" implementation meant, it was anticipated that the target products for cost-effectiveness requirements are not only existing ones but also expanded to new ones in preparation for the National Formulary listing.

Furthermore, alongside the ICER appreciation at the fourth step of appraisal, two viewpoints were established to be examined, i.e., (1) scientific validity and (2) ethical and social impacts. The more details are described as follows:

1. Criteria for testing scientific validity:
   (a) Whether the analysis by the company and reanalysis group is conducted in accordance with the Chuikyo guideline [10] as the standard method of analysis
   (b) Whether the method of analysis is reasonably selected when it is difficult to use the standard method of analysis
   (c) Whether the data used are appropriate
   (d) Whether the assessment of validity is appropriate
2. Factors to be considered in assessing the ethical and social impacts:
   (a) Benefits in terms of public health (such as infection control)
   (b) Significant improvement in cost-effectiveness with the additional cost incurred
   (c) Improvement in survival of patients with serious illnesses
   (d) Therapy for patients with rare and incurable illnesses for which no alternative therapy is available

2.3.3 Methods for Cost-Effectiveness Judgment and Price Adjustment

The scope of price adjustment was defined as follows [13]:

1. Additional premium for prices determined based on the similar efficacy comparison method.
2. Entire drug price for prices determined based on the cost accounting method (although under the pilot implementation, only those products for which the operating profit has been adjusted are to be evaluated, the price after adjustment is not to fall below the sum of operating profit, overall cost, and marketing cost).

The evaluation of cost-effectiveness was classified into alternative cases in which the ICER can or cannot be calculated [14]. In cases where the ICER can be calculated (the product is more effective and more costly), the price will be maintained if the ICER equals to or is below the threshold of JPY 5 million (Euro38,500; 1 Euro = 130 JPY)/QALY and will be reduced if the ICER exceeds the threshold. On the other hand, in cases where the ICER cannot be calculated (the product is more effective (or equivalent in effectiveness) and less costly, where the product is dominant), the price is raised (Fig. 2.3). Considering products for which both the results of analysis at the company and by the reanalysis group are available, the results that

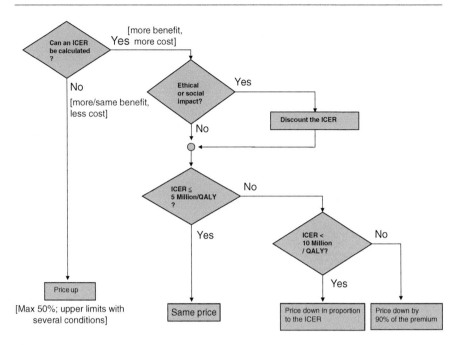

Fig. 2.3 Algorithm for price adjustment

require a smaller change in price will be adopted and incorporated in price adjustment.

1. Cases in which the ICER can be calculated:

For cases in which the ICER can be calculated, the rules proposed by Chuikyo for price adjustment based on the assessment of cost-effectiveness are as detailed in Fig. 2.4. The process of price adjustment can be roughly organized into the following three steps.

Step 1. Discount the ICER in consideration of the ethical and social impacts
The ICER is discounted by 5% once each of the four factors is met by the product under evaluation.

Step 2. Determine the weighted average where multiple ICERs are calculated
Considering products for which multiple ICERs are obtained, such as for multiple indications, the weighted average of all the ICERs obtained in the analysis is determined by assigning a weight to each ICER based on attributes, such as the percentage of patients being treated with the product. In the example of Drug A shown in Table 2.7 where the ICER is calculated to be JPY8M (i.e., million)/QALY and 4M/QALY for indications X and Y, respectively, and the percentages of patients with the respective conditions that are treated with this drug are 70% and 30%, respectively, the weighted average of the two ICERs is determined as:

$$(8 \times 0.7) + (4 \times 0.3) = JPY\ 6.8\ million\ /\ QALY.$$

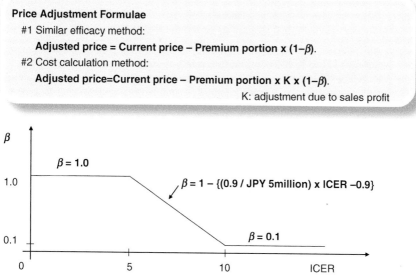

Price Adjustment Formulae

#1 Similar efficacy method:

   Adjusted price = Current price – Premium portion x (1–β).

#2 Cost calculation method:

   Adjusted price=Current price – Premium portion x K x (1–β).

                                                K: adjustment due to sales profit

Fig. 2.4 Calculation method and formulae for price adjustment. Source: CMC Ref. [14]

Table 2.7 Example of the weighted average of multiple ICERs combined with discounting of an ICER

	Proportion of the patients (%)	ICER without discount (JPY million/QALY)	ICER with discount (JPY million/QALY)
Disease X	70	800	800 (0%)
Disease Y	30	400	380 (5%)
Weighted average of multiple ICERs		680	674

Source: Chuikyo Ref. [7]

Table 2.7 further proposes two approaches to take into account the ethical and social impacts considered in Step 1. Considering the first approach, the weighted average is obtained first, after which the ICER is discounted by 5% that provides the ICER of JPY 6.46 (=6.89 × 0.95) M/QALY. Considering the second approach, 5% discount is applied to the ICERs for the respective indications, after which the weighted average is obtained that provides the ICER of JPY 6.74 (= (8 × 0.7) + (4 × 0.95) × 0.3) M/QALY. The Chuikyo has adopted the second approach.

Step 3. Evaluate the ICER at three levels and adjust the price accordingly

Once a single ICER is obtained through the first two steps, the price is adjusted at the following three levels according to the estimate of ICER (Fig. 2.4):

Level 1. If the ICER equals or is below JPY5M/QALY, the price is not adjusted (the price adjustment coefficient $\beta = 1.0$).

Level 2. If the ICER is in the range JPY5–10M/QALY, the premium price is reduced with the price adjustment coefficient β reduced linearly according to the estimate of ICER.

#1 Formula to determine the coefficient:

$$\beta = 1 - \{((0.9 / \text{JPY5M}) \times \text{ICER}) - 0.9\}.$$

#2 Formula for pricing (similar efficacy method):

$$\text{Adjusted price} = \text{Current price} - \{\text{Premium portion} \times (1 - \beta)\}.$$

In case of cost calculation method, the formula for similar efficacy method is slightly modified based on a profit rate for the product.

Level 3. If the ICER equals or exceeds JPY10M/QALY, the price is reduced by 90% of the premium price subject to adjustment (at a constant price adjustment coefficient of $\beta = 0.1$).

2. Cases in which the ICER cannot be calculated:

In cases where the target product provides more health benefit (or equivalent in health benefit) at a reduced cost in comparison to its comparator, the price of the target product is to be raised. When the product is equivalent to its comparator in terms of effectiveness, the incremental effectiveness becomes zero. It makes the denominator of ICER being zero, which provides an ICER estimate of infinity for a given value of incremental cost. When the cost of the target product is reduced, the incremental cost takes a negative value. Here, the ICER will also take a negative value as a result of dividing a negative incremental cost by a positive incremental effectiveness. Such cases where the ICER is infinity or takes a negative value are referred to at Chuikyo as cases in which the ICER cannot be calculated [14].

The Chuikyo states that the price is raised when both the following two prior requirements are met:

Requirement 1. *The product (technology) is demonstrated to be more health benefit (or equivalent in health benefit) in comparison to its comparator, such as in clinical trials.*

Requirement 2. *The product (technology) is one that is entirely distinct from its comparator or one that is distinct in basic structure and mechanism of actions beyond the extent of general improvement.*

In addition, the Chuikyo requires the following conditions for the details on the rate and amount of increase:

• *The method of calculation for price adjustment will be in accordance with the method employed in cases where the product (technology) is both more costly and more effective in comparison to its comparator, with a maximum rate of increase of 50% (a coefficient β of 1.5) and the amount of increase not exceeding 10% of the price before adjustment.*

- *Simultaneously, in line with the purpose of the policy on cost containment, the amount of increase should not exceed the amount that is equivalent of half of the reduction in cost per patient in comparison to the comparator. If the amount of increase determined based on the preceding requirement exceeds the amount equivalent of half of the reduction in cost per patient, the price will be increased by the amount equivalent of half of the reduction in cost per patient.*
- *The approach to identifying the products for which the price is to be adjusted and the steps in applying price adjustment will be in accordance with those employed in cases where the product (technology) is both more costly and more effective in comparison to its comparator.*
- *For these products, the ethical and social impacts will not be considered in price adjustment.*

2.3.4   Excerpts from MHLW Materials

Listed below are excerpts from the Chuikyo materials entitled "The provisional implementation of cost-effectiveness evaluation," from the Chuikyo's meeting (December 16, 2015).

2.3.4.1 Excerpt 1: The Repricing Process Under Provisional Implementation

1. Criteria for the selection of products to be evaluated
   (a) Basic policy of selection criteria
      Pharmaceuticals and medical devices with high financial impact, innovativeness, and usefulness will be considered for assessment, based on the fact that the need for cost-effectiveness considerations was recognized in light of concerns over the impact of more costly and advanced health technologies on health insurance funding.
   (b) Selection criteria when repricing products
      Products will be selected and publically announced by the Special Committee on Cost-Effectiveness, according to the following criteria:
      - The price of the product has been determined by the cost accounting method or has been determined by the similar efficacy (or functional category for medical devices) comparison method and was assigned a certain premium level.
      - The estimated peak sales of the product are high.
        However, for medical devices the reimbursement price will be used as their peak sales have not been hitherto published.
      - The price of the product has been reviewed for repricing once or twice since listing.

- The product is not a pharmaceutical or medical device intended for use in therapy for patients with rare illnesses with insufficient treatment approaches (e.g., specified intractable diseases, hemophilia, and HIV infection).
- The product is not a pharmaceutical or medical device for which a request for development or public invitation has been issued by the MHLW's Committees for Unapproved Drugs or High Medical Needs.

2. Submission of Data by Companies

(a) Companies will be required to submit data for the selected products.
For pharmaceuticals and medical device products that are not selected, if companies desire, they may submit data voluntarily. However, the assessment of selected products will be given priority when data are submitted by a large number of companies and the order of evaluation and such will be considered by the Special Committee on Cost-Effectiveness.

(b) Companies will conduct and submit their assessment in accordance with the Guideline for Preparing Cost-Effectiveness Evaluation for the Central Social Insurance Medical Council.[1]

(c) If, before the start of the assessment, it is predicted that methods other than the standard method of analysis need to be employed or that it may be difficult even for the reanalysis group to select a method, etc. due to reasons such as lack of data or difficulty for the analysis group to select appropriate methods, the Special Organization for Cost-Effectiveness Evaluation (tentative name) may be consulted in advance for the approval of analysis methods used in order to maintain the efficiency of the evaluation process.

3. Reanalysis of Submitted Data

(a) Data submitted by companies will be reanalyzed by an official, independent body.

(b) The reanalysis will be conducted primarily by independent experts, in cooperation with the official body (hereafter, reanalysis group), who will submit the reanalysis results to the Ministry of Health, Labour and Welfare.

(c) Members of the reanalysis group will conduct reanalyses in accordance with a predetermined conflict of interest policy.

4. Appraisal

(a) Analysis results submitted by companies and the reanalysis group will be appraised by the Special Organization for Cost-Effectiveness Evaluation (tentative name) from the following two viewpoints:

- Viewpoint of verifying the scientific validity of the results

---

[1] Prepared as part of the "Research for the establishment of evaluation methods, data standardization methods, and an evaluation framework geared the application of economic evaluation of healthcare technologies for public policy" supported by a 2015 Health and Labour Science Research Grant (Strategic Integrated Scientific Research Project) (team leader: Takashi Fukuda, Director, Department of Health and Welfare Services, National Institute of Public Health).

The scientific validity of the results will be verified with consideration of the following points:

- Whether the company and the reanalysis group used the standard analysis method in their analysis
- Whether the analysis method that was selected was rational (when it is difficult to use the standard method of analysis)
- Whether the data used are appropriate

• Viewpoint of ethical and social impacts

Evaluation will be conducted from the viewpoint of the ethical and social impacts from the analysis results.

Factors to be considered in the evaluation will continue to be discussed in preparation for the full-scale implementation based on data accumulated during the provisional implementation and with broad reference to points considered in other countries such as the UK, France, Sweden, and Australia.

(b) During the appraisal process, if the Special Organization for Cost-Effectiveness Evaluation (tentative name) deems it necessary, companies that have submitted their data may present themselves at the Special Organization and express their views.

(c) If, based on the results of the appraisal, it is determined that the analysis needs to include analysis from additional perspectives, such as a more detailed analysis of the target patients and usage of the technology, an analysis of productivity loss, etc., then a reanalysis should be conducted.

(d) The product will ultimately be evaluated qualitatively as being either "cost-effective" or "not cost-effective" based on submitted analysis results such as ICER.

(e) An ICER threshold, based on which the product is evaluated as being "cost-effective" or "not cost-effective," will not be specified at this time of provisional implementation. However, since the research group has already presented their views on the threshold to use, the organization will use these as a reference in its decisions and will continue discussions based on the data accumulated during the provisional implementation. Additionally, measures of willingness to pay will be examined based on data available in Japan, which will also be discussed in preparation for the full-scale implementation.

(f) The results of the appraisal by the Special Organization for Cost-Effectiveness Evaluation (tentative name) will be submitted to the Drug Pricing Organization or Special Organization for Insured Medical Materials and will be used to adjust the price determined by the standard pricing (repricing) process by each of the two organizations. The specific method of the price adjustment will be determined during the FY 2018 reimbursement policy revisions.

2.3.4.2 Excerpt 2: Requirements When Pricing Newly Listed Products

1. Criteria for the selection of products to be evaluated
   (a) Basic policy for selection criteria
      Similar to the repricing of products, pharmaceuticals and medical devices considered to have a high financial impact, innovativeness, and usefulness will be considered for assessment.
   (b) Selection criteria when pricing newly listed products
      Products will be selected according to the following criteria, and companies should submit data for pharmaceuticals and medical devices that satisfy the criteria based on the content included in requests for entry in the NHI List when companies submit a request for entry in the NHI list.
      Pharmaceuticals and medical devices that are newly listed and satisfy the selection criteria will be reviewed by the Special Committee on Cost-Effectiveness to ensure that they meet the criteria, before the selection is publicly announced.
      - The price of the product has been determined by the cost accounting method or has been determined by the similar efficacy (or functional category) comparison method and was assigned a certain premium level.
      - The estimated peak sales of the product are high.
        The reimbursement price will be used for medical devices, as their peak sales have not been hitherto published.
      - The product is not a pharmaceutical or medical device intended for use in therapy for patients with rare illnesses with insufficient treatment approaches (e.g., specified intractable diseases, hemophilia, and HIV infection).
      - The product is not a pharmaceutical or medical device for which a request for development or public invitation has been issued by the MHLW's Committees for Unapproved Drugs or High Medical Needs.
2. Submission of data by companies
   (a) Along with the submission of the request for entry in the NHI List, companies are required to submit the results of their analysis for products that satisfy the selection criteria, by following the Guideline for Preparing Cost-Effectiveness Evaluation to the Central Social Insurance Medical Council as closely as possible. For pharmaceuticals and medical device products that are not selected, if companies desire to, they may submit data voluntarily. However, the assessment of selected products will be given priority when data are submitted by a large number of companies and the order of evaluation, and such will be considered by the Special Committee on Cost-Effectiveness.
3. Reanalysis of submitted data
   (a) As a general rule, data submitted by companies will be reanalyzed by an official, independent body, as in the case when repricing products.
4. Appraisal
   (a) As a general rule, similar to repricing, analysis results submitted by companies and the reanalysis group will be appraised by the Special Organization for Cost-Effectiveness Evaluation (tentative name) with a qualitative evaluation.

(b) Similar to the repricing process, the results of cost-effectiveness evaluation will be considered after the price has been determined by using the standard calculation method for the products to be listed. However, since the framework for assessment has not been fully established, the assessment by the Special Organization for Cost-Effectiveness Evaluation (tentative name) will likely not be completed in time for the listing of the new product. Therefore, the results of the assessment will not be used in pricing decisions during the provisional implementation.

(c) Regarding the full-scale implementation, the Special Committee on Cost-Effectiveness will continue its consideration about the design of a framework that allows for a quick assessment and the quality of data and the content to be included with the request for entry in the NHI list, based on the data submitted during the provisional implementation.

2.3.4.3 Excerpt 3: The Special Organization for Cost-Effectiveness Evaluation (Tentative Name)

1. The Special Organization for Cost-Effectiveness Evaluation (tentative name) will consist of a panel of health experts, including healthcare professionals, insurers and patient representatives, and economists, and will discuss technical matters related to the conducting of cost-effectiveness evaluations for pharmaceuticals and medical devices.

2. Meetings of the Special Organization for Cost-Effectiveness Evaluation (tentative name) will be closed to the public as they will include a discussion of specific products.

2.3.5 Self-Check!

1. Does the Chuikyo use an ICER threshold for cost-effectiveness evaluations?
2. What are the two viewpoints considered for the appraisal?
3. Are the results of the appraisal used as reference in coverage decisions or pricing decisions?
4. Are medical devices also subject to evaluation?
5. Who determines the selection criteria?
6. Are companies allowed to submit data for products not among the selected products?
7. Are there guidelines for the analysis?
8. Who will reanalyze the submitted data?
9. Are companies able to present their views after the data submission?
10. What is the qualitative evaluation given as the outcome of appraisal?
11. What is the specific process of using the results of the cost-effectiveness evaluation in price adjustments?
12. What is the name of the organization responsible for carrying out the appraisal?
13. Will the results of the appraisal be used in price adjustments for newly listed products?

2.4   Controversial Issues on the Methodology in 2016–2018

The primary aim of the pilot implementation was supposed to apply pharmacoeconomic methodology to the cost-effectiveness evaluations of health technology.
Certainly, the introduction of the following policies in the pilot period so far deserves
recognition as a pharmacoeconomically appropriate approach:

1. To calculate and use the ICER as an indicator of pharmacoeconomic value of the
   product
2. To take into account not only the ICER but also the ethical and social impacts for
   appraisal in terms of cost-effectiveness

However, as discussed in the preceding section, the Chuikyo proposed an
approach to price adjustment that simultaneously integrates both of ICER and ethi-
cal/social impacts, venturing into "value-based pricing" for which scientific methods are not well established in pharmacoeconomics. Therefore, while the methods
proposed by Chuikyo was a challenging attempt, its approach seemed to lack scientific validity in terms of pharmacoeconomics. It offered an impression that the estimate of ICER was merely used to conjure up convenient rules for calculation for the
purpose of price reduction. Here the following three problems should be noted
regarding the methodology which Chuikyo proposed:

2.4.1   Discounting of ICER

While the Chuikyo proposed to discount the ICER in consideration of the ethical
and social impacts, the idea of discounting the ICER has never existed in pharmacoeconomics. The concept of discounting in economics originated in the time preference of humans that the value of cost varies over time. For instance, one may
consider that the value of JPY1000 one year from now will not be equivalent to the
value of JPY1000 at present and that it is equivalent to approximately JPY950, with
a 5% discount, at present. As the ICER is defined by the incremental cost in the
numerator divided by the incremental effectiveness in the denominator, discounting
the cost in the numerator has been accepted as a concept in economics in cases
where a long-term cost is being evaluated. On the other hand, controversy has traditionally existed regarding whether the denominator, that is, the effectiveness,
should also be discounted, although the principle of equal discount rate for the
numerator and denominator has since been established in pharmacoeconomic
theory.

As such, the question was how the policy of discounting adopted by Chuikyo
should be interpreted. In Table 2.7, for instance, the ICER of JPY4M/QALY is
discounted at a rate of 5% to provide an ICER of JPY3.8M/QALY. This ICER is
obtained by merely multiplying JPY4M/QALY by 0.95, which is essentially
equivalent to multiplying the numerator (i.e., the cost) of the original ICER by
0.95. In other words, the discounting of ICER in this case is equivalent in

calculation of the "discounting of cost," where only the cost is discounted by 5%. Consequently, it would be reasonable to interpret that the Chuikyo approach of taking into account the ethical and social impacts by means of discounting of cost only based on time preference lacks pharmacoeconomic foundation. The discount rate of 5% per criterion met for ethical and social impacts was also employed on insufficient grounds. In any case, the calculation of discounting the ICER proposed by Chuikyo violates the principle of equal discount rate for the numerator and denominator of ICER.

The Chuikyo argued that the discounting of ICER is merely for the purpose of manipulation to reduce the numerical value of ICER and therefore does not require to conform to the pharmacoeconomic concept of discounting. If it is in fact such manipulation of numbers for convenience, the use of the term "discounting" should be carefully avoided to prevent confusion with the pharmacoeconomic concept of discounting.

Then, the question was how ethical and social impacts could be incorporated into the assessment of cost-effectiveness, other than by the false discounting of ICER estimate. Pharmacoeconomically, the answer is clear. That is, the threshold for the assessment of cost-effectiveness can be adjusted according to the degree of ethical and social impacts, considering the change of the level of societal willingness to pay (WTP). As the proposal by Chuikyo adopted a threshold of JPY5M/QALY, positive ethical and social impacts could be taken into account by adopting a looser threshold (a threshold value larger than JPY5M/QALY) according to the degree of impacts. As the threshold reflects the society's WTP, it is reasonable to assume an increase in WTP where positive ethical and social impacts are recognized.

2.4.2   Calculation of Weighted Average of the ICER

For products under evaluation with multiple indications or comparators, multiple estimates of the ICER are obtained. Accordingly, Chuikyo proposed to determine a weighted average on a pro rata basis according to the percentage of patients with the respective conditions who are treated with the product (or patients treated with the respective comparators).

Similar to the case of discounting of the ICER, the idea of weighted average of the ICER proposed by Chuikyo has never existed in pharmacoeconomics. This is owing to the fact that the ICER, by definition, is an indicator whose value is estimated with respect to a specific comparator, and thus combining multiple ICERs estimated with respect to different comparators appears to be misleading or meaningless. Unless the same comparator is used, it would be very hard to interpret what the weighted average means.

Hence, assume that multiple estimates of the ICER were obtained with respect to the same comparator, and we continue to intend to determine the weighted average of these ICER estimates. Even for this case, two approaches would be available if we should stick to the idea of the weighted average. One is to take the weighted average of the pre-calculated ICER estimates as proposed by Chuikyo, and the other is to calculate the weighted average of the numerator of the ICER, the cost, and the denominator, the effectiveness, individually prior to division. The weighted averages obtained by the two approaches, either weighting the estimates of the ICER before or after division, do not necessarily take the same value.

For instance, Table 2.8 illustrates an example of disparity of the weighted averages between different approaches. With the approach employed by Chuikyo, where the ICER is calculated as JPY8M/QALY and 4M/QALY for indications X and Y, respectively, and the percentages of patients with the respective conditions who are treated with this drug are 70% and 30%, respectively, the weighted average of the two ICERs was determined to be JPY6.8M/QALY.

Now, let us suppose that the ICERs of JPY8M/QALY and 4M/QALY were obtained by the equations JPY16M ÷ 2 QALYs and JPY20M ÷ 5 QALYs, respectively. Here, the results of weighting the numerator and denominator prior to division are as shown in Table 2.8. This provides the weighted cost of JPY17.2M and weighted effectiveness of 2.9 QALYs, the division of which provides the ICER of JPY5.93M/QALY. The weighted average obtained here indeed takes a value distinct from the weighted average of JPY6.8M/QALY determined by the approach of Chuikyo. As such, the question is which of these weighted averages is appropriate. While it is challenging to interpret what Chuikyo's weighted average of JPY6.8M/ QALY essentially indicates, the estimate of JPY5.93M/QALY could be interpreted as the average ICER for population, because it is the quotient obtained from dividing the average cost for population by the average effectiveness for the same population.

Table 2.8 Example of disparity between two estimates of weighted average

ΔC	ΔE	ICER	Weight	ICER× Weight	ΔC× Weight	ΔE× Weight
1600	2	800	0.7	①560	1120	1.4
2000	5	400	0.3	②120	600	1.5
					③1720	④2.9
Weighted Average				①+② =680		③÷④ =593
				An estimate By Chuikyo		Another Estimate

In the proposal by Chuikyo, the weighted average of the ICER is further discounted at a rate of 5% per one criterion met for ethical and social impacts as shown in Table 2.7. This adds to further confusion in the methodology. Discounting of ICER and also the rate of 5% both lack foundation as previously discussed, and so it is seriously concerned that the approach to combining 5% discount of ICER with the weighted average might further diminish the theoretical validity.

2.4.3 An Arbitrary Formula for the Association of ICER and Price Adjustment Coefficient

With respect to pharmacoeconomic methodology, it is well-grounded and valid to adopt an ICER threshold for assessing the cost-effectiveness of the product under evaluation. However, the theoretical association between price and the ICER has not been well-established in pharmacoeconomics. Although the term "value-based pricing (VBP)" is frequently being quoted in HTA, it is not too much to say that the relationship between "value" and "price" is still a challenging frontier in pharmacoeconomics.

This is based on two reasons. One is that even if we consider the ICER as "value" in a narrow sense, the association between the ICER and price cannot be easily formulated in theory. The other is that the ICER is not the only indicator of "value" and that "value" encompasses a wide range of factors. Accordingly, the process referred to as VBP in Europe is based on price adjustment by means of multidisciplinary discussions among parties concerned, and hence VBP does not mean just an algorithmic method in which the price of target product is determined by simply substituting numbers into equations.

However, possibly to avoid the black boxing of the process of price adjustment based on subjective discussions, the Chuikyo has devised a formula to associate the ICER with the price adjustment coefficient β, as shown in Fig. 2.4. Once the weighted average of ICER is established, price adjustment coefficient β can be automatically estimated according to the formula #1: $\beta = 1 - \{(0.9/\text{JPY 5 million}) \times \text{ICER} - 0.9\}$ in case of JPY 5 million < ICER < JPY 10 million/QALY. Consequently, the adjusted price can be determined by the formula #2: Adjusted price = Current price − (Premium portion × (1 − β)). For example, if the ICER is JPY 8 million/QALY, then

$$\beta = 1 - \{((0.9/\text{JPY 5 million}) \times \text{JPY 8 million}) - 0.9\} = 0.46$$

Hence, the adjusted price is determined by subtracting 54% portion of the premium from the current price.

The price adjustment proposed by Chuikyo, as shown in this example, is apparently an algorithmic approach to get a solution through mechanical operations, which should be avoided from the viewpoint of conventional wisdom of pharmacoeconomics. In addition, this formula has been developed arbitrarily to be consistent with two anchoring, (JPY5M, $\beta = 0.9$) and (JPY10M, $\beta = 0.1$), on the $X–Y$ plane, merely to fit the discounting policy of Chuikyo. Although it certainly contributes to ensuring the transparency of rules, the implementation of algorithmic approach without firm scientific grounds cannot avoid the criticism of being premature.

On the other hand, some may argue that price adjustment is not necessarily a scientific but a "political" decision, and thus the arbitrarily developed formula, such as the one in Fig. 2.4, would be perfectly acceptable. However, if it were to be a political decision, then it would be significantly more "politically correct" to rely on price adjustment by means of deliberative approach to get consensus among parties concerned, rather than merely employing a formula whose validity is questionable. Essentially, the use of methods that lack pharmacoeconomic foundation should be avoided by all means. Considering the situation as described here, one may be concerned that the Chuikyo, who emphasizes the need for scientific validity in the process of appraisal, in fact might intend to take inconsistent policy with respect to adopting new rules whose scientific validity is questionable.

2.5 Summary of HTA Institutionalization in 2019

2.5.1 Key Points

- The cost-effectiveness requirements for drug/device pricing provisionally implemented in April 2016 were institutionalized at full scale in April 2019.
- The methodological guidelines are revised to Version 2.0 in March 2019, maintaining the basic frame despite extensive change of conditions.
- The Japanese new HTA highlights ICER-based pricing with an algorithmic approach.

2.5.2 Essential Knowledge

Following the pilot implementation which began in April 2016, the new policy was implemented on a full scale in fiscal 2019. There were three focuses in methods of pros and cons as seen in Sect. 2.4: (1) discounting of an ICER, (2) the weighted average of ICERs, which arises when multiple ICERs are obtained, and (3) the arbitrary (or random) relational expression between the ICER and the price adjustment coefficient. Certain negative views and questions concerning the weighted average of ICERs were raised and discussed by a group of pharmacoeconomics experts in Japan. Regarding the relational expression between the ICER and the price adjustment coefficient, Chuikyo eventually invented and adopted a "step" approach, not a "slope" approach described in Sect. 2.3.3. At the same time, the methodological MHLW guidelines are revised into Version 2.0, maintaining the basic frame of the initial version despite extensive change of conditions.

Thus, the new HTA policy effective from April 2019 is characterized by the following properties.

- Full-size implementation (institutionalization) in April 2019
- Applied for medical products including drugs and medical devices
- Conventional decision processes for pricing and listing of new products are not changed: price adjustment based on economic evaluation is applied only after official prices are determined and the products are listed on the National Formulary.
- Selected products expensive or with a large market size, not for all the products, are targeted for price adjustment based on economic evaluation.
- The products for orphan diseases in which no sufficient treatment exists or the products utilized only for pediatric diseases are excluded.
- The primary threshold for price adjustment is set at 5 million JPY (USD45K)/QALY, while JPY7.5M/QALY for some selected medicines such as cancer drugs.
- Special considerations in the appraisal committee regarding socio-ethical factors, features of products, etc. are further developed.

2.5.3   Key Changes from the Provisional Implementation 2016 to Full-Scale 2019

If the nature of the Japanese new HTA system is described in a single word, it certainly highlights "ICER-based pricing" with an algorithmic approach. This feature was proposed in the provisional implementation 2016, and further enhanced in the full-scale institutionalization in April 2019. The major changes are summarized as follows:

- Target products are classified into five categories from H1 to H5 with each selection criteria according to the properties of products, whether new product or existing one, and whether the similar efficacy method or the cost calculation method is applied (refer to Table 2.9).
- The decision processes from target selection to price adjustment by CMC are revised as shown in Fig. 2.5. The general outline of the decision flow has not changed much from the one in the trial program. However, consultation prior to analysis between a company and MHLW is newly created. Also, the confirmatory analysis by experts' group is renamed for "public analysis." The involvement of the National Institute of Public Health (Center for Outcomes Research and Economic Evaluation for Health: CORE2-Health for short) is officially announced. The standard term is described with 15 months total (at least 12 months).
- Reduction of ICER (the Chuikyo use the term "discount of ICER") with 5% for each ethical/social aspect is discarded since no scientific rationale of reduction can be found.
- The weighted averaging method of multiple ICERs for multiple indications or multiple subgroups was discarded, and as an alternative, each ICER is converted to the price adjustment coefficient first, and then the resultant multiple coefficients are averaged out, weighted by patient population size of each indication, ignoring different comparators for the ICER estimation.

Table 2.9 Selection criteria

	Category	Similar efficacy method (comparator pricing method)	Cost calculation method	Selection criteria
(a) New product: listed after April 2019	H1	With premiums of innovation, usefulness, etc.	With premiums of innovation, usefulness, etc. or with disclosure less than 50% of the total product costs	• Predicted amount of sales at a peak period: Over 10 billion JPY (90 million USD)
	H2			• Predicted amount of sales at a peak period: 5 to 10 billion JPY (45 to 90 million USD)
	H3			• Products which the CMC (Chu-i-kyo) regards the price as being too expensive
(b) Existing product in the market: listed before April 2019	H4	Regardless of calculation method, products with premiums of innovation, usefulness, etc.		• Total amount of sales over 100 billion JPY • Products which the CMC (Chu-i-kyo) regards the price as being too expensive
Similar product	H5	Similar product included in Category H1 to H4		• Drugs whose price is determined compared to a drug targeted for cost-effectiveness assessment in either of Category H1 to H4 • Medical devices to which the same rule above as for drugs is applicable within a same function category

- The "threshold-slope" method (refer to Fig. 2.4) is changed into "threshold-step(or stair)" method shown in Fig. 2.6. Three thresholds—JPY5M, 7.5M, and 10M/QALY (Chuikyo calls it a "standard," not a threshold)—are introduced according to the three levels of price adjustment rate (coefficient): 0.7, 0.4, and 0.1. This adjustment rate is applied only for the premium portion of the whole price of a target product based on the following formula:

  Adjusted Premium = Prior premium − (Prior premium × (1 − Price adjustment rate)).

- It means that the premium portion is reduced with 30%, 60%, and 90% according to the price adjustment rate of 0.7, 0.4, and 0.1 in the case of "JPY5M<ICER<7.5M," "7.5M<ICER<10M," and "ICER>10M/QALY," respectively. Special consideration is reserved for anticancer drugs (where the approved indication is a malignant tumor, and the cost-effectiveness analysis is conducted for cancer patients). That is, the thresholds are shifted to more generous levels: JPY7.5, 11.25, and 15M/QALY. The price adjustment is not applied for the case of orphan diseases such as designated incurable diseases, hemophilia, and HIV infection, for which no effective treatment exists, or pediatric diseases for which the dose and administration for a child is approved in Japan.

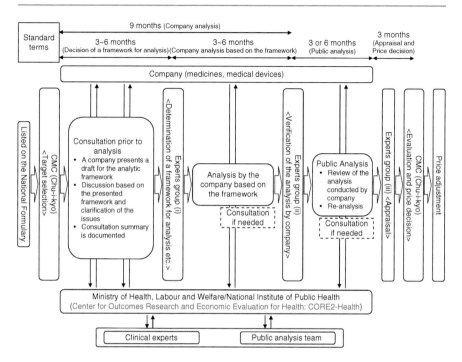

Fig. 2.5 New decision processes

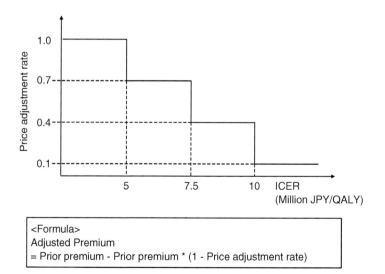

Fig. 2.6 Thresholds-step method for price adjustment

Table 2.10 Conditions and rate for upward pricing

	(a) Dominant	(b) ICER under 2 million JPY/QALY
Condition 1: RCT evidence shows clinical benefit greater than (or equal to) in a comparator	OK	OK If published in the journal with IP > 15, and also statistically significant benefit for Asian patients including the Japanese
Condition 2: Products totally different from a comparator, or beyond ordinary improvement regarding basic structures or functions	OK	OK
Upward pricing rate	50% (within less than 10% of the total price)	25% (within less than 5% of the total price, not exceeding 2M JPY/QALY)

- Conditions and the rate for upward pricing are clarified as shown in Table 2.10, according to the case whether ordinary technology (condition 1) or innovative technology (condition 2) by either case of goodness: dominant or ICER under JPY2M/QALY with upward rate of 50% and 25%, respectively, although some additional conditions are reserved, considering the certain budget impact.

Japan initiated a quite ambitious challenge for ICER-based pricing. The key changes from the provisional implementation 2016 to full-scale 2019 reveal continuing efforts to improve the systems. However, the methods seem to be too algorithmic, mixed up with science and art. The "threshold-slope" method in the pilot program in 2016–2018 was arbitrary with no scientific rationale. The discussions have not yet matured on whether public pricing may go beyond WTP or not. Regarding the contradiction to VBP as expressed by WHO, the challenge of ICER-based pricing in Japan might be too extreme without any space to consider deliberative decision making. Apparently, it excludes alternative methods such as rebates, reward rules, and so on. Even though being changed into "threshold-stair" method in 2019, it does not solve the problem of no scientific rationale as well as rigidity for pricing decisions. The discussion on MCDA (Multiple Criteria Decision Analysis) has not been included in Chuikyo so far, although it must be a key challenge to consider multiple factors based on a wider concept of value. The roadmap to attain the final goal: how we could make the Japanese universal health coverage affordable and sustainable to the future is not adequately addressed in the reform of HTA institutionalization 2019.

2.5.4   Self-Check!

1. Which method is the threshold-slope method changed into?
2. For which portion of the price is the price adjustment rate applied?
3. Is there any allowance of price adjustment for cancer medicines?
4. What is the nature of the Japanese new HTA system if described in a single word?

2.6   Issues for Further Development of HTA in Japan[2]

2.6.1   Key Points

- The Chuikyo suggests five focus points for its discussion about the future full-scale implementation of HTA in Japan in addition to the development of a framework.
- The use of evaluation results in reimbursement decisions is also to be considered with the full-scale implementation of HTA in Japan.
- HTA issues in Japan should not be trivialized as a minor revision of the pricing system, and further discussion from a global viewpoint is desired.

2.6.2   Essential Knowledge

According to Chuikyo materials (December 16, 2015), the Chuikyo announced to continue its discussion of the following points, in addition to the development of a framework:

1. Revision of the selection criteria
2. Factors to be considered specifically in Japan for the appraisal from the viewpoint of ethical and social impacts
3. Design of a framework that allows for quick assessment and the quality and content of data to be submitted at the time of the request for entry in the NHI list
4. Promotion of a framework associated with data management for Japan
5. The specific scheme to be used when deciding whether reimbursement is possible or not based on the evaluation results
   The first four points above may seem reasonable. Actually those points were more clarified in the institutionalization 2019. However, the fifth point is left for future discussions. The reason for that is that the provisional implementation of HTA that began in FY 2016 was about using the evaluation results for pricing decisions. The full-scale implementation of HTA followed the same policy as that in provisional program for using the results in pricing decisions. The Ministry of Finance Japan has been proposing the policy that the evaluation results should be properly used for reimbursement decisions in listing or not listing on the National Formulary.
   Needless to say, the adoption of an ICER threshold needs to be considered if evaluation results are to be used in reimbursement decisions as they are by the UK's NICE. The Chuikyo decided to limit the use of evaluation results to pricing decisions for the 2016 provisional implementation to avoid discussing the issue of an ICER threshold. Subsequently, it was not included as a focus point in discus-

---

[2] This section is a revised version of the following original article: *Kamae I. Perspective on pharmacoeconomic approaches to health technology assessment (1): recent development in assessing innovation*. Pharmaceutical and Medical Device Regulatory Science 2012; 43(1):39–44.

sions about the full-scale implementation by the Chuikyo. Therefore, while the discussion about the use of evaluation results for reimbursement decisions is not to be disregarded, the following point should precede the fifth point in the list of focus points:
6. More scientific methods when making pricing adjustments based on evaluation results

Looking at the issues to be considered from a broader point of view, the foremost question to be asked is for what purpose HTA is to be adopted. Table 2.11 presents four questions and six pitfalls to be considered in this discussion. The first question is, why healthcare innovation should be evaluated. Even if the evaluation is based on the assumption that innovation creates value, questions such as what is its incremental value and how it does relate to society's willingness to pay still need to be addressed. Additionally, identifying the association with the efficiency frontier concept, introduced in Germany, is also important for the Japanese quasi-VBP. The second question is whether or not the aim of the policy to adopt HTA is to reduce healthcare spending. There is a lot to learn from European countries who have experienced both hope and disillusion with regard to spending cuts when introducing HTA. Moreover, the discussion should not be limited to pricing decisions but should also make clear the approach for addressing the price-volume issue. The third question is whether the new HTA policy aims to strengthen the ability of domestic pharmaceutical companies to compete internationally. The new premium rules introduced in FY 2010 worked to the advantage of foreign pharmaceutical companies, suggesting to the contrary that the introduction of new policies do not necessarily assist in increasing the international competitiveness of domestic companies. Therefore, whether the HTA policy will lead to such inconsistencies needs to be considered. This is also related to whether the country aims to develop and expand the Japanese quasi-VBP or to follow the British VBP approach. The fourth question is whether to consider the adoption of HTA as an international strategy to respond to globalization. Japan's position in terms of its leadership in the current global trend toward HTA is consistently brought into question. The questions of whether Japan's healthcare industry is ready to embark on the creation of new fields and markets and how to develop human resources capable of leading

Table 2.11 Arguments and pitfalls

Arguments
• Why do we assess health innovation?
• Is introduction of HTA aiming at medical expenditure reduction?
• Do we intend to increase international competitiveness of domestic pharmaceutical industry?
• Is it an international strategy responding to globalization?
Pitfalls
• Trivialization of the problems
• Negative effects of similar efficacy comparison method
• Uncertainty of data
• Foreign price adjustment
• International comparison of the thresholds
• Collaboration among ministries

such efforts need to be discussed regarding healthcare as a nation-building pillar for the twenty-first century.

The following pitfalls to the usage of HTA should also be sufficiently discussed. For instance, it is of course important to discuss how to apply pharmacoeconomic methodology to the existing pricing system in Japan. However, there is concern that narrowing the issue to simply question of finding a position for HTA in the healthcare system trivializes it and in particular neglects the third and fourth questions raised above. In addition to the question of where to "use" HTA, whether the system can "make use of" HTA also needs to be addressed. Regarding methodology, attention needs to be paid to the issue of cost (price) for the pricing comparator. In the Japanese quasi-VBP system, the similar efficacy comparison method, which allows for premium pricing for new drugs, starts with the assumption of equivalence with the comparator in terms of daily cost. In terms of pharmacoeconomic evaluation, issues remain with this approach and the rules to be used moving forward will need to be discussed. The issue of data uncertainty, traditionally undervalued, can now be considered in light of the recent advances in modeling using computers. Therefore, questions such as how to address uncertainty in modeling and randomized clinical trials, cost-effectiveness analyses, and how to reflect the differences in uncertainty between Phase III trials and post-marketing surveillance in evaluations should not be overlooked.

Discussion is also needed about how to handle the current foreign reference price adjustment. Even if evidence-based pricing is achieved using pharmacoeconomic methods, ultimately the question remains of whether to allow foreign price adjustment subjectively or according to a rule that is influenced by political circumstances. Moreover, making the implementation of HTA in Japan, the prerogative of the Ministry of Health, Labour and Welfare (MHLW) alone would clearly be insufficient in view of the third and fourth questions above. Collaboration among at least three ministries (the MHLW, the Ministry of Economy, Trade and Industry, and the Ministry of Education, Science, Sports and Culture) and the Cabinet Office is expected, as in the case for the 5-year Clinical Trial Activation Plan.

Recently, leadership in the implementation of HTA in Asia has been shown by South Korea, who has also offered some lessons for Japan. First, South Korea has expressed its aim to lead other nations in Asia in the implementation of HTA, requesting that those involved in its implementation view the policy as an international strategy. This could be viewed as an indication of its determination to take its universal healthcare coverage system, which is learned from Japan, further. South Korea's efforts began with the establishment of the Health Insurance Review and Assessment Service (HIRA), which led the implementation of HTA in South Korea. It has subsequently set up as its scientific base, the National Evidence-Based Healthcare Collaborating Agency (NECA), a body within the government that also carries out pharmacoeconomic research. Being among the first in Asia to implement HTA as a national policy, South Korea continues to face challenges with some political and business-related confusion.

2016–2019 marked evolving years for Japan to show its strength. The provisional implementation of cost-effectiveness evaluation was started in FY 2016, which was followed by the annual meeting of Health Technology Assessment international (HTAi) being held in Tokyo in May 2016. HTAi 2016 Tokyo served as a major opportunity to

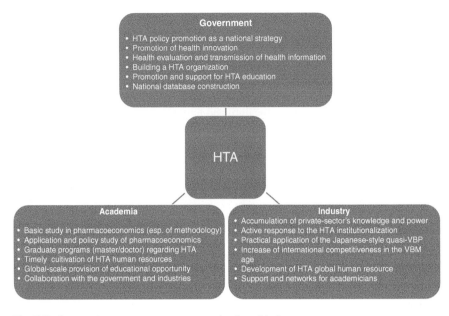

Fig. 2.7 Cooperation among government, academia and industry

present the world with Japan's HTA initiatives. In addition, the ISPOR Asia-Pacific Conference 2018 Tokyo boosted them to the next level of HTA in Japan. The industry is expected to change its passive stance of not doing anything unless required to by the government and to consider the government's implementation of HTA as a business opportunity by calling upon the expertise of the private sector. For this purpose, the industry must have a vision to use pharmacoeconomic evidence even within the existing Japanese quasi-VBP scheme. Additionally, it should request the government to lay out clear rules for HTA in Japan. The government should lead the HTA efforts by following the principle of "no agency, no policy," as in the example of South Korea, while at the same time encouraging research to address methodological issues. During such time of change, the academic sector is also expected to undertake a restructuring and to establish an environment to support world-class pharmacoeconomic research and education to achieve empirical research and practical education (see Fig. 2.7).

Regarding the definition of "value," the ISPOR Special Task Force reported twelve elements of value [16]:

1. Four elements commonly known so far: QALYs gained, net costs, productivity, adherence-improving factors.
2. Eight elements additionally identified: reduction in uncertainty, fear of contagion, insurance value, severity of disease, value of hope, real option-value, equity, scientific spillovers.

The ISPOR experts group encouraged to conduct an augmented cost-effectiveness analysis based on those twelve elements of value. It is left for an important challenge in the future.

2.6.3   Expectations on Wise Spending and Evidence-Based Policy Making

It would be useful for us to know the broader vision and policy of the government beyond the trial implementation of cost-effectiveness policy in MHLW. The 2017 Big-Boned Policy approved by the cabinet states that "…in FY2018, the plan will continue without loosening the reins to push ahead with the efforts in terms of both expenditure and revenue, including the development of more efficient system of social security. In doing so, 'visualization,' promotion of advanced and best practices, and wise spending will be emphasized, as well as promoting evidence-based policy making…" (Chapter 3, Sect. 3.1. On the steady implementation of economic and financial reform) [15], which highlights the concepts of "wise spending" and "evidence-based policy making."

With regard to the reform of drug pricing system, the policy states that the government will "…undertake the fundamental reform of drug pricing system, such as the full implementation of cost-effectiveness evaluation, balance the 'sustainability of universal health care' and 'promotion of innovations,' …and establish a drug pricing scheme that reflects the assessment of cost-effectiveness based on evidence…".

Considering it briefly, the Big-Boned Policy of the government states that "wise spending" is critical in balancing the sustainability of universal healthcare and promotion of innovations, and that a new drug pricing scheme will be established so that it can reflect the cost-effectiveness for VBP as an example of "evidence-based policy making." Accordingly, it appears logical for CMC to act in accordance with this policy and focus on health technology assessment that is based on "wise spending" and "evidence-based policy making," aiming at implementation of VBP on a trial basis as the first in the world.

However, the new rules for price adjustment proposed by CMC, which allows price increase only in case of dominance or a low estimate of ICER (smaller than JPY2M/QALY) with regard to cost-effectiveness, apparently lack pharmacoeconomic rationality, because the number of such cases for new technology is quite a few and hence most of the new technologies may increase health benefit, while at the same time may increase the cost. Consequently, most of innovative technologies with a positive number of ICER higher than JPY2M/QALY will have no chance to get the price adjustment upwards even if the product under evaluation succeeds to attain the ICER as good with the range lower than JPY5M/QALY. On the contrary, even in case of extraordinarily high number of ICER, say JPY30M/QALY, the same discount rate of 90% for premium portion as one in case of JPY10M/QALY will be applied as a flat rate without any discount below the current price.

This situation is not desirable from the perspective of promoting innovations, and it simultaneously violates the principle of pharmacoeconomics that the price of health technology should reflect its value. Also the methods to set an adjustment coefficient, β, with an arbitrary number of 0.1, 0.7, and 0.9 are clearly lacking scientific basis. Thus, the price adjustment introduced by CMC in the institutionalization 2019 is not an ideal implementation of "wise spending" and "evidence-based policy making."

As can be seen, the CMC's insufficiency to understand the principle of VBP has caused the current situation of methodological turmoil. It is certainly a brave but risky attempt to venture into the domain of VBP, despite the theory of VBP not being well established in the world. Therefore, it may be allowed to learn by trial and error to improve the rules for price adjustment, and the adoption of independent "Galapagos" (i.e., the system with unique evolution detached from the world) approaches might also be acceptable under the pilot implementation and even early stage of the full-scale implementation since April 2019. However, the current rules for price adjustment as of FY2019 need to be re-examined from scratch, in order to develop a methodology with strong academic foundation.

As part of this process, the following two-phase approach may be considered, which are based on the idea of making a clear distinction between the two phases of scientific evaluation and interdisciplinary deliberation, instead of reaching a final decision on pricing solely based on algorithmic calculations as proposed by CMC:

1. *The first phase (scientific evaluation)*: development of methodology for price adjustment and formulation on the basis of pharmacoeconomics
   Point 1. Establish multiple levels of thresholds that take into account the ethical and social impacts as well as financial impacts.
   Point 2. Determine which threshold is to be specifically applied to the product under evaluation, in consideration of its ethical, social, and financial impacts (such as by means of multiple-criteria decision analysis).
   Point 3. Evaluate the cost-effectiveness of the product by comparing the ICER estimated based on its current (expected) price with the threshold determined in Point 2. Also, calculate the threshold price that satisfies the evaluation threshold.
   Point 4. For a product with multiple indications (or conditions), perform the above Points 2 and 3 for each indication (or condition) and calculate the threshold price for each indication (or condition).
2. *The second phase (deliberation)*: decision on a tentative price based on discussions at the committee
   Point 1. For a product with single indication (or condition), compare the current price with the threshold price to decide which of the prices should be adopted, or whether to take the average of the two prices, from multiple perspectives before making a decision on a price to be adopted.
   Point 2. For a product with multiple indications (or conditions), compare the current price with the threshold price for each indication (or condition) to decide which of the prices should be adopted, or whether to take the average of the two prices, from multiple perspectives before making a decision on a price to be adopted. Combine the prices determined for multiple indications into a single price as required (e.g., take the weighted average on a pro rata basis according to the percentage of patients with the respective conditions who are treated with the product).

Obviously, the two-phase approach is based on the assumption that the calculation of ICER is essentially required in coverage decision and price adjustment in order to achieve "wise spending." Simultaneously, the development of methodology and its formulation requires deep expertise. Regarding the limited number of HTA experts in Japan, it is a matter of urgency toward full-scale implementation to establish a government-related HTA agency as a national center for the HTA management with highly specialized professionals. Once established, the mission of the HTA agency will then be to study how the new policy and methods on cost-effectiveness currently implemented by CMC could be improved into a future system of "wise spending" that ensures the sustainability of universal health coverage in Japan. In April 2018, the Center for Outcomes Research and Economic Evaluation for Health (for short, CORE2Health or C2H) was established in the National Institute of Public Health in Japan. This center is expected to work for HTA systems development to the future in Japan.

2.6.4 Self-Check!

1. What are the major HTA-related international conferences recently held in Tokyo?
2. What is two-phase approach in pricing decisions?
3. What are the four questions and six pitfalls to be considered in discussions about HTA in Japan?

References

1. Mahlich J, Kamae I, Rossi B (2017) A New Health Technology Assessment System for Japan? Simulating the potential impact on the price of Simeprevir. Int J Technol Assess Health Care 33(1):121–127
2. Kamae I, Kobayashi M (2010) Value-based pricing of new drugs in japan using the principle of incremental cost-effectiveness ratio. ISPOR Connect 16(4):9–10
3. Kamae I, Murata T, Suman D, Yamabe K, Sugimoto T, Kobayashi M (2013) The survey of the japan-style premium scheme in pharmaceutical pricing decisions. ISPOR 16th annual European congress, Dublin, 5 Nov 2013
4. Central Social Insurance Medical Council Special Committee on Cost-Effectiveness. Pilot implementation of cost-effectiveness evaluation, cost-1, 16 Dec 2015 (in Japanese). http://www.mhlw.go.jp/file/05-Shingikai-12404000-Hokenkyoku-Iryouka/0000107178.pdf. Accessed 21 Jul 2017
5. Kamae I (2017) New system on health technology assessment in Japanese Ministry of Health, Labour and Welfare: (1) pilot introduction of 'cost-effectiveness' evaluation. Pharm Med Device Regulat Sci 48(2):82–88. (in Japanese)
6. Kamae I (2017) New system on health technology assessment in Japanese Ministry of Health, Labour and Welfare: (2) how to make a decision on whether cost-effective or not. Pharm Med Device Regulat Sci 48(4):215–220. (in Japanese)
7. Kamae I (2017) New system on health technology assessment in Japanese Ministry of Health, Labour and Welfare: (3) how to reflect the cost-effectiveness in pricing. Pharm Med Device Regulat Sci 48(7):452–459. (in Japanese)
8. Kamae I (2017) New system on health technology assessment in Japanese Ministry of Health, Labour and Welfare: (4) how to attain the sustainability of the system. Pharm Med Device Regulat Sci 48(9):588–593. (in Japanese)

9. Shiroiwa T, Fukuda T, Ikeda S, Takura T, Moriwaki K (2017) Development of an official guideline for the economic evaluation of drugs/medical devices in Japan. Value Health 20(3):372–378

10. The Study Team (2016) (Team Leader: Fukuda T) for "Establishing evaluation methods, data standardization, and assessment systems toward the application of economic evaluation of healthcare technologies to governmental policies." Guideline for preparing cost-effectiveness evaluation to the Central Social Insurance Medical Council. Version 1.0. https://www.ispor.org/PEguidelines/source/Japanese_PE_Guideline.pdf. Accessed 9 Mar 2018

11. Central Social Insurance Medical Council Special Committee on Cost-Effectiveness (2017) Special Committee on Drug Pricing, Special Committee on Health and Medical Devices (the 5th meeting). Response to the issues raised in the pilot implementation of cost-effectiveness evaluation (other issues). Cost/Drug/Device-2 (in Japanese). http://www.mhlw.go.jp/file/05-Shingikai-12404000-Hokenkyoku-Iryouka/0000184180.pdf. Accessed 8 Jan 2018

12. Central Social Insurance Medical Council Special Committee on Drug Pricing (2017) (The 140th meeting). Fundamental reform of the drug pricing system (proposal), Drug-1 (in Japanese). http://www.mhlw.go.jp/file/05-Shingikai-12404000-Hokenkyoku-Iryouka/0000185617.pdf. Accessed 8 Jan 2018.

13. Central Social Insurance Medical Council Special Committee on Drug Pricing (2017) Outline of the fundamental reform of the drug pricing system: appendix (proposal), drug-2. The 143th meeting, 20 Dec 2017 (in Japanese). http://www.mhlw.go.jp/file/05-Shingikai-12404000-Hokenkyoku-Iryouka/0000188705.pdf. Accessed 8 Jan 2018

14. Central Social Insurance Medical Council Special Committee on Drug Pricing (2017). Fundamental reform of the drug pricing system (proposal), drug-2. The 140th meeting, 22 Nov 2017 (in Japanese) http://www.mhlw.go.jp/file/05-Shingikai-12404000-Hokenkyoku-Iryouka/0000188612.pdf. Accessed 8 Jan 2018

15. Cabinet Office. The 2017 Basic Policy on Economic and Fiscal Management and Reform: increasing productivity through investment on human resources" (Big-Boned Policy), outline of the 2017 Basic Policy on Economic and Fiscal Management and Reform (in Japanese). http://www5.cao.go.jp/keizai-shimon/kaigi/cabinet/2017/2017_basicpolicies_ja.pdf. Accessed 5 Jan 2018

16. Lakdawalla DN, Doshi JA, Garrison LP, Phelps CE, Basu A, Danzon PM: Defining Elements of Value in Health Care—A Health Economics Approach: An ISPOR Special Task Force Report [3]. Value in Health 21(2):131-139, February 2018. https://www.valueinhealthjournal.com/article/S1098-3015(17)33892–5/pdf [Accessed December 24, 2018]

MHLW Guidelines for Cost-Effectiveness Analysis

3

3.1 Objectives

Ministry of Health, Labour and Welfare (MHLW) Guidelines Ver. 2.0

1.1. This guideline presents standard methods to perform cost-effectiveness evaluations of medicines and medical devices selected by the Central Social Insurance Medical Council ("selected technologies").

1.2. This guideline is applied to manufacturers' submissions and academic analysis (review and re-analysis).

Pharmacoeconomic (PE) evaluation has evolved rapidly in recent years in Europe and the USA as a method of analysis to assist with decisionmaking for the funding and management of pharmaceuticals and, more broadly, medical devices and services, in order to address issues related to national healthcare systems and health insurance programs. PE guidelines provide guidelines for that process and can be used as a standard format for decisionmaking by the government, as a guide for designing and conducting patient outcome studies and providing guidance for treatment recommendations, or as a template for evaluating publications and reports on economic evaluations.

The Guideline for Preparing Cost-Effectiveness Evaluation to the Central Social Insurance Medical Council [1, 2] issued on January 20, 2016 (hereafter, MHLW Guidelines), provides a standard for conducting economic evaluations to inform the decisionmaking of the Central Social Insurance Medical Council (CMC (or CSIMC) or Chuikyo), as well as a template for assessing submitted evaluation reports. The version 2.0 was approved by Chuikyo on February 20, 2019. It covers the topics listed in Table 3.1.

The original version of this chapter was revised. A correction to this chapter can be found at
https://doi.org/10.1007/978-981-13-5793-0_8

© Springer Nature Singapore Pte Ltd. 2019
I. Kamae, *Health Technology Assessment in Japan*,
https://doi.org/10.1007/978-981-13-5793-0_3

Table 3.1 The table of contents in the analysis guideline of the Ministry of Health, Labour and Welfare

1. Objectives	2. Analysis perspective	3. Target population
4. Comparator(s)	5. Additional benefit	6. Methods of analysis
7. Time horizon	8. Choice of outcome measure	9. Sources of clinical data (except costs)
10. Calculation of healthcare costs	11. Public long-term care costs and productivity loss	12. Discounting
13. Modeling	14. Uncertainty	

Table 3.2 The items to include

1. Type	9. Target drug	17. Rationale for cost data	25. Discount rate of outcome
2. Tile and fiscal year	10. Target population	18. Analysis model	26. Sensitivity analysis of parameters
3. Affiliation of authors	11. Subgroup analysis	19. Systematic review	27. Sensitivity analysis of method
4. Principal objective	12. Selection of comparators	20. Concept of effect	28. Result display
5. Standard report format	13. Time axis	21. Outcome measurement method	29. Incremental analysis
6. Fund disclosure	14. Assumption	22. Utility measurement method	30. Overall cost effectiveness ratio
7. People to present	15. Appropriate analytical method	23. Fairness of the problem presentation	31. Generality of result
8. Analytical position	16. Cost to be included	24. Discount rate of cost	32. Impact on finance

Partially revised: Kamae I, Ikeda T: Draft of Socio-economic Evaluation Guideline for Pharmaceuticals and Medical Devices Based on Japanese Experts Consensus: Potentials and Issues. Jpn J Pharmacoepidemiol, 16(1):24, 2011

Although the content of PE guidelines varies by country, topics required or recommended include those listed in Table 3.2.

3.1.1 Self-Check!

1. What is the role of PE guidelines? List three roles.
2. Do the guidelines issued by the Chuikyo cover all of the topics listed in Table 3.2?

3.2   Analysis Perspective

Ministry of Health, Labour and Welfare (MHLW) Guidelines Ver. 2.0
2.1. The perspective of the analysis should be specified. In particular, the analysis should consider the range of costs corresponding to this perspective.
2.2. "Public healthcare payer's perspective" is a standard perspective that pertains to factors such as costs, comparator(s), and target populations within the range of the public healthcare insurance in Japan.
  2.2.1. Even when an analysis is conducted from a perspective other than the "public healthcare payer's perspective," an analysis from the "public healthcare payer's perspective" should also be submitted.
  2.2.2. There are some healthcare technologies that are not covered by the public healthcare insurance but are publicly funded, such as some prophylactic procedures (e.g., health checkups, vaccinations). Analyses including these technologies should be submitted from the "public healthcare payer's perspective."
2.3. If the effect on public long-term care costs is important with regard to the selected technology, it is acceptable to perform an analysis from the "public healthcare and long-term care payer's perspective."
2.4. If the introduction of a selected technology has a direct influence on productivity, it is acceptable to perform an analysis that considers the broader costs and counts productivity loss as a cost.

Perspectives of analyses generally include the following four levels: (1) patients and families, (2) service provider institutions such as hospitals, (3) insurers (in Japan, the public health insurance system), and (4) society. The range of costs associated with each perspective widens as the perspective shifts from (1) to (4). For cost-effectiveness analyses conducted in recent years, perspectives (1) and (2) have rarely been adopted, and the focus is whether to choose between perspectives (3) and (4). The costs associated with lost productivity as an opportunity costs are typically not included in perspective (3) but are considered in perspective (4). The MHLW Guidelines adopt the perspective of the public healthcare payer, and thus the costs of lost productivity are typically excluded. According to 2.4 of the MHLW Guidelines, as necessary, a wider perspective that includes the costs of lost productivity is permitted (see Terminology: Productivity loss). Additionally, while the perspective of public healthcare does not in principle include long-term care costs, the "perspective of the public healthcare and long-term care payer" may be adopted as a variation of perspective (3) where long-term care costs are considered to have a significant impact.

3.2.1   Self-Check!

1. List the four basic perspectives of evaluation.
2. If productivity costs are to be considered, which perspective should be adopted?

3.3   Target Population

Ministry of Health, Labour and Welfare (MHLW) Guidelines Ver. 2.0
3.1. Patient populations that meet the indications for the selected technology when the manufacturer's analysis is performed should be considered the target population of the cost-effectiveness evaluation.
    3.1.1. In the case that a new indication (or addition of a new dose and administration) is approved between the time of the selection of target technology and the manufacturer's submission of analysis, the new indication (or dose and administration) is also included in the target population.
3.2. If the technology has multiple indications or even in single-indication subpopulations which differ in outcome, application method/dose and administration or comparator of cost-effectiveness evaluation, an analysis should be conducted for each population in principal.
    3.2.1. However, if item 3.2 is difficult to achieve, it is acceptable to perform analyses of limited population(s) considering factors such as the number of patients or features of the illness. The exemption is determined based on agreement between the manufacturer and the National Institute of Public Health/public academic group in consultation.

The target population for analyses must be clearly defined based on objective criteria. Specifically, it is recommended the criteria consist of clinical indices accepted by clinicians, such as specialists. In cases where values for a clinical index and qualitative assessments are measured based on the results of a clinical test, evidence supporting the accuracy of the clinical test such as its sensitivity and specificity is required. The target population may not always be defined easily in terms of clinical epidemiology. Item 3.2 of the MHLW Guidelines suggests that if there are n primary populations and m interventions (or indications) are to be used for each of them, then $n \times m$ analyses would be conducted. Conducting multiple analyses like that can lead to various practical difficulties with conducting randomized clinical trials-cost-effectiveness analyses (RCT-CEA) as well as in modeling the required $n \times m$ or more combinations parameters, which is expected to lead to difficulties concerning data availability. In this regard, Item 3.2.1 of the MHLW Guidelines offers flexibility by allowing for prior arrangements to be made in terms of the choice of the target population.

3.3.1 Self-Check!

1. In what situations may preliminary consultations be made?
2. May the target population be defined qualitatively?

3.4 Comparator(s)

Ministry of Health, Labour and Welfare (MHLW) Guidelines Ver. 2.0

4.1. The comparator(s) should be principally selected from among technologies which are expected to be replaced by the selected technology at the time when the technology was introduced to treat the target population. Among them, technologies which are widely used in clinical practice and which result in a better outcome should be selected.

    4.1.1. Non-treatment or watchful waiting can also be used as comparators.

    4.1.2. Except for the cases described in item 4.1.1, comparator(s) should be selected from among technologies reimbursed by public healthcare insurance.

    4.1.3. If single comparator cannot be determined based on item 4.1, the comparator(s) should be selected considering the comparators in randomized controlled trials (RCTs), referred technology when determining the official price, cost-effectiveness, and other factors, based on agreement in consultation.

4.2. Sufficient explanation of the reasons underlying the selection of the comparator(s) is needed.

In principle, a standard of care (SOC) should be chosen as the comparator according to Item 4.1 of the MHLW Guidelines. However, the guidelines do not use the term "standard of care" as it may not always be clear what that refers to.

According to Item 4.1.1 of the MHLW Guidelines, no treatment or watchful waiting may also be used as comparators. Generally, the value of the incremental cost-effectiveness ratio for the technology being evaluated will vary depending on the comparator chosen (see Sect. 7.4, Chapter 3 to know more details in theory). When no treatment or watchful waiting is selected as comparators, the range of costs and effectiveness to be estimated comes into question, which is often referred to as the "do nothing" problem.

3.4.1   Self-Check!

1. What in principle is selected as the comparator?
2. "No treatment" was chosen as the comparator and its cost and effectiveness were estimated to be zero. Is this appropriate?

3.5   Additional Benefit

Ministry of Health, Labour and Welfare (MHLW) Guidelines Ver. 2.0

5.1. When a cost-effectiveness evaluation is conducted, the additional benefit of the selected technology to the comparator(s) should first be evaluated.

5.2. Evaluations of the additional benefit should be conducted on the basis of a systematic review (SR) of RCTs. The RCTs should be directly compared with the technology selected in Sect. 4. The results of unpublished clinical studies/trials may also be included in the SR if they are deemed appropriate.

    5.2.1. When an SR is conducted, clinical questions (CQs) should be clearly presented. For example, a definition of structured CQs according to PICO (P: patient, I: intervention, C: comparator, O: outcome) may be provided.

    5.2.2. There may be technologies with similar action mechanism or function category to the selected technologies or comparator(s) determined in Sect. 4, which will be expected to show equivalent outcomes to them. These technologies can be included as an intervention (I) or comparator (C) in the SR if they are deemed appropriate in consultation.

    5.2.3. As outcome (O) in item 5.2.1, the most appropriate clinical outcomes (e.g. a "true outcome") should be used to evaluate selected technology from the viewpoint of clinical effectiveness, safety, and health-related quality of life (HRQOL).

    5.2.4. A description of the inclusion/exclusion criteria, databases used, search algorithm, and research selection process (inclusion flow of information) is required in accordance with the PRISMA (Preferred Reporting Items for Systematic Reviews and Meta-Analyses) statement.

    5.2.5. It is acceptable to utilize any existing reliable SR. In such cases, the existing review will be used directly or in combination with a new additional study. In this case, it should confirm the consistency of the existing review by considering the CQs and coverage of the most recent literature.

    5.2.6. If deemed appropriate, pooled results by meta-analysis should be presented. In such cases, the required reporting factors include the employed statistical method, assessment of heterogeneity, forest plot, pooled results, and confidence interval, among others.

5.2.7. When it is obvious that no RCTs have been performed, the process described in Sect. 5.2 can be skipped upon agreement in consultation.

5.2.8. A time point between determining the framework of analysis and manufacturer's submission can be used as a cut-off date for the literature search in the SR.

5.2.9. There may be cases in which the results of new clinical trials are published after the cut-off date defined in item 5.2.8 but are regarded as important information for cost-effectiveness evaluation (e.g., clinical trials with large sample size or reliable results different from current knowledge). Inclusion of these trials in the SR should be considered. In that case, additional SR is not necessarily required.

5.3. When no studies or only insufficient studies are available based on the result of SR described in Sect. 5.2, additional benefit is evaluated by SR of comparative non-RCT (e.g. observational) studies based on Sect. 5.2, if agreed upon in consultation. In that case, sufficient explanation on research quality is needed (e.g., study design, differences in background factors between groups, methods of statistical analysis, sample size, and number of institutions).

5.4. When more reliable results are obtained, additional benefit can be evaluated by re-analysis of existing observational study and/or registry data, if agreed upon in consultation. In that case, sufficient explanation on research quality is needed (e.g., study design, differences in background factors between groups, methods of statistical analysis, sample size, and number of institutions).

5.5. When there are no RCT studies using the same comparator selected in Sect. 4, but there are RCT studies of the selected technology compared to others, additional benefit is evaluated by indirect comparison using SR results, if agreed upon in consultation.

5.5.1. The applicability of item 5.5 depends on the quality of study on the indirect comparison. If an indirect comparison is conducted, sufficient explanation on the prerequisites for the indirect comparison (e.g., heterogeneity of illness, severity, and patient background or similarity of the studies) is also needed.

5.6. When there are only single-arm clinical studies of selected technologies, SR results of the selected technologies (and comparator(s) if needed) should be shown.

5.6.1. In such cases, the evaluation of additional benefit has to consider a number of factors such as the characteristics of the technology and/or disease, background of the participants, and the quality of the studies. Therefore, whether an additional benefit is shown is judged by agreement in consultation.

5.7. There may be cases in which the results obtained by the methods in Sects. 5.3–5.6 have serious problems regarding the quality of the studies and it is expected that the selected technology is not inferior to the comparator. In such cases, the analysis described in Sect. 6 can be performed, assuming the outcome of selected technology is equivalent to that of the comparator(s).

5.8. When there are not any available clinical data on the selected technology in humans, the analysis described in Sect. 6. can be performed, assuming the outcome of the selected technology is equivalent to that of the comparator(s) and considering the approval of the Pharmaceuticals and Medical Devices Agency (PMDA), if agreed upon in consultation.

5.9. When results obtained by the methods in Sect. 5.2–5.6 show that outcomes of the selected technology are inferior to that of the comparator(s), no cost-effectiveness analysis is performed.

Additional benefits refer to the net benefits obtained by subtracting the benefit of the comparator from that of the technology being evaluated. The additional benefits can naturally have a negative value, although in practice only positive values are worth considering, unless the additional cost is also negative (i.e., a cost reduction).

The MHLW Guidelines state that the assessment of additional benefits should be based on a systematic review of randomized control trials (see Terminology: Systematic review), conducted in accordance with the Preferred Reporting Items for Systematic Reviews and Meta-Analyses (PRISMA). Although not required, the results of a meta-analysis (see Terminology: Meta-analysis) may be presented where appropriate. Additionally, indirect comparisons (see Terminology: Indirect comparisons) may be synthesized from the results of a systematic review (see Sect. 6.7, Chapter 6 to know more details in theory). Consultation with biostatistics experts or their participation in the study is recommended for the selection and use of these analysis methods.

3.5.1   Self-Check!

1. Is a meta-analysis required for the assessment of additional benefits in terms of effectiveness?
2. May data from unpublished studies be included for the assessment of additional benefits in terms of effectiveness?
3. What does PICO refer to?
4. What is a true (or final) outcome measure?
5. May existing systematic reviews be used?
6. List five features that should be reported when conducting meta-analysis.
7. What does PRISMA stand for?
8. List three requirements to conducting an indirect comparison.
9. In what situation may an indirect comparison be conducted?
10. What should be done when no comparative studies are available?

3.6 Methods of Analysis

Ministry of Health, Labour and Welfare (MHLW) Guidelines Ver. 2.0

6.1. A cost-effectiveness analysis should be used. In this guideline, cost-effectiveness analysis is defined as an analysis that calculates cost and effectiveness separately without converting effectiveness into monetary units.

6.2. If the analysis described in Sect. 5 allows a judgment that reveals additional benefit, the incremental cost-effectiveness ratio (ICER) should be calculated from the expected cost and effectiveness in each treatment group.

6.3. In the following cases, only the expected cost and effectiveness in each group need to be presented and the ICER should not be calculated.

6.3.1 In cases where the technology is equivalent or superior in terms of effectiveness (non-negative incremental effectiveness) and lower in terms of cost, relative to the comparator, the technology is considered "dominant" without a calculation of ICER.

6.3.2 A cost comparison with the comparator (so-called "cost minimization analysis" [CMA]) should be performed if the analysis described in Sect. 5 does not demonstrate an additional benefit compared to the comparator, but the outcome of the selected technology appears equivalent to that of the comparator.

6.4. If the selected technology has multiple indications or sub-populations defined in item 3.2 and/or 3.2.1, ICER should be calculated for each indication or sub-population.

6.5. If a cost-effectiveness analysis for a selected technology published in an academic journal or an evaluation from a major public health technology assessment (HTA) agency are available, these results should also be presented.

An economic evaluation compares the costs incurred and the resulting clinical effectiveness from adopting the health technology being evaluated. Our focus is the method of comparison used, and there are four basic types of methods (see Fig. 3.1).

The first is a cost-minimization analysis (CMA), in which only the costs of the two health technologies are compared based on the assumption that the alternatives are equivalent in terms of clinical effectiveness. Although comparison of only the costs is the simplest type of comparison, demonstrating that the criterion that the two alternatives being compared are equivalent in terms of clinical effectiveness has been met is needed. A CMA would not be appropriate if there are differences between the alternatives in terms of effectiveness.

The second is the cost-effectiveness analysis (CEA), which is used when there are differences between the alternatives in terms of both clinical effectiveness and cost. A CEA compares alternatives in terms of the costs associated with a unit of effectiveness divided by the costs for each alternative. For

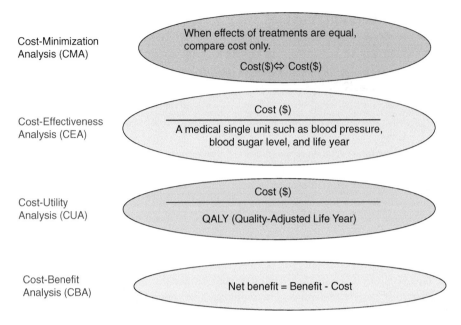

Fig. 3.1 Four methods of analysis

instance, in a CEA of hematopoietic stem cell transplantation (HSCT) and chemotherapy, as shown in Fig. 3.2, the average cost per life year gained can be calculated for each intervention by dividing the cost incurred with the intervention by the expected life years. In a CEA, the incremental cost-effectiveness ratio (ICER, calculated by dividing the difference in the cost of the two alternatives by their difference in effectiveness) is more important than the average cost. In this example, the ICER is 1.80 million JPY per life year gained. Assuming that a ratio of 5 million JPY per life year gained is adopted as an indicator of cost-effectiveness, HSCT is determined to be superior to chemotherapy in terms of cost-effectiveness. Since an absolute standard of cost-effectiveness has not been established, a specific value needs to be separately assigned as a guide to determining cost-effectiveness. This is often referred to as the threshold issue.

As much as possible, a commonly used clinical measure is desirable as the outcome measure used. Types of outcome measures include intermediate outcomes (treatment success rate, lives saved, etc.), outcomes measured in terms of time (disease-free survival, life years saved, and person years saved), and final outcomes (quality-adjusted life years: QALYs). Generally, a CEA that uses QALYs as an outcome is referred to as a cost-utility analysis (CUA).

The only difference between CUA and CEA is in the measure of health outcomes. In CUA, the health-related quality of life (HRQOL) of a patient is first weighed on a scale of 0–1. For example, an HRQOL weight of 0.8 may be assigned to a patient with chronic hepatitis. The HRQOL weight (generally referred to as

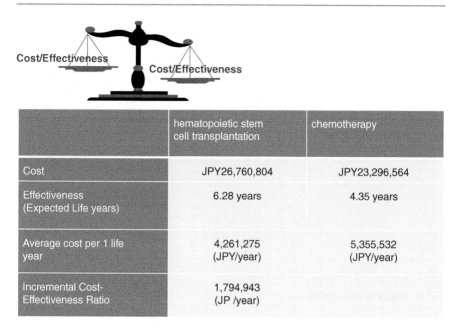

	hematopoietic stem cell transplantation	chemotherapy
Cost	JPY26,760,804	JPY23,296,564
Effectiveness (Expected Life years)	6.28 years	4.35 years
Average cost per 1 life year	4,261,275 (JPY/year)	5,355,532 (JPY/year)
Incremental Cost-Effectiveness Ratio	1,794,943 (JP /year)	

Fig. 3.2 An example of cost-effectiveness analysis

utility) is then used to adjust the life years lived by patients in that particular state of health to determine the QALY. The QALY is thus calculated as the sum of products between life years lived and utility. For example, if a patient has 10 life years, of which 6 are lived with chronic hepatitis (utility of 0.8) and the remaining 4 with cirrhosis (utility of 0.4), then their QALY would be calculated as 6.4 $((6 \times 0.8) + (4 \times 0.4) = 6.4)$.

A cost-benefit analysis (CBA) values health outcomes in monetary terms. Since both the costs incurred and outcomes (benefits) are compared in monetary units, a CBA allows for the evaluation of cost-effectiveness by subtracting costs from benefits. CBAs are often used to evaluate long-term disease control and prevention programs. CBAs are straightforward in that cost-effectiveness is measured in monetary units only, although they are not used as frequently as CEAs due to difficulties in converting health outcomes into monetary values.

Selection of the appropriate evaluation type is done on a case-by-case basis, but as a general rule, the MHLW Guidelines recommend the use of CEA (see Sect. 1.3, Chapter 1 to know more details of CEA). However, the term "cost-effectiveness analysis" is used here in a broad sense to refer to CMA, CEA, and CUA. Generally, a study needs to be designed based on the ten steps shown in Table 3.3. The MHLW Guidelines also require the calculation of the ICER, except in the following two cases, for which an ICER calculation can be omitted:

1. Dominant (more effective and less costly)
2. Additional benefit is not demonstrated

Table 3.3 Ten steps for a research project

1. Set a research theme
2. Design an analytic frame
3. Collect data
4. Organize data
5. Check data error
6. Construct a mathematical model of analysis
7. Assess outcome measures (e.g. QALY) and conduct the analysis
8. Improve the modeling structure
9. Sensitivity analysis
10. Report research results

It is clear that the ICER has no significance in case (1) above.

For case (4), the use of a CMA may be allowed as a practical approach when the additional benefits of a technology compared to the comparator are not demonstrated, even though evidence of equivalence or non-inferiority is not clearly demonstrated and the requirement for conducting a CMA (i.e., equivalence in terms of effectiveness) is not satisfied.

3.6.1 Self-Check!

1. Calculate the average cost per life year gained for HSCT and chemotherapy in Fig. 3.2 and confirm that the values match those in the figure.
2. Calculate the ICER of HSCT compared to chemotherapy in Fig. 3.2 and confirm that the value matches the one in the figure.
3. What should be done when no statistically significant difference in clinical effectiveness is demonstrated?
4. List two cases when the calculation of an ICER is not required.

3.7   Time Horizon

Ministry of Health, Labour and Welfare (MHLW) Guidelines Ver. 2.0

7.1. The time horizon should be sufficiently long to evaluate the influence of the technology on cost and effectiveness.

7.2. The same time horizon should be applied for both cost and effectiveness.

7.3. The reason for setting this time horizon should be specified.

The appropriate period of analysis depends on the study design, with the following two main approaches for cost-effectiveness studies:

• Randomized clinical trials–cost-effectiveness analysis (RCT-CEA)
• Modeling research

In the former approach, both effectiveness and cost data are collected and analyzed within a clinical trial.

The period of analysis will thus be short term, a few years at the longest, including several weeks for the trial period and a subsequent follow-up period. This type of study is sometimes referred to as a piggyback study or simply a randomized clinical trials–cost-effectiveness analysis (RCT-CEA).

In the latter approach, the evaluation is based on mathematical modeling using computer simulations. The Chuikyo thus specifies appropriate approaches to modeling in its guidelines (see Sect. 3.13, Chapter 3 to know more details in theory of modeling).

In addition to the period of analysis, differences between the two approaches regarding other features should be recognized. An RCT-CEA study allows for a swift conclusion, and its advantages are that it is based on evidence from actual collected data, the validity of the results, and the transparency of the analysis. By contrast, a modeling study allows for desktop analysis using computer simulations and has the advantage of incorporating a long-term analysis (e.g., lifetime follow-up), although a longer-term period of analysis requires that attention be paid to the model validity and the results of the modeling. Additionally, given that the behavior of computer simulations is somewhat of a black box, the transparency of the analysis can also come into question. A modeling study is generally superior in terms of analysis effort and cost (Table 3.4). From a scholarly perspective, the ISPOR good practice guidelines presented in Table 3.5 are well-recognized internationally.

Table 3.4 Comparison of two analytic approaches

	RCT-CEA	Modeling
Assessment of new drugs	Clinical trials	Desk analysis
Statistical test	Implemented	Not implemented
Data	Actual data	Literature data
Cost, work	Large	Relatively small
Time horizon	Short-term only	Possibly long-term
Validity of results	High	Caution needed
Transparency of analysis	High	Caution needed

Table 3.5 The ISPOR's principles of clinical trials and modeling studies for cost-effectiveness

• Ramsey S, Willke R, Briggs A, Brown R, Buxton M, Chawla A, Cook J, Glick H, Liljas B, Petitti D, Reed S. Good research practices for cost-effectiveness analysis alongside clinical trials: the ISPOR RCT-CEA Task Force report. Value Health. 2005 Sep–Oct;8(5):521–33
• Weinstein MC, O'Brien B, Hornberger J, Jackson J, Johannesson M, McCabe C, Luce BR; ISPOR Task Force on Good Research Practices—Modeling Studies. Principles of good practice for decision analytic modeling in health-care evaluation: report of the ISPOR Task Force on Good Research Practices—Modeling Studies. Value Health. 2003 Jan–Feb;6(1):9–17
Principles from 2003 to 2016 are available at the following sites: http://www.ispor.org/research_initiatives/hs_initiatives.asp

3.7.1   Self-Check!

1. Which of the two approaches, RCT-CEA or modeling studies, generally use a longer-term period of analysis?
2. What problems can arise when using a longer-term period of analysis?

3.8   Choice of Outcome Measure

Ministry of Health, Labour and Welfare (MHLW) Guidelines Ver. 2.0

8.1. Quality-adjusted life years (QALY) should be used in principle.

    8.1.1. When it is difficult to calculate QALY and CMA is applied, other outcome measures can be used, upon agreement in consultation.

8.2. When QALY is calculated, the QOL score should be reflective of the value in a general population (using preference-based measure [PBM] or direct methods such as the standard gamble [SG] and the time trade-off [TTO]). However, systematic difference may exist between QOL scores measured by SG and by TTO.

    8.2.1. If Japanese QOL scores are newly collected for a cost-effectiveness analysis, the use of PBMs with a value set developed in Japan using TTO (or mapped onto a TTO score) is recommended as the first choice.

    8.2.2. If data corresponding to item 8.2" are unavailable, it is acceptable to use mapping of other appropriate HRQOL data. When using a QOL score obtained from mapping, the conversion into a QOL score via an appropriate method should be explained.

8.3. When the QOL score is assessed by PBM, the subjects' own QOL responses should be used.

    8.3.1. In the case of using PBMs, responses from a proxy (e.g., family member or caregiver) may be used only when the subject cannot respond.

    8.3.2. In the case of using PBMs by proxy responses from a healthcare professional, possible discrepancies from subjects' own responses should be explained.

    8.3.3. If it is difficult to directly collect QOL scores from subjects, it is acceptable for general people to evaluate the presented health scenario by direct methods. It is better for the validity of the presented scenario to be confirmed by clinicians. In this case, use of the TTO method is recommended.

8.4. As long as a QOL score that satisfies Sects. 8.2 and 8.3 is available, the use of Japanese results is preferentially recommended.

    8.4.1. If Japanese research is absent or insufficient but high-quality research is available overseas, it is acceptable to use the data collected overseas.

The term "effectiveness" in cost-effectiveness evaluations can include a wide range of outcome measures such as the following measures, in addition to narrowly defined clinical effectiveness.

3.8.1   Clinical Effectiveness

Clinical effectiveness refers to objective data expressed as clinical endpoints. For example, blood pressure measured for the management of daily health is one such measure. They can be classified into intermediate outcomes (including blood pressure, treatment success rate, and lives saved) and final outcomes (mortality, expected life years, and life years saved). Outcomes such as disease-free survival, life years saved, and person years saved are also referred to as clinical effectiveness which takes time into consideration.

3.8.2   Utility

Utility refers to the preferences or desires of an individual for a specific health state, measured quantitatively given some degree of uncertainty. Specifically, a particular health state is assigned a score on a scale from 0 to 1, whereby death is 0 and perfect health is 1. Approaches to measuring utilities include the visual analogue scale (VAS), in which subjects are asked to intuitively value specific disease states on a scale from 0 to 1; the standard gamble method, which involves subjects making a hypothetical wager where they are asked whether or not to wager against death; the Time-Trade-Off (TTO) method, in which subjects weigh the value of returning to perfect health against trading years of remaining life expectancy; as well as instruments that measure health status with questionnaires (well-known examples include EQ-5D and EQ-5D-5L).

3.8.3   Health-Related Quality of Life (HRQOL)

HRQOL is a measure that comprehensively evaluates the individual satisfaction that is perceived for a given health state including things like the ability to perform activities of daily living (ADL). The measurement of HRQOL involves a number of difficulties, but a typical approach is to use patient-reported outcomes (PRO) as defined by the US Food and Drug Administration (FDA). Utilities obtained with EQ-5D are also a measure of HRQOL.

3.8.4   Benefit

Benefit refers to the outcome of adopting a health technology, measured in monetary terms, such as the amount of life insurance benefits received. It often involves the estimation of the statistical value of a life. However, it should be noted that the term "benefit," when used in the concept of risk and benefit, simply refers to clinical benefits relative to risk, including efficacy and effectiveness. The term benefit is often used in a broader sense and requires careful attention to the context that it is used in. The MHLW Guidelines regard the term of benefit in a broader sense, implying "effectiveness" (see Item 5, Additional Benefit).

In a health economic evaluation, the use of a common clinical endpoint even for different conditions is desired, and the UK's NICE has adopted QALYs as a final outcome measure. QALY is useful as a unified measure that captures changes in both the quantity and quality of life lived, calculated by weighting life years by utility (or HRQOL measured on an interval scale).

Conceptually, QALY is defined as the difference in quality-adjusted life expectancy (QALE) between two interventions (e.g., administration of a new drug and a comparator drug). QALE refers to the number of life years remaining at a given age, adjusted for the state of health at the time, and is calculated using the following formula:

$$QALE = \text{life expectancy} \times \text{average HRQOL}.$$

QALE thus reflects the impact of illnesses and interventions on the quantity (life expectancy) and quality (HRQOL) of life lived. Since HRQOL is a quality weight between 0 and 1, QALE is generally shorter than life expectancy. Once QALE is obtained, QALYs can be calculated using the following formula:

$$QALYs = QALE_{\text{intervention1}} - QALE_{\text{intervention2}}$$
$$= \text{life expectancy}_{\text{intervention1}} \times \text{average HRQOL}_{\text{intervention1}}$$
$$- \text{life expectancy}_{\text{intervention2}} \times \text{average HRQOL}_{\text{intervention2}}.$$

Many illnesses impact the quality of life of patients in varying degrees depending on the patient's health state. Therefore, data on changes in health status over a long period for the cohort of interest are needed. For instance, by following a group of patients with heart disease classified into five categories of health status (S_1, healthy; S_2, mild; S_3, moderate; S_4, severe; and S_5, death) and recording the number of years patients remain in each status, a lifetime health pathway can be drawn (see Fig. 3.3) from which QALE can be obtained with the area under the curve representing the lifetime health pathway.

In practice, the summation method and Markov models are often used for calculations. The summation method calculates QALYs for a particular cohort by obtaining, for each period of a particular health status, the product of the difference in utility between two treatments and the length of time patients live with that particular level of utility, and then summing all products. The steps are summarized in Table 3.6.

QALYs can also be calculated using a life table for the cohort of interest. Moreover, disability-adjusted life years (DALYs) can also be used as a measure that considers the health effects of an intervention in terms of averting the loss of health. Conceptually, DALYs can be calculated using the following formula:

$$DALYs = \text{years of life lost}\left(YLL\right) + \text{years lived with disability}\left(YLD\right)$$

(where YLD is the disability weight of a specific disease × number of years disabled and the disability weight is 1 − HRQOL).

DALYs differ from QALYs in that while QALYs consider the relative "gain" from the health effects of an intervention, DALYs consider the ability to "avert" loss of health. The two approaches are complementary, and DALYs and QALYs are

Utility values

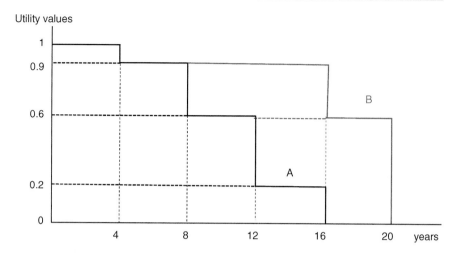

The utility values of health states S1, 2, 3, 4, and 5 are respectively 1, 0.9, 0.6, 0.2, 0. The treatment effect is the same for both A and B for the first 8 years; however, B can survive for 4 years longer.

Fig. 3.3 Difference of lifelong health paths between treatments A and B

Table 3.6 Steps for summation

1. Describe the change in health conditions of a cohort group in detail
2. Calculate the time span spent in each health condition
3. Obtain the utility (or health-related QOL) for each health condition
4. Calculate the difference between the utilities of two groups multiplied by the time span of the different health conditions
5. Aggregate all the values for each health condition obtained at Step 4

essentially equivalent. DALYs, however, have not been used as frequently in cost-effectiveness analysis in recent years, being mainly used as a tool to evaluate health programs in developing countries.

The MHLW Guidelines, in principle, adopt QALYs as the outcome measure. The use of an outcome measure other than QALYs requires prior consultation (Sect. 8.1.1 of the MHLW Guidelines) if it is difficult to calculate QALY and CMA is applied.

Item 8.2 of the MHLW Guidelines accepts different methods to measure quality of life. In calculating QALYs, two big issues are whether a valid interval scale is used and the possibility of inconsistency resulting from the concomitant use of different methods (see Sect. 6.2, Chapter 6 to know more details in theory). The MHLW Guidelines mention to pay careful attention to a discrepancy in scores measured by SG and TTO. Also, the use of TTO tariff developed in Japan is recommended as the first choice of PBMs (see Item 8.2.1). Moreover, it is not always simple what is considered "appropriate" in terms of PRO and the "appropriate" conversion method with the mapping mentioned in Item 8.2.2 of the MHLW Guidelines, and its validation is not always simple.

3.8.5   Self-Check!

1. What would the QALE be when the population of a country in FY 2010 has an average life expectancy of 77.6 years at one year of age and an average HRQOL of 0.832?
2. In congenital joint malformation, the average HRQOL is 0.67 for no treatment and can be improved to 0.72 with surgery (life expectancy is equivalent for the two groups at 76.5 years). In this case, what would be the QALYs gained from the surgery?
3. What is the QALE for treatments A and B in Fig. 3.3, and what are the QALYs?
4. How would DALYs be calculated with Fig. 3.3?

3.9   Sources of Clinical Data (Except Costs)

Ministry of Health, Labour and Welfare (MHLW) Guidelines Ver. 2.0

9.1. Calculations of the ICER should preferentially use effectiveness, safety, and QOL data (inclusion of parameters such as transition probability for model analysis) derived from high-quality research, with a high evidence level reflective of practical clinical results in Japan.

9.1.1. The selection of effectiveness, safety, and QOL data on the basis of an SR of Japanese and overseas clinical research is recommended. This review may also include unpublished clinical study/trial data if deemed appropriate.

9.1.2. Data with a high evidence level should be used preferentially. The use of data deemed appropriate from the viewpoints of research quality, target population, and external validity is recommended (for example, it is possible that the results of an RCT may differ markedly from practical clinical results).

9.1.3. Data by re-analysis of existing study and/or registry data can be used if deemed appropriate. In that case, detailed information on patient background, statistical methods, etc. must be provided.

9.2. Japanese data should be used preferentially if there is evident heterogeneity between Japanese and overseas data.

9.3. If the data do not differ statistically significantly between the selected technology and the comparator(s), pooled data of both groups should be applied. Otherwise, the rationale that additional benefit is shown by the process described in Sect. 5 etc. must be explained.

9.4. Regarding evaluation of medical devices, if there are reliable and quantitative data, analysis reflecting "learning effect" (i.e., improvement of treatment effect by the accumulation of clinicians' experience) or "product improvement effect" can be submitted in addition to analysis not considering the effects, upon agreement in consultation.

In the above citation, the recommended data sources are specified, and it can be summarized as follows:

- High-quality and high evidence level studies.
- A preference for sources that reflect actual clinical performance.
- Domestic and international systematic reviews are recommended.
- Indirect comparisons are acceptable in some cases.

In terms of actual clinical performance, an RCT-CEA may be conducted. In such cases, one issue related to the quality and evidence level of a study is the handling of missing and censored data. In this regard, the ISPOR guidelines (see Table 3.5) make the following recommendations:

- It is not recommended to eliminate cases with missing data, for it may introduce bias or severely reduce the power to test hypotheses.
- Small amounts of missing data may be ignored if doing so does not introduce bias.
- Statistical approaches should be used for inputting missing data.
- Censoring should be reported.

Regarding data management in an RCT-CEA, cost data should be collected and managed together in the case report form. When collecting cost data from an insurer's database or pre- and post-clinical trial records, the analyst must obtain prior written consent from the patients being studied or the insurer.

3.9.1   Self-Check!

1. When the level of the evidence is nearly equal but there is a difference in findings for domestic and overseas studies, which findings should be prioritized?
2. Is it acceptable to reanalyze an existing study and/or registry data?
3. Is it acceptable to consider "learning effect"?

3.10   Calculation of Healthcare Costs

Ministry of Health, Labour and Welfare (MHLW) Guidelines Ver. 2.0
10.1. Only public healthcare costs should be included in the case of analysis from the public healthcare payers' perspective.
10.2. Healthcare costs of each health state include only related costs that are directly affected by the selected technology and do not include unrelated costs.
10.3. Healthcare costs of each health state should reflect the average resource consumption and standard clinical practices in Japan.

10.4. It is recommended that claims databases established in Japan, which reflect actual clinical practice from the viewpoint of Sect. 10.3, should be used to estimate the costs of each health state, if deemed appropriate. However, this recommendation does not apply to cases in which it is difficult to define health states using only information from claims data, insufficient data have been accumulated in the database, and so on.

    10.4.1. Definition of each health state and its rationale is required when claims data are used for cost estimation.

    10.4.2. The methods and rationale for handling outliers and unrelated costs should be shown.

10.5. Micro-costing (by medical fee schedule etc.) based on the definitions of the standard clinical process can be used, if it is difficult to estimate the costs of each health state by claims database or if micro-costing is more appropriate.

    10.5.1. In the case of the application of micro-costing, the rationale for costing should be shown from the viewpoint of item 10.3. It may be better to identify relevant items and/or estimate the amount of medical resource consumption in the claims database.

    10.5.2. When micro-costing is used, the medical resource consumption and unit costs should be reported separately.

    10.5.3. In principle, for the estimation of resource consumption in item 10.5.2, the amount of injection products consumed should be defined by the number of vials rather than by patient dosages.

10.6. The estimation should include not only the costs of the selected technology and the comparator(s) but also the costs of factors such as adverse events and related future events.

10.7. An analysis of the public healthcare costs should include not only the portion of costs paid by the insurer but also those paid by the government and patients as copayment (i.e., the total public healthcare expenses).

    10.7.1 Based on the principal in item 2.2.2, the analysis should include the costs of health checkups, vaccinations, or similar procedures that are funded publicly and not reimbursed by Japan's public healthcare insurance.

10.8. Unit costs should be derived from the latest medical fee schedule, drug price lists, or similar resources. It is particularly essential to use the latest unit costs for the selected technology or comparator(s).

    10.8.1. Even if existing cost-of-illness studies or analyses of claims data are used, unit costs at the time of evaluation, not at the time that the medical resources consumed, should be applied. It is acceptable to make adjustments such as multiplication by the medical payment system revision rate.

    10.8.2. Such adjustments may be omitted if the influence on results is minimal.

10.9. If generics of the comparator(s) are already on the market, analysis using these costs should be also submitted.

10.10. If the costs of selected technology and/or comparator(s) are included in bundled payment, the estimation should be based on fee-for-service payment.

10.11. Future costs should also be estimated on the basis of current medical resource consumption and unit costs.

10.12. Calculations of medical resource consumption based on overseas data will require attention regarding possible differences in healthcare technology use between Japan and overseas countries. The unit costs in Japan should be applied in the analysis.

In health economic evaluations, cost refers to opportunity cost. Generally, when engaging resources for a particular good or service, benefits that could have been received through alternative resource uses are forgone. Therefore, the opportunity cost is the value of the best forgone benefits. For instance, by engaging health resources (human and physical), such as surgeons, anesthesiologists, surgical nurses, and operating rooms in an emergency surgery for appendicitis, the next best service that can be provided at the same time using the same resources (e.g., cholelithotomy) must be given up (see Fig. 3.4). The benefit forgone in that case is the opportunity cost.

There are three types of costs to be considered in analysis: (1) direct costs, (2) indirect costs, and (3) intangible costs. Direct costs are costs that are directly associated with the delivery of medical care and can be classified into direct medical costs (including costs of drugs, surgeries, screening services, hospital stays, and visits) and direct nonmedical costs (including costs of travel to the hospital, babysitter costs, time costs associated with caregivers and undergoing treatment, etc.). Indirect costs refer to the costs associated with lost productivity, such as lost work time and leisure time that results from morbidity and mortality. Intangible costs are costs associated with pain and emotional distress, which are obscure and difficult to

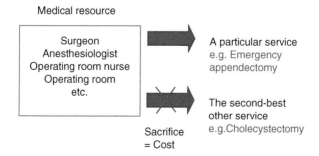

Fig. 3.4 Opportunity costs

measure. They cannot be objectively quantified and are, thus, generally excluded from cost estimation.

Cost estimation involves the following three steps:

1. Resource identification: First, events that occur along the timeline of a condition of interest are listed, and resources that are utilized during that timeline are identified.
2. Resource measurement: Utilization of identified resources is quantified.
3. Resource valuation: Resource utilization is valued in monetary terms.

Micro-costing is a method of resource use estimation in accordance with these three steps. With gross costing, on the other hand, Steps 2 and 3 above are omitted, and an all-inclusive estimation of the costs for the individual items identified in Step 1 above, such as in-patient services, pharmaceutical uses, etc. (see Table 3.7), is conducted. Sources of such data include the MHLW's Survey of Medical Care Activities in Public Health Insurance (by the Social Statistics Division, Statistics and Information Department, Minister's Secretariat), the Estimates of National Medical Care Expenditure (by the Health Statistics Office, Vital and Health Statistics Division, Statistics and Information Department, Minister's Secretariat), and the Medical Fee Information Service (by the MHLW Health Insurance Bureau).

Although gross costing is a relatively simple approach that utilizes databases and literature, the obtained cost estimates may be too general and may not adequately capture all incurred costs. Micro-costing is thus useful when specific cost data are not available through databases and literature, although precise estimates require a lot of work and may lack external validity.

Costs can also be divided into variable and fixed costs. Variable costs refer to the value of resources whose utilization varies depending on the intervention used, and they are always included in the estimation. On the other hand, fixed costs refer to the value of resources whose utilization remains constant when two interventions are being compared, such as equipment and administrative costs. Fixed costs can generally be excluded from a CEA that estimates an ICER, as they cancel out in the calculation of incremental costs (see Sect. 1.4, Chapter 1 to know more details in calculation). When the impact of an intervention on fixed costs is substantial or the analysis is long term, then the fixed costs associated with an intervention may differ from those of the comparator, in which case they need to be included in the cost estimation.

Table 3.7 Difference between micro- and gross costing

Micro-costing	Gross costing
• Identify, measure, and evaluate resource to use, following three steps for value estimation	• Comprehensive estimate on each service (hospital treatment, medicine, etc.)
• Useful when specific cost data is not available on database or literature	• Use cost data from database and literature
• Need labor	• Use diagnostic classification codes
• Frequently produce error	• Simple (only Step 1)
• Deficient in outer validity	• Not always properly cover target costs

Special types of costs include friction and transfer costs. Friction costs are costs incurred by the employer due to the patient's absence from work or termination of employment as a result of ill health (e.g., differences between the productivity of the patient and the replacement worker and costs associated with training replacement workers). Transfer costs refer to the administrative costs incurred in the process of making transfer payments, such as social security payments (e.g., from individuals to the government to individuals), and the money being transferred itself is not considered. Friction and transfer costs are generally excluded from the analysis unless they are significant.

There is also the consideration of how to handle future costs. It is generally said that an effective intervention will reduce future healthcare costs, while, conversely, some argue that avoiding an early disease could lead to an increase in healthcare costs due to the risk of another disease occurring later in life. At the same time, premature death due to ill heath will result in a reduction of future medical costs. Therefore, the cost of treating a disease in the future that arises when avoiding the disease of interest and the cost incurred as a result of premature death are excluded from the estimation but may be considered in a sensitivity analysis (see Sects. 1.3, Chapter 1 and Sect. 3.14, Chapter 3 to know more details of sensitivity analysis in theory), as needed.

The range of costs to be included in the estimation also varies with the perspective of evaluation. Perspectives include (1) patients and families (which estimates costs such as out-of-pocket payments, costs for over-the-counter drugs and caregivers), (2) service provider institutions (which estimates costs incurred within a particular healthcare facility), (3) insurers (which estimates costs incurred within a health insurance system), and (4) society (which estimates all costs). The societal perspective considers a broad range of costs in the estimation, including indirect costs such as lost productivity, whereas the insurer's perspective does not always require that direct nonmedical costs and lost productivity be included. It is important to always clearly specify the range of cost estimation as it may have an impact on the ICER. Ideally, an economic evaluation would use the societal perspective and consider opportunity costs instead of market prices. However, where official economic evaluation guidelines are issued, the recommended perspective should be adopted (e.g., in the case of the UK's NICE, insurance payments by the NHS).

Item 10.1 of the MHLW Guidelines specifies the range of public healthcare costs to be included in public healthcare payers' perspective. In terms of public healthcare costs, Item 10.7 of the MHLW Guidelines requires that "total public healthcare expenses" be considered. The cost of preventive care such as health checkups and vaccinations should be included, and the handling of public healthcare expenses is defined as follows:

Total public healthcare expenses = costs incurred by the insurer, government, and patients + public healthcare costs such as the cost of health checkups and vaccinations, etc.

The MHLW Guidelines, as a general rule, recommend to use "claims databases" in Japan and also accept that unit costs and quantities of resources consumed be specified in the data analysis and reporting of results. This is for the purpose of identifying the price-volume relationship in the costs.

South Korea's HIRA adopts a similar approach for cost accounting. Regarding the discrepancy of consumption data between domestic and international sources, domestic data are required for unit costs. Moreover, the unit costs that are current at the time of analysis are desired. However, obtaining unit costs at the same timing might be difficult, and therefore such adjustments for the same timing may not be necessary if the impact of adjustment is practically negligible (Item 10.8.2 of the MHLW Guidelines). Generally speaking, costs should be estimated on a fee-for-service basis and not as flat payment, such as the case in the diagnosis procedure combination (DPC) payment system in Japan.

For a new health technology, information on current costs may be insufficient. For example, the variability of the data may be high, there may be a lack of credible data, or it may include "protocol-driven costs" from clinical trials. In such cases, an additional survey questionnaire may be required to derive model cost estimates. When collecting cost data from physicians, survey questions must be carefully designed, and the results should be validated.

If generics are on the market, the analysis with the prices of generics should be submitted (Item 10.9).

3.10.1 Self-Check!

1. What is opportunity cost?
2. For what perspective of cost estimation would indirect costs be considered?
3. Name the types of costs included in public healthcare expenses in Japan.
4. Where cost = A × B, identify A and B.
5. May all-inclusive costs, such as those based on the DPC system in Japan, be used in a cost estimation?

3.11 Public Long-Term Care Costs and Productivity Loss

Ministry of Health, Labour and Welfare (MHLW) Guidelines Ver. 2.0

11.1. Public long-term care costs and productivity losses arising from an inability to perform work should not be included in the base-case analysis.

    11.1.1. It is acceptable to include public long-term care costs and productivity losses in additional analyses only if they can be estimated by Japanese data. However, judgments regarding the appropriateness of including productivity losses should consider the possibility of working in the context of the illness characteristics.

11.2. When public long-term care costs are included in the analysis, it is recommended that these costs should be calculated based on the care level.

11.3. The amount utilized under public long-term care insurance should be based on the actual quantity of resources consumed. If this quantity is difficult to determine, it is acceptable to use the average amount utilized per beneficiary or similar data.

11.4. Decreases in productivity losses may be classified as follows:

(A) Decreases arising directly from healthcare technology (e.g., treatment-related shortening of hospital stay).

(B) Decreases arising indirectly from outcome improvements (e.g., alleviation of illness, survival period extension).

When productivity loss is included in an analysis, only (A) should be included in the calculation of costs.

11.5. Productivity losses should be estimated using the human capital method. This method was designed to generate estimations based on the expected earned wage in the absence of illness.

11.5.1. The unit wage used for estimations of productivity loss should be the average wage across all industries, all ages, and both genders or the average wage for each age group in all industries and both genders derived from the latest "Basic Survey on Wage Structure" (Wage Census) and not discriminate by income.

11.5.2. Estimations of productivity loss require an actual investigation of the employment status in the target population (i.e., a measure of the days or hours of work missed). The actual measured number of days or hours should then be multiplied by the average wage across all industries, all ages, and both genders to estimate the productivity loss.

11.5.3. If the item described in item 11.5.2 is difficult to perform, productivity loss should be calculated by multiplying the expected number of days (excluding holidays) or hours of work missed in the target population by the average wage across all industries, all ages, and both genders. A 100% employment rate should be assumed for those aged 18 years and older. However, note that this method may overestimate productivity losses.

11.6. If other individuals (e.g., family members) experience productivity losses due to the provision of nursing or informal patient care, it is acceptable to count these productivity losses as costs under the same conditions and using the same methods as those used to calculate the patient's productivity loss.

11.7. Time costs that are unrelated to a decrease in work should not be included in the cost estimations.

Items 2.3, 2.4, and 11.1.1 of the MHLW Guidelines state that long-term care costs and productivity loss may be included in an additional analysis only if they can be estimated by Japanese data, so the adoption of the perspective of public healthcare and long-term care payers or a wider perspective is allowed. Accordingly, the guidelines specify the requirements in estimating long-term care costs and productivity loss. The general rule is as follows:

Base case analysis: the perspective of public healthcare payer
Additional analysis: the perspective of public healthcare and long-term care payers
    or a wider perspective

However, analysts should carefully consider the following two points in deciding whether an additional analysis is required.

1. How meaningful would it be to consider a wider range of costs in the estimation?
2. If the purpose of the cost-effectiveness evaluation is to inform the decision on price adjustments in the fee schedule, should long-term care costs and productivity loss be considered?

The first point relates to the calculation of the ICER where the numerator is the difference in costs between two compared interventions. As for the fixed costs in the previous section, costs that are identical in two interventions cancel out by subtraction and thus need not be included in ICER calculations. Even when long-term care and productivity costs are included, they may not have a significant impact on the ICER if the difference between two interventions is negligible, as in the case of fixed costs. Item 11.4 of the MHLW Guidelines requires that a reduction in productivity loss resulting from improved outcomes be excluded from the analysis (B). If only (A) is considered, the difference in productivity loss between two interventions might be minimal.

The second point above requires further discussion, as the estimate of an ICER is eventually used for pricing decisions with respect to adjusting the premium portion of the public price. An additional CEA with wider costs might clarify the value of the premium better. Generally, the perspective of the public healthcare payer would be sufficient to inform pricing decisions under the health insurance system.

3.11.1 Self-Check!

1. Which perspective should be used in the base case analysis?
2. What are the requirements in terms of necessary care levels when estimating long-term care costs?
3. Which wage rates should be used as a unit cost in estimating productivity loss?

3.12 Discounting

> **Ministry of Health, Labour and Welfare (MHLW) Guidelines Ver. 2.0**
> 12.1. Future costs and effectiveness must be discounted and converted into present values.
>   12.1.1. Discounting is not needed if the time horizon is 1 year or less or is otherwise sufficiently short to ignore the influence of discounting.
> 12.2. Both cost and effectiveness should be discounted at a rate of 2% per year.
> 12.3. The discount rate should be subjected to sensitivity analysis and should be changed at the same rate of 0–4% per year for both costs and effectiveness.

Discounting is required in the MHLW Guidelines. However, there is no absolute standard in terms of the correct discount rate to use. The concept of discounting reflects the time preference of individuals when they believe that monetary values decline over time. As such, although the discount rate is often confused with the rate of inflation or interest rate, the principle is different.

The preferences of people are influenced by the period of time, the state of the national economy, and their cultural and social values, thus making the establishment of an absolute standard impossible. Accordingly, the discount rate specified in the MHLW Guidelines can be viewed as a guide for a reasonable range of the rate to be used in practice. The Chuikyo set the standard rate for the base case analysis at 2% per year and requires that a sensitivity analysis with the rate varying within a specified range from 0% to 4% be conducted. The MHLW Guidelines also require that both costs and outcomes be discounted at the same rate. Although controversy exists regarding whether outcomes should be discounted, discounting of only costs and not outcomes can selectively lower an ICER. It is therefore reasonable, in theory, to discount both costs and outcomes.

The discounting formula given in the Glossary, $C_p = \dfrac{C_i}{(1+d)^{i-1}}$, only considers a time point of i years later.

If a multi-year program is designed, for which the estimation of a cumulative cost is required, the sum of all costs calculated for the respective years must be obtained.

It should be noted that when $i = 1$ in this formula (i.e., 1 year later), then $C_p = C_1$ and discounting would not be considered.

3.12.1 Self-Check!

1. Would a larger discount rate result in an increase in present value or a decrease?
2. Present a discounting formula for estimating the cumulative cost of a 3-year program.

3.13   Modeling

Ministry of Health, Labour and Welfare (MHLW) Guidelines Ver. 2.0

13.1. To predict prognosis and future expenses, it is acceptable to conduct a model analysis using a decision analytic model, Markov model, and/or other models in accordance with the principle described in Sect. 7.

13.2. Model analysis should present the validity of the model. For example:

(A) Internal validity: This addresses why a model with a given structure has been created, whether or not the natural course of illness has been sufficiently evaluated, whether or not the parameters used are appropriate, and other factors.

(B) External validity: This addresses whether the estimation yielded from the model is appropriate in comparison to existing other clinical data, and other factors.

13.3. The assumption used to create the model should be described clearly.

13.4. All parameters and data sources used for model creation should be shown.

13.5. The model used and the calculation processes should be submitted in the form of electronic files. The model must be easily understood by third-party experts and all main parameters (transition probability, QOL score, and healthcare costs) must be able to be changed.

13.5.1. It is better that not only total costs but also the breakdown (in the case of micro-costing, the medical resource consumption and unit costs of each item) can be changed. Especially, the unit costs of the selected technology and comparator(s) must be able to be changed by academic analysis group in the model.

13.6. Half-cycle correction should be used in the Markov model if the length of the Markov cycle is long and its influence on the results is not negligible.

Modeling may use approaches such as decision trees and Markov models. Although decision tree modeling is a fundamental approach used in cost effectiveness analysis as described in Sect. 1.3, a decision tree does not always clearly model changes in conditions over time. By contrast, Markov modeling represents such changes over time and is thus suitable for predicting long-term outcomes of chronic illnesses as well as illnesses that involve complicated changes in the disease state over time. Let us consider a simple Markov model involving three clinical states: healthy, disabled, and dead (Fig. 3.5). This model can be illustrated by a state transition diagram, where circles (○) represent clinical states and arrows (→) represent transitions that occur between states during a specific period (generally 1 year). Termination of a Markov model requires at least one absorbing state, which is usually death. States other than death that satisfy certain conditions may also be defined as absorbing states.

Estimation using a Markov model requires that transition probabilities be defined between states. For instance, Table 3.8 shows the state transition probabilities of the Markov model introduced in Fig. 3.5. Here, values in each column represent the

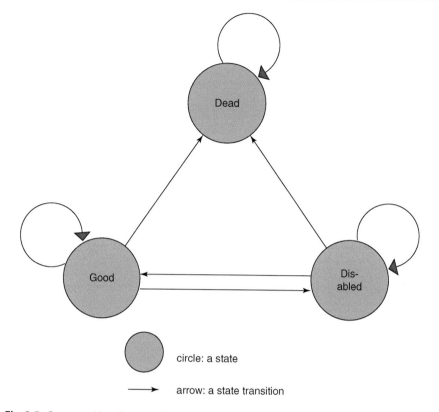

circle: a state

arrow: a state transition

Fig. 3.5 State transition diagram of Markov model

Table 3.8 State transition probability matrix

		Current state		
		Good	Disabled	Dead
Next state	Good	0. 9	0. 2	0
	Disabled	0. 1	0. 6	0
	Dead	0	0. 2	1

e.g. 20%: probability from the state with disability to death

probabilities of transitioning from the state indicated in the column title to other respective states. For example, the probabilities of transitioning from the disabled state to the healthy, disabled, and dead states are 20%, 60%, and 20%, respectively. The probability of transitioning from the dead state to the dead state is indicated as 1. When the transition probability is zero, arrows are omitted from the state transition diagram.

- Markov cycle
  - The time axis of analysis is separated by discrete time units
  - E.g. the first year, the second year …
- Markov property
  - Repeat state transitions according to the transition probabilities in any cycle

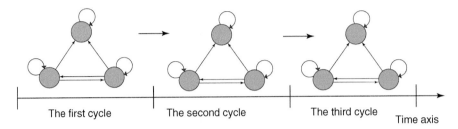

Fig. 3.6 Features of Markov model

Table 3.9 State transition table

		Markov cycle			
		First year	Second year	Third year	Fourth year
State	Good	100	90	83	78
	Disabled	0	10	15	17
	Dead	0	0	2	5

State transition probabilities must be determined within the same specific period, known as the Markov cycle. As shown in Fig. 3.6, state transitions in any Markov cycle (generally specified in years) are repeated based on the transition probabilities assigned to that cycle. The property of a process that is independent of this cycle and whose state transition probabilities remain constant is termed the Markov property. Although this Markov property represents an advantage of Markov models, it also is a limitation that diminishes the validity of models whose state transition probabilities vary over time. Accordingly, time-dependent Markov models that do not satisfy the Markov property have been increasingly employed in recent years. In such cases, cycle-dependent variations in state transition probabilities must be expressed by one method or another, generally using exponential functions. As such, when it comes to the internal validity of a Markov model (Item 13.2(A), MHLW Guidelines), the question of whether the model satisfies the Markov property is an important point. Although the question on Markov property is relevant to the external validity of a model, no algorithms and methods for testing the external validity of Markov models exist. The MHLW Guidelines (Item 13.2(B)), from a practical standpoint, require to justify the external validity of the resultant estimates, compared to existing clinical data.

If given a transition diagram with the transition probabilities defined, then the outcomes of state transitions over time and along Markov cycles can be fully calculated, as shown in Table 3.9. Such a calculation of a Markov process may use matrix algebra or, more commonly, computer simulations such as cohort and Monte Carlo simulations. Table 3.9 shows the outcomes of the Markov model presented in Table 3.8 up to the fourth year.

- In Markov model, analysis is possible allocating a attribute-value to each state.
- Examples of attribute-values
  - Utility of patients (QOL)
  - Cost

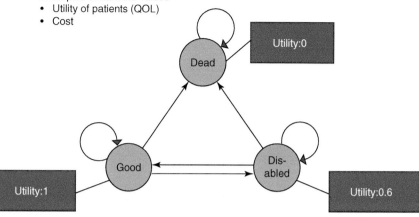

Fig. 3.7 Allocation of attribute-values to states

Table 3.10 State transition table: allocating utilities

Markov cycle

States (Utility)	1st yr	2nd yr	3rd yr	4th yr	Accumulative utility (QALYs)
Good (1)	100 / 100	90 / 90	83 /83	78 /78	351
Disabled (0.6)	0 / 0	10 /6	15 / 9	17/ 10.2	25.2
Dead (0)	0 / 0	0 / 0	2 / 0	5 / 0	0

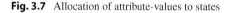

Headcount   One year×Utility×Headcount

A Markov model can be evaluated by assigning, to each state, values representing patient quality of life (utilities, when calculating QALYs) or costs, which becomes the basis for evaluating cost-effectiveness using such a model. For example, Fig. 3.7 shows a transition diagram where utilities of 1, 0, and 0.6 are assigned to the healthy, dead, and disabled states, respectively, and Table 3.10 shows the calculation of cumulative utilities over four Markov cycles. Since cumulative costs can also be obtained for each state in the same manner, the calculation can ultimately derive the cost per QALY per patient.

A model that combines features of a decision tree and a Markov model may also be used in the analysis. A Markov model can be presented as a decision tree, as in

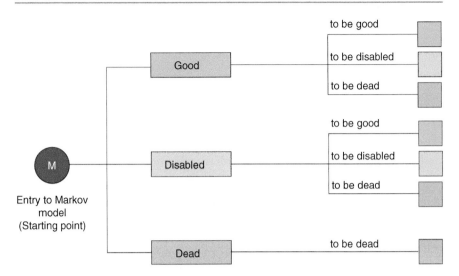

Fig. 3.8 Expression of Markov model in decision tree

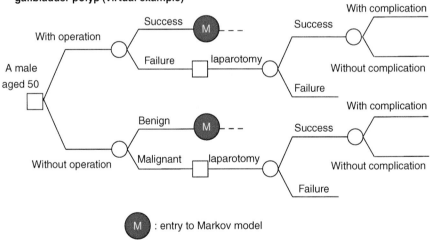

Fig. 3.9 Incorporating Markov model into decision tree model

Fig. 3.8, and thus can be integrated into a decision tree, as shown in Fig. 3.9, in which Markov nodes are specified to allow for the analysis based on the Markov model for these nodes. The hypothetical model in Fig. 3.9 may already look complicated, but actual modeling may hold added complexity.

Item 13.5 of the MHLW Guidelines requires to submit the analytic model in the form of electronic files, which enables the third-party experts to manage to change all the main parameters such as transition probabilities, QOL scores, and healthcare costs. Also, half-cycle correction should be conducted if the Markov cycle is substantially too long (Item 13.6). However, the criteria for appropriate length of Markov cycle are not clear.

3.13.1 Self-Check!

1. What is a Markov cycle?
2. What are the limitations of a Markov model?
3. What steps can be taken when the Markov property is not satisfied?
4. Is it possible to test the validity of a Markov model?

3.14 Uncertainty

Ministry of Health, Labour and Welfare (MHLW) Guidelines Ver. 2.0

14.1. If the patterns of clinical practice or other factors are not uniform and this discrepancy could affect the results, analyses based on multiple scenarios should be conducted.

14.2. For situations in which the uncertainty is large because of a long time horizon, a shorter-term analysis is necessary, such as an analysis of the period for which clinical study data are available.

14.3. If no available studies involve a comparison with the comparator according to Sect. 5, particularly when a comparison has been made concerning results between single-arm studies, a sensitivity analysis with a sufficiently wide range is required because of the large uncertainty.

14.4. Sensitivity analyses are needed for parameters with large variances, those based on assumptions rather than actual data, those with possible heterogeneity between overseas and domestic data, and others.

14.5. When the variance of the estimator should be considered (parametric uncertainty), the range moving parameter in the sensitivity analysis can refer to the 95% confidence interval of the estimator.

14.6. A probabilistic sensitivity analysis (PSA) is also desirable. In such cases, the distribution used for analysis, scatter plots of the cost-effectiveness plane, and cost-effectiveness acceptability curves (CEAC) must be presented.

Collection of data through observation involves uncertainty, to which clinical data are no exception. Even for a healthy person, values of blood pressure measured every morning will generally vary from day to day. Such random differences in data are referred to as variability and can be observed as differences in the outcomes measured for a target population. Moreover, the average body weight may differ for Japanese and US individuals. Such differences in characteristics within a population are referred to as heterogeneity. In clinical practice, decisions are constantly made in terms of appropriate screening and treatment strategies. Even if decisions are made rationally based on data, to the extent that there is uncertainty in the data, then errors cannot be avoided. This intrinsic property that decisionmaking is based on is referred to as decisionmaking under uncertainty.

Two approaches to addressing uncertainty include statistical and sensitivity analyses (see Table 3.11).

In statistics, variability and heterogeneity are addressed as follows: when a population has a normal distribution with mean μ and variance σ^2, the mean m and variance s^2 of a random sample are known to be

$$m = \mu, s^2 = \sigma^2 / n \left(\text{where } n \text{ is the sample size}\right).$$

That is, a random sample from the population $N(\mu, \sigma^2)$ will have a normal distribution $N(\mu, \sigma^2/n)$. Here, the 95% confidence interval is given as:

$$\text{sample mean} \pm 1.96\sigma / \sqrt{n}.$$

Statistical calculation of a 95% confidence interval is also recommended in health economic evaluations. In an economic evaluation, the ICER calculation is required as a final output. Since the ICER is derived from multiple parameters related to cost and effectiveness, the uncertainty of those parameters is reflected in its estimation.

The ICER is defined by the division between two variables, incremental cost ($\triangle$C), and incremental effectiveness ($\triangle$E), so its estimation requires an approach using a two-dimensional function. Figure 3.10 shows an example of a 95% confidence region and a 95% confidence ellipse on the incremental cost-effectiveness plane.

- *95% confidence region*: is the rectangular area shaped by the combination of the 95% confidence intervals of $\triangle$E and $\triangle$C. Of the two lines joining the origin to a tangent point on the rectangle, the one with a larger slope gives the upper limit of the ICER's 95% confidence region, and the other gives the lower limit. However, this 95% confidence region does not always capture the interaction

Table 3.11 How to cope with uncertainty	Statistical analysis
	• 95% confidence interval
	• 95% confidence ellipsoid
	• Analytical method: delta method, etc.
	Sensitivity analysis
	• Deterministic sensitivity analysis
	– Structural sensitivity analysis
	– Parameter sensitivity analysis: one-/two-/multi-way sensitivity analysis
	• Probabilistic sensitivity analysis
	– Second-order Monte Carlo simulation
	– Nonparametric bootstrap

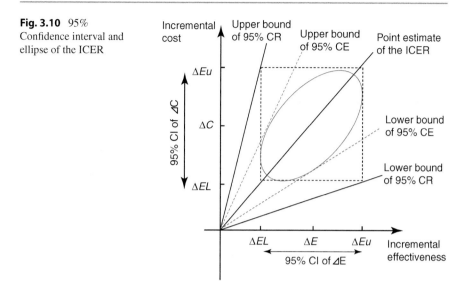

Fig. 3.10 95% Confidence interval and ellipse of the ICER

between the two variables, $\triangle E$ and $\triangle C$, and tends to overestimate the true 95% confidence interval. It is thus preferred that confidence intervals be obtained using a scatter plot of cost and effectiveness.

- *95% confidence ellipse*: models the covariation of cost and effectiveness, based on their scatter plot. The ellipse is positively sloped when cost and effectiveness are positively correlated and negatively sloped when they are negatively correlated. Of the two lines in Fig. 3.10 that join the origin to a point on the inscribed ellipse of the rectangle, the one with a larger slope gives the upper limit of ICER's confidence ellipse, and the other gives the lower limit. The 95% confidence ellipse allows for a narrower ICER confidence interval compared with the 95% confidence region.

The delta method estimates the 95% confidence interval of the ICER analytically. It approximates the ICER variance by applying the Taylor expansion and also allows for consideration of the covariation of cost and effectiveness. Moreover, Fieller's theorem allows for consideration of deviations in the distribution of ICERs, assuming that $\triangle E$ and $\triangle C$ are normally distributed. Recently, however, computer simulations are increasingly employed to estimate uncertainty in ICERs, and the use of statistical analysis in handling uncertainty is less common.

Another approach to handling uncertainty is a sensitivity analysis (see Table 3.11). A sensitivity analysis examines the behavior of the results when the point estimate of a parameter varies within a specific range. When the weather forecast reports a 50% chance of rain, we still assume a 30–70% chance and be dressed for both rain and shine. Such situations are common in daily life and can be considered our daily sensitivity analyses.

In a sensitivity analysis, if changes are observed in the results, the thresholds of key parameters that contribute to these changes can be identified. In contrast, if no changes are observed, it demonstrates that the results obtained are robust. This test of robustness can also be used in model validation. Sensitivity analyses can be classified into deterministic and probabilistic analyses. The former is a more classical approach, but most recent studies employ the latter.

Item 14.1 of the MHLW Guidelines requires that variability in clinical practice patterns be handled through further analysis based on different scenarios, which suggests the use of structure sensitivity analysis. According to 14.4 of the MHLW Guidelines, the following parameters must be tested through a sensitivity analysis:

1. Parameters with large variability (the degree of variability is not specified)
2. Parameters based on assumptions
3. Parameters from studies in other countries (consideration of heterogeneity)

There are one-, two-, and multi-way sensitivity analyses, in which, one, two, or more than two parameters are varied, respectively. Up to a two-way analysis is generally used, due to the complexity involved in varying multiple sets of parameters in a multi-way analysis. Figure 3.11 shows a hypothetical example of a one-way sensitivity analysis. Here, the graph represents changes in the expected costs of treatment $Y (= 2000 + 9000p)$ when one parameter (the probability p of a patient having cancer) is varied from 0% to 100%. This analysis helps determine that if, for instance, the expected cost is to be kept below JPY 3800, then the probability of a patient having a cancer needs to be below 20%. A tornado diagram (see Fig. 3.12) can be used to display the results of multiple one-way sensitivity analyses performed independently with different parameters. Here, the parameters are ordered from the greatest to smallest impact on the results. The ranges of variation in parameters can be randomly assigned, as there are no absolute standards. Accordingly, the ranges should be specified in the diagram, as shown in Fig. 3.12.

Item 14.2 of the MHLW Guidelines notes the possible increase in uncertainty in evaluations with longer-term time horizons. For instance, long-term analysis such as 30 years with a model having a 1-year Markov cycle may not justify the Markov property. This can of course be addressed through alternate methods, such as the use of time-dependent Markov models. The MHLW Guidelines require that an analysis with a shorter-term time horizon for which data from clinical studies are available also be performed. According to 14.3 of the MHLW Guidelines, a simple comparison of single-arm studies can involve a large degree of uncertainty and must be tested through a sensitivity analysis with a sufficiently wide range. However, the MHLW Guidelines do not specify what represents a sufficiently wide range of

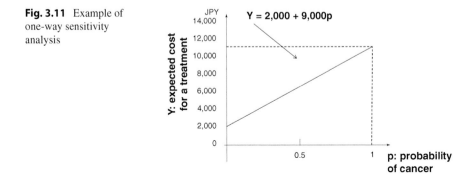

Fig. 3.11 Example of one-way sensitivity analysis

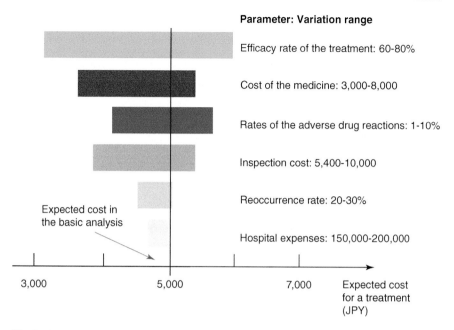

Fig. 3.12 Tornado diagram

variation or how to handle interactions between parameters if a two- or multi-way analysis is performed. The following limitations should be carefully noted when performing a sensitivity analysis:

1. Possible bias in the selection of parameters to be included in the sensitivity analysis
2. Validity of the ranges of parameter variation
3. Possibility of not capturing interactions between parameters

Attention must be paid to the validity of the range of variation assigned to each parameter, particularly when a tornado diagram is used. Although such a diagram is useful in identifying the degrees of impact of individual parameters, it does not reflect the impact of combined variations in multiple parameters. Moreover, the degree of impact can be altered by modifying the ranges of variation (i.e., the degree of impact of a specific parameter can be intentionally controlled).

As such, the question of how to assign an appropriate range of variation is consistently raised for sensitivity analysis. Although there are no standard rules, some principles do exist:

1. Parameters estimated based on expert opinions are expected to have greater uncertainty due to biases in opinions, and their impact should be tested through sensitivity analyses using a wide range.
2. A 95% confidence interval should be used where observational data collected through random sampling are available.
3. Where multiple estimates are available, they should be combined through a meta-analysis, and a 95% confidence interval should be used.

4. Where parameters are obtained through a database search, the range of uncertainty in the data used should be estimated by carefully referring to the errors reported in the data sources.

Item 14.5 of the MHLW Guidelines specifies the use of 95% confidence interval for sensitivity analysis.

Additionally, the degree of impact from the variation of one parameter on the results should be examined using approaches such as a structure sensitivity analysis and consideration of the points below:

1. The overall significance of the parameter in the real world
2. Uncertainty in the baseline estimates used in the base case analysis
3. The relative position that the parameter is assigned in the model
4. The number of times the parameter is used in the model

Recently, probabilistic sensitivity analysis (PSA) through computer simulations is increasingly employed. PSA uses a probability distribution for analyzing sensitivity and includes second-order Monte Carlo simulations, which use parametric probability distributions such as triangular and binomial distributions, and nonparametric bootstrapping that does not use any specific probability distribution (see Table 3.11).

A second-order Monte Carlo simulation is the most commonly used PSA and is sometimes confused with a first-order Monte Carlo simulation. A first-order Monte Carlo simulation consists of the following steps: patients from a cohort are entered into the model one at a time; each patient is followed along the probabilistic choices made within the model (such as the selection of outcomes that occur at chance nodes on a decision tree or transition to the next state in a Markov model); and the results for all patients entered into the model are accumulated to predict the behavior of the whole cohort. This is also called a micro-simulation, as it follows the behavior of individual patients along the model. A second-order Monte Carlo simulation follows the same process as a micro-simulation and additionally applies a probability distribution to the probabilistic choices made within the model. Therefore, while in a first-order Monte Carlo simulation a patient transitions to the next state based on a state transition probability that is selected probabilistically (e.g., rolling a dice) from predetermined state transition probabilities, in a second-order simulation, a patient transitions to the next state based on a state transition probability determined by random sampling for each patient from a probability distribution with a predetermined state transition probability as the mean. Since a second-order Monte Carlo simulation allows for assigning a probability distribution to all parameters in the model, the impact that variations in the parameters have can be simultaneously evaluated.

Figure 3.13 illustrates the process of a second-order Monte Carlo simulation described above, involving the following steps:

Step 1: Patients from a hypothetical cohort are entered into the decision model one at a time.
Step 2: At the first chance node (at each state in the Markov model), the patient is given a probability based on the probability distribution assigned to the parameter and then moves to the next chance node.

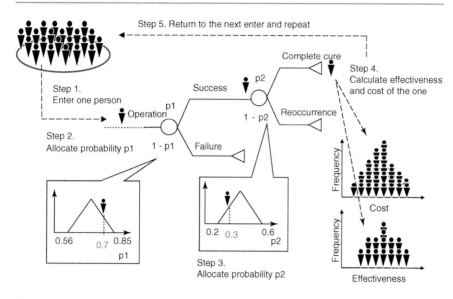

Fig. 3.13 Second-order Monte Carlo simulation

Step 3: As in Step 2, a probability distribution is assigned to the next chance node (which can be a different probability distribution from the one assigned in Step 2), and the patient continues to move along the model.

Step 4: At terminal nodes, incurred costs and effects are tallied and recorded.

Step 5: The next patient is entered into the model and the same process is repeated for all patients, from which cost and effectiveness of each alternative and an experimental distribution of ICERs are obtained.

The example in Fig. 3.13 uses a triangular distribution, although there are no rules for assigning a probability distribution and the analyst should decide on a case-by-case basis.

In terms of the range of parameter variation, when parameter estimates are obtained from literature, they tend to be used as such estimates tend to be based on normal distributions and the 95% confidence interval and standard deviation are known. If parameters are obtained from electronic data, then statistical software can be used to obtain an approximate distribution. For parameters estimated based on assumptions and expert opinions, their distribution and variability must be considered carefully.

The advantages of using a Monte Carlo simulation include the mean and standard deviation of cost and effectiveness being obtainable for individual alternatives (e.g., new and standard drug), based on which a scatter plot of cost and effectiveness and a cost-effectiveness acceptability curve can be graphed to evaluate uncertainty. Item 14.6 of the MHLW Guidelines recommends the use of probabilistic sensitivity analysis and that the (1) probability distribution, (2) scatter plot, and (3) cost-effectiveness acceptability curve be presented.

There are no standard rules for the number of simulations to be performed, and they do not need to equal the number of patients studied. Generally, around 10,000

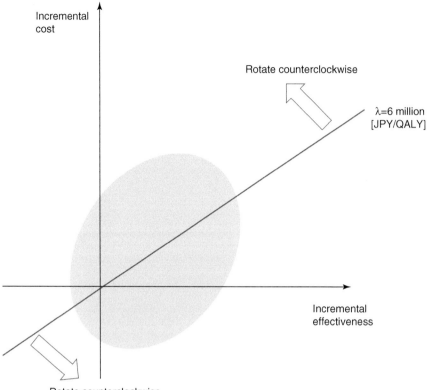

Fig. 3.14 Scatter plot and image of scanning by a threshold line

patients are used as a guide for a simulation using a decision tree with 5–10 terminal nodes. Generated cost and effectiveness datasets may also be statistically tested. Regardless, it is recommended that the criteria for termination of the simulation be determined prior to the start of the analysis.

A cost-effectiveness acceptability curve (CEAC) shows the probability that the ICER for a new technology falls below the allowable threshold. A scatter plot of cost and effectiveness is thus drawn based on a Monte Carlo simulation or bootstrapping, which is then used to derive a curve (Fig. 3.14). As shown in Fig. 3.14, on the scatter plot of incremental cost and effectiveness, the straight line through the origin representing the threshold (λ) is rotated counterclockwise from a slope of 0 (parallel to the x-axis) to ∞ (parallel to the y-axis), and the plot is scanned.

During this rotation, the number of points on the scatter plot that fall onto the area under a given threshold line λ is counted to obtain its ratio to the total number of points on the plot. This pair of λ and corresponding ratios is then plotted on an XY plane. For example, if the percentage of points under the threshold line λ is determined as 53% for a threshold λ of 6 million JPY/QALY, this combination can be shown as per Fig. 3.15. The y-axis of the CEAC represents the percentage of points under the line representing a given threshold λ but can also be viewed as the probability of the net monetary benefit (NMB; see Sect. 6.3, Chapter 6 to know more

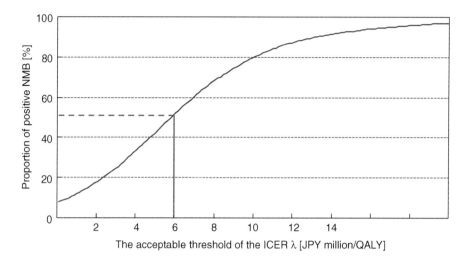

Fig. 3.15 Cost-effectiveness acceptability curve (CEAC)

details in theory) being positive. The threshold line is scanned over the first, third, and fourth quadrants, and the results in the second quadrant (dominated region) are not reflected in the CEAC. Additionally, the results in the fourth quadrant (dominant region) are always included in the scan and thus are always reflected in the CEAC to a certain extent.

As inferred from the process of generating the curve, the CEAC shows the probability that the technology under investigation (e.g., a new drug) is cost-effective at each ceiling ratio (or willingness-to-pay threshold). For example, Fig. 3.15 illustrates that there is an 80% probability that the technology is cost-effective at a threshold of 10 million JPY/QALY. The presentation of results as a CEAC has multiple applications. For example, the results for uncertainty when it comes to differences in patient strata, such as by clinical stages or genetic conditions, and the impact of varying parameters, such as the discount rate, can be shown.

The limitations of CEAC include that it cannot clearly distinguish between different shapes of distributions. For example, CEACs obtained from two scatter plots with different sizes but similar distributions will have identical curves (see Sect. 5.2.10, Chapter 5 to know more details of the example). That is, there is no one-to-one correspondence between the shape of a scatter plot and the CEAC. It has also been argued that CEACs are not necessary if a neutral perspective is taken in terms of uncertainty. When there are risks to be avoided, they may not always be identified using CEACs. Other issues that have been raised include that a hypothesis cannot be tested with CEACs as their statistical precision is not known and that CEACs do not reflect the expected value of perfect information (EVPI) (see Sect. 6.5, Chapter 6 to know more details in theory), which is a measure of uncertainty, as well as information related to clinical significance and urgency.

As another PSA method, nonparametric bootstrapping has been increasingly employed in recent years. This method uses computer simulations to perform random sampling of observational data with replacement (see Fig. 3.16) and uses the obtained statistics to experimentally generate ICER distributions. As shown in

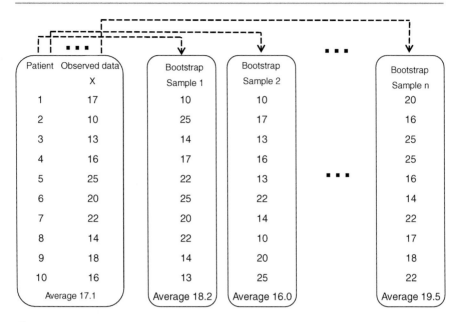

Fig. 3.16 Example of repeated sampling

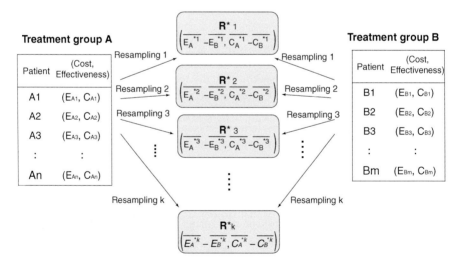

Fig. 3.17 Estimating ICERs by bootstrapping

Fig. 3.16, bootstrapping can be easily performed given observed data from clinical trials and is thus a useful method in RCT-CEA where patient data on costs and effectiveness are available. This allows 95% confidence intervals as well as means to be estimated.

Figure 3.17 illustrates the estimation of an ICER through bootstrapping, involving the following steps:

Step 1: An n number of samples are drawn from observed data (cost-effectiveness pairs) for Treatment A group allowing for duplication, following which the mean is calculated for both effectiveness and cost. That is, (E_A^{*1}, C_A^{*1}) is obtained.

Step 2: An m number of samples are drawn from observed data for Treatment B group; from the mean (E_B^{*1}, C_B^{*1}) is obtained in the same manner as above.

Step 3: Based on the results in Steps 1 and 2, a bootstrap estimate of the ICER is calculated:

$$R_1^* = (C_A^{*1} - C_B^{*1}) / (E_A^{*1} - E_B^{*1}).$$

Step 4: Steps 1–3 are repeated k times ($k = 5000$ as a rough guide). As a result, a k number of ICER estimates, $R_1^*, R_2^*, \ldots, R_k^*$ are obtained.

Similar to the approach used for the Monte Carlo simulation, the set of k number of ICERs obtained above can be presented as a scatter plot consisting of a k number of points on the incremental cost-effectiveness plane. Once the scatter plot is obtained, a CEAC can then be graphed.

3.14.1 Self-Check!

1. What can be done to address data uncertainty?
2. What are the measures of uncertainty used in statistical estimations?
3. List two types of sensitivity analysis.
4. What are the three types of parameters that are subject to sensitivity analysis that are mentioned in the MHLW Guidelines?
5. What are the points to note when comparing single-arm studies that are mentioned in the MHLW Guidelines?
6. Is PSA required in the MHLW Guidelines? If so, what results need to be presented?
7. What are the two methods of PSA?
8. What is the difference between first- and second-order Monte Carlo simulations?
9. Given a specific cost-effectiveness threshold, what information can be obtained from a CEAC?
10. May bootstrapping be applied to data from clinical trials?

References

1. Guideline for preparing cost-effectiveness evaluation to the Central Social Insurance Medical Council. http://www.mhlw.go.jp/file/05-shingikai-12404000-Hokenkyoku-Iry-ouka/0000109789.pdf. Accessed 30 May 2016.
2. Guideline for preparing cost-effectiveness evaluation to the Central Social Insurance Medical Council. https://c2h.niph.go.jp/tools/guideline/guideline_en.pdf. Accessed 15 Apr 2019.

How to Appraise

4

4.1 What Is "Appraisal"?

4.1.1 Key Points

- The process of cost-effectiveness evaluation consists of (1) data submission, (2) reanalysis, (3) appraisal, and (4) decision-making based on the results.
- Viewpoints of (1) validity and (2) ethical and social impacts were used in the appraisal in the pilot period of 2016–2018.
- The appraisal Committee in Chuikyo evaluates the estimate(s) of ICER, which is submitted by company and re-analyzed by the experts group, and determines a price-adjustment rate for each ICER, considering three ICER thresholds: JPY5M, 7.5M, and 10M/QALY.
- In case of the multiple estimates of ICER for multiple indications, the overall average of the price-adjustment rates determined for each ICER is calculated in a way weighted by population size for each indication.

4.1.2 Essential Knowledge

The process for cost-effectiveness evaluation of Chuikyo consists of the following four steps: (1) submission of data by companies, (2) reanalysis, (3) appraisal, and (4) decision-making based on the results. Steps 1 and 2 refer to "assessment," which is followed by the appraisal established by the UK's NICE.

4.1.2.1 Historical Discussions in the Pilot Period 2016–2018

- Evaluations were appraised by the Task Force for Cost-Effectiveness Evaluation (provisional name) from the following two viewpoints.

© Springer Nature Singapore Pte Ltd. 2019
I. Kamae, *Health Technology Assessment in Japan*,
https://doi.org/10.1007/978-981-13-5793-0_4

   – Validity: whether the standard (or reasonable) method of analysis is used and
     the data are appropriate.
   – Ethical and social impacts: points to be considered will be discussed further
     by referring to practices in countries such as the UK, France, Sweden, and
     Australia.
- When the Task Force for Cost-Effectiveness Evaluation deems necessary, com-
panies may attend the meeting and express their views.
- Depending on the appraisal results, a reanalysis may be conducted.
- A qualitative assessment of being "cost-effective" or "not cost-effective" was
initially suggested without any explicit threshold of cost-effectiveness.
- The results of the appraisal was used to adjust the price determined by the stan-
dard pricing (repricing) process. A slope relation between ICER and price-
adjustment rate was invented utilizing two ICER standards: JPY5M and 10M/
QALY.

Of the two viewpoints above, validity can be assessed in accordance with
MHLW's Guidelines. However, in terms of ethical and social impacts, the development of standards for objective and independent assessments cannot be easily
developed. The difficulty was also recognized in Chuikyo's handout, in which international practices was outlined as reference (Table 4.1).

Table 4.1 Examples of foreign countries considering ethical and social impacts

(3) Perspectives on ethical and social impacts

In the appraisal, how to recognize the other aspects to be considered in addition to scientific analysis.

- The view points for appraisals in other countries are as described below; however, the method for utilizing the results and also the social/cultural background differ from country to country.
- Due to such diversity, it may be difficult to clarify the common viewpoints that can be made into rules.

(Extract from/added to the handout 【hi-2】 in the General Assembly of Central Social Insurance Medical Council in April 10, 2013)

UK	Sweden	Australia	France	Germany
• Disease severity • Life-prolonging treatment for fatal diseases • Opinions from stakeholders • The degree of innovation • Consideration for groups of people with disabilities • Pediatric diseases	Three basic principles of reimbursement • All people are treated equally/No discrimination based on age, race, sex, etc. • People with high severity has priority • Redeem a cost-effective medicine	• The degree of usefulness relative to a comparator • Economic burden of patients with no reimbursement by insurance • Financial Impact on total insurance budget etc.	Example of the concept "fairness": • Efficacy • Equity • Discrimination • Geographical imbalance • Social injustice • Ease of use • Compensation * Quotation from the general principles of action by HAS because any public document does not indicate view points in the appraisal.	Any public document does not indicate the viewpoints
Reimbursement decisions/ To reflect on price	Reimbursement decisions	Reimbursement decisions/ To reflect on price	To reflect on price	To reflect on price

(Handout in Special Committee on Cost-Effectiveness, Central Social Insurance Medical Council.
October 28, 2015)

The problem with conducting an appraisal under the provisional implementation was that, on one hand, Chuikyo initially chose not to specify the standards for assessment by saying that:

1. The assessment of ethical and social impacts cannot be standardized
2. An ICER threshold will not be specified

while on the other hand, it required a final assessment of being either "cost-effective" or "not cost-effective." If the grounds for assessment are not clear, the result becomes inevitably subjective. Hence, the "comprehensive (*sogoteki*)" aspect of appraisal was emphasized.

Although an ICER threshold was initially not adopted in the provisional implementation, Chuikyo provided a reference (Table 4.2) for the ICER interpretation. Here, different threshold ranges were presented, such as JPY5–6M/QALY from Japanese studies, one to three times GDP per capita by WHO, GBP20–30K/QALY in the UK, and USD50–100K/QALY in the USA. Although this is a useful reference for a beginner, given that no specific standards are provided under the provisional implementation, these threshold ranges could possibly influence the assessment of cost-effectiveness. Hence, the Chikyo eventually introduced two thresholds (they called two standards): JPY5M and 10M/QALY, which were utilized for price-adjustment decisions, not for reimbursement decision. These thresholds were used as benchmark for the price reduction: no reduction if the ICER estimate < JPY5M/QALY, reduction of premium portion with 10% to 90% in proportion to the ICER estimate, and reduction of 90% if the ICER estimate > JPY10M/QALY.

Table 4.2 Interpretation of ICER

Interpretation of incremental cost effectiveness ratio (ICER)
• One of the interpretations regarding ICER is to compare it with a reference threshold, and judge the cost-effectiveness which the ICER conveys.
• No country mechanically operates a constant value of threshold, but some countries use standard values.
• Standard values are almost set in the following methods.
– To estimate the cost of an existing medical treatment which is widely accepted as a standard.
– The extent to which the public can pay. (= willingness to pay)
For example, some surveys represent 5–6 million yen per QALY in Japan.
– Economic indicators such as GDP per capita
For example, once to three times amount of GDP per capita.
GDP per capita in Japan is 3.8 million yen in 2013.
The standard of 20K to 30K pounds per QALY in the UK NICE is equivalent to 0.8–1.2 times amount of the UK GDP per capita, 25K pounds in 2013.
USD 50K to 100K often referred in the US corresponds to 0.9 to 1.9 times amount of the US GDP per capita, USD 53K in 2013.

(Handout in Special Committee on Cost-Effectiveness, Central Social Insurance Medical Council. June 24, 2015)

4.1.2.2 New Appraisal in the Institutionalization 2019

Despite the multi-aspect discussions on the roles of appraisal committee in Chuikyo, substantial changes were proposed and approved for new appraisal in the full-scale program (institutionalization from) April 2019. The policy that the appraisal committee dichotomously judges whether the cost-effectiveness is "good" or "not good" without any threshold of ICER was completely discarded. Instead, three ICER (Chuikyo calls "standards.") are introduced for price adjustment with JPY5M, 7.5M, and 10M/QALY. The new role of cost-effectiveness appraisal 2019 in Chuikyo is more focused rather than in the pilot 2016, and summarized as follows:

1. Scientific validity
   (a) If it is difficult to determine a single estimate, multiples estimates or a range of ICERs are considered,
   (b) For multiple populations for analysis, an ICER is estimated for each population,
   (c) For multiple estimates of ICER, price adjustment by population for each ICER is conducted first based on three ICER thresholds: JPY5M, 7.5M, and 10M/QALY, and the revised price is subsequently adjusted by the weighted average method considering the population size.
2. Special considerations for orphan diseases and serious diseases, etc.
   (a) One of indications for the target technology includes orphan diseases (designated incurable diseases, hemophilia and HIV infection) for which treatment does not exist,
   (b) One of indications for the target technology includes pediatric diseases for which a dose and administration is approved for Japanese children in Japan,
   (c) Anticancer medicines (the efficacy for malignant tumor(s) is confirmed among cancer patients at approval),
   (d) Special considerations are reflected as an allowance, shifting of three ICER thresholds upwards to JPY7.5M, 11.25M, and 15M/QALY,
   (e) An additional analysis to the baseline CEA may include public long-term care costs and productivity losses only if data estimated in Japan is utilized. The results of the additional analysis are not used for price adjustment, but left for further investigations to reform the current HTA systems.

4.1.3 Self-Check!

1. Name the four steps of cost-effectiveness evaluation.
2. Are companies allowed to present their views on evaluation?
3. Is the assessment of cost-effectiveness possible without the standards for evaluating ICER?

4.2 Basics on Critical Appraisal of CEA Studies

4.2.1 Key Points

- Critical appraisal refers to the assessment of elements required in health economic evaluations.
- Critical appraisal is useful in learning, reading, and writing economic evaluations.
- Drummond's ten key principles provides a well-known and useful standard for critical appraisal.

4.2.2 Essential Knowledge

Critical appraisal addresses the question of how to assess the results of health economic evaluations. The significance of critical appraisal is not limited to its use in assessing economic studies but also as an introduction for beginners to learn the conceptual framework of economic evaluation and as a tool in reading published economic studies and interpreting their results, as shown in Table 4.3. It may also serve as a guide for researchers in writing their own papers, by highlighting the elements that require attention, such as the study design, method of analysis, choice of outcome measures, and focus of argument.

Drummond's ten key principles are well known [1] as a standard method for critical appraisal. It is perhaps way the constitution of economic evaluation of comprising of ten key principles and additional questions that supplement the principles. Table 4.4 summarizes the key principles.

Table 4.3 Significance of a critical appraisal

Purpose	How useful
Learn (learning)	Standard format for beginners
Read (interpretation)	Template for evaluating papers/ reports of economic evaluations
Write (paper writing)	Study design, methods for analysis, outcome measures, and guidance of issues to discuss

Table 4.4 Drummond's ten key principles

1. Question definition
2. Description of alternatives
3. Evidence of effectiveness
4. Costs and consequences: identification
5. Costs and consequences: appropriateness of measuring
6. Costs and consequences: credibility in valuing
7. Cost and outcome: time adjustment
8. Incremental analysis
9. Uncertainty of estimates
10. Study results and user concerns

1. Was a well-defined question posed in answerable form?
   1.1 Did the study examine both costs and effects of the service(s) or programme(s) over an appropriate time horizon?
   1.2 Did the study involve a comparison of alternatives?
   1.3 Was a perspective for the analysis stated and was the study placed in any particular decision-making context?
   1.4 Were the patient population and any relevant subgroups adequately defined?
2. Was a comprehensive description of the competing alternatives given (i.e., can you tell who did what to whom, where, and how often)?
   2.1 Were any relevant alternatives omitted?
   2.2 Was (Should) a 'do-nothing' alternative (be) considered?
   2.3 Were relevant alternatives identified for the patient subgroups?
3. Was the effectiveness of the programmes or services established?
   3.1 Was this done through a randomized controlled clinical trial? If so, did the trial protocol reflect what would happen in practice?
   3.2 Were effectiveness data collected and summarized through a systematic overview of clinical studies? If so, were the search strategy and rules for inclusion or exclusion outlined?
   3.3 Were observational data or assumptions used to establish effectiveness? If so, were any potential biases recognized?
4. Were all the important and relevant costs and consequences for each alternative identified?
   4.1 Was the range wide enough for the research question at hand?
   4.2 Did it cover all relevant perspectives? (Possible perspectives include those of patients and third-party payers; other perspectives may also be relevant depending on the particular analysis.)
   4.3 Were capital costs, as well as operating costs, included?
5. Were costs and consequences measured accurately in appropriate physical units prior to valuation (e.g., hours of nursing time, number of physician visits, lost work-days, gained life-years)?
   5.1 Were the sources of resource utilization described and justified?
   5.2 Were any of the identified items omitted from measurement? If so, does this mean that they carried no weight in the subsequent analysis?
   5.3 Were there any special circumstances (e.g., joint use of resources) that made measurement difficult? Were these circumstances handled appropriately?
6. Were the cost and consequences valued credibly?
   6.1 Were the sources of all values clearly identified? (possible sources include market values, patient or client preferences and views, policy makers' views, and health professionals' judgements.)
   6.2 Were market values employed for changes involving resources gained or depleted?
   6.3 Where market values were absent (e.g., volunteer labor) or market values did not reflect actual values (e.g., clinic space donated at a reduced rate), were adjustments made to approximate market values?

6.4 Was the valuation of consequences appropriate for the question posed (i.e., has the appropriate type or types of analysis – cost-effective, cost-benefit – been selected)?

7. Were costs and consequences adjusted for differential timing?

7.1 Were costs and consequences that occur in the future 'discounted' to their present values?

7.2 Was any justification given for the discount rate(s) used?

8. Was an incremental analysis of costs and consequences of alternatives performed?

8.1 Were the additional (incremental) costs generated by one alternative over another compared to the additional effects, benefits, or utilities generated?

9. Was uncertainty in the estimates of costs and consequences adequately characterized?

9.1 If patient-level data on costs and consequences were available, were appropriate statistical analyses performed?

9.2 If a sensitivity analysis was employed, was justification provided for the form(s) of sensitivity analysis employed and the ranges or distributions of values (for key study parameters)?

9.3 Were the conclusions of the study sensitive to the uncertainty in the results, as quantified by the statistical and/or sensitivity analysis?

9.4 Was heterogeneity in the patient population recognized, for example by presenting study results for relevant subgroups?

10. Did the presentation and discussion of study results include all issues of concern to users?

10.1 Were the conclusions of the analysis based on some overall index or ratio of costs to consequences (e.g., cost-effectiveness ratio)? If so, was the index interpreted intelligently or in a mechanistic fashion?

10.2 Were the results compared with those of others who have investigated the same question? If so, were allowances made for potential differences in study methodology?

10.3 Did the study discuss the generalizability of the results to other settings and patient/client groups?

10.4 Did the study allude to, or take account of, other important factors in the choice or decision under consideration (e.g., distribution of costs and consequences or relevant ethical issues)?

10.5 Did the study discuss issues of implementation, such as the feasibility of adopting the 'preferred' programme, given existing financial or other constraints, and whether any freed resources could be redeployed to other worthwhile programmes?

10.6 Were the implications of uncertainty for decision-making, including the need for future research, explored?

4.2.3 Self-Check!

1. What is referred to as the "do-nothing" problem, and why does it need to be considered?
2. How are the operating costs and capital costs treated in MHLW's Guidelines?
3. Is it valid to discount only the costs or the consequences as well? If so, why?

4.3 Appraisal for HTA Agency

4.3.1 Key Points

- Drummond et al. proposed 15 key principles for the improved conduct of health technology assessments.
- These principles are organized into four sections.
- The principles are useful in the conduct and assessment of HTA activities in Japan.

4.3.2 Essential Knowledge

Drummond et al. have proposed a basic framework for the improved implementation and conduct of HTA worldwide [2]. Their 15 key principles, as shown in Table 4.5, are organized into the following four sections:

Table 4.5 15 basic principles for improving HTA practice

Structure of HTA program (KP 1 to 4)
1. The goal and scope of the HTA should be explicit and relevant to its use.
2. HTA should be unbiased and transparent exercise.
3. HTA should include all relevant technologies.
4. A clear system for setting priorities for HTA should exist.
Method of HTA (KP 5 to 9)
5. HTA should incorporate appropriate methods for assessing costs and benefits.
6. HTAs should consider a wide range of evidence and outcomes.
7. A full societal perspective should be considered when undertaking HTAs.
8. HTAs should explicitly characterize uncertainty surrounding estimates.
9. HTAs should consider and address generalizability and transferability.
Process on HTA implementation (KP 10 to 12)
10. Those conducting HTAs should actively engage all key stakeholders groups.
11. Those undertaking HTAs should actively seek all available data.
12. The implementation of HTA findings needs to be monitored.
Use of HTA in decision making (KP 13 to 15)
13. HTA should be timely.
14. HTA findings need to be communicated appropriately to different decision makers.
15. The link between HTA findings and decision-making processes needs to be transparent and clearly defined.

1. Structure of HTA programs (principles 1–4)
2. Methods of HTA (principles 5–9)
3. Processes for conduct of HTA (principles 10–12)
4. Use of HTA in decision-making (principles 13–15)

Based on these 15 principles, studies have been reported where HTA activities are included for each of the four sections, examining whether there are differences between two groups of programs, with and without official guidelines for economic evaluation in place. The key principles of Drummond et al. are often referred to as a global standard for the worldwide assessment of HTA agencies.

In Japan, with the provisional implementation of HTA in the pricing system in FY2016–2018, the Chuikyo reached consensus on the need for establishing a HTA-specific public institute or HTA agency at no distant date, for which the principles of Drummond et al. offer valuable insights.

4.3.3 Self-Check!

1. Which of the key principles relates to cost-effectiveness?
2. How should principle 10 be achieved?
3. Which principle refers to transparency?

References

1. Drummond MF, Sculpher MJ, Claxton K et al (2015) Methods for the economic evaluation of health care programmes, 4th edn. Oxford University Press, Oxford
2. Drummond M, Schwartz JS, Jönsson B et al (2008) Key principles for the improved conduct of health technology assessments for resource allocation decisions. Int J Technol Assess Health Care 24(3):244–258

Exercises for Powerful Assessment

5

5.1 Basics of Biostatistics and Clinical Epidemiology

5.1.1 Monthly Cost of Pharmaceutical Treatment

Example

The monthly cost of pharmaceutical treatment for nine patients with disease X was found to be JPY 150, 190, 220, 260, 210, 100, 130, 120, and 150K, respectively.

   Question 1. Find the mean, variance, and median.

   Question 2. What is the standard deviation?

   Question 3. What is the standard error?

   Question 4. Find the 95% confidence interval for the mean.

   Question 5. Assuming the national average of monthly cost for the pharmaceutical treatment of disease X is known to be JPY 120K in Japan, how do you interpret the treatment cost for this patient group?

   Question 6. Would it be appropriate to use the national average, JPY 120K, as an estimate in the base case analysis and the 95% confidence interval determined in Question 4 as the range of variation in sensitivity analysis?

Solutions

   Question 1. Mean = $(150 + 190 + 220 + 260 + 210 + 100 + 130 + 120 + 150)/9 =$ JPY 170K

   Variance = sum of squared deviations from the mean/(sample size − 1)

$$= \{(150 - 170)^2 + (190 - 170)^2 + (220 - 170)^2 + (260 - 170)^2 + (210 - 170)^2$$
$$+ (100 - 170)^2 + (130 - 170)^2 + (120 - 170)^2 + (150 - 170)^2\}/(9 - 1)$$
$$= 22400\text{M}/8 = \text{JPY2800M}$$

   Median = the middle (fifth) value when arranged in numerical order, JPY 150K

   Question 2. Standard deviation = square root of the variance = $\sqrt{2800M}$ = 52.9K

© Springer Nature Singapore Pte Ltd. 2019
I. Kamae, *Health Technology Assessment in Japan*,
https://doi.org/10.1007/978-981-13-5793-0_5

Question 3. Standard error = standard deviation/$\sqrt{n}$ = 52.9K / $\sqrt{9}$ = 17.6K

Question 4. 95% confidence interval using the t-distribution = sample mean ± 2.306 × standard error

= 170K ± 2.306 × 17.6K
= (JPY 130K, 210K)

Question 5. The obtained 95% confidence interval does not contain the national average JPY 120K. That is, a significant difference is observed at the 5% significance level. The mean monthly treatment cost of JPY 170K reported for this patient group is therefore different from the national average.

Question 6. When using the national average of JPY 120K as an estimate in the base case analysis, it is not appropriate to use the range (JPY 130K, 210K) as the range of variation, since a significant difference is observed. However, when using the mean monthly treatment cost of JPY 170K reported for this patient group as an estimate in the base case analysis (assuming this is appropriate), it is acceptable to use the 95% confidence interval (JPY 130K, 210K) for the range of variation of the mean.

5.1.2 Epidemiological Survey

Example
In an epidemiological survey of a region, the percentage of smokers diagnosed with lung cancer was 70% in a group of 40 patients and 40% in a group of 30 subjects without lung cancer.

Question 1. What type of study is this?
Question 2. What is the risk ratio?
Question 3. What is the odds ratio?
Question 4. Find the 95% confidence interval for this odds ratio.
Question 5. Is it appropriate to conclude that smoking is associated with lung cancer?

Solutions
Question 1. A case-control study.

Question 2. A case-control study is a retrospective study, in which the risk of onset cannot be determined. Therefore, the risk ratio (relative risk) cannot be estimated either.

Question 3. A two-by-two table can be drawn as follows:

	Lung cancer	No lung cancer
Smoker	28 (a)	12 (b)
Non-smoker	12 (c)	18 (d)
	40	30

Odds ratio = $a \times d/b \times c$
= (28 × 18)/(12 × 12) = 3.5

Question 4. The 95% confidence interval of the odds ratio is

$$OR * e^{\pm 1.96\sqrt{V}} \text{ where } V = \frac{1}{a} + \frac{1}{b} + \frac{1}{c} + \frac{1}{d} = 1/28 + 1/12 + 1/12 + 1/18 = 0.258$$

$$= 3.5 \times e^{\pm 1.96\sqrt{0.258}}$$

$$= (1.29, 9.47)$$

Question 5. Since the 95% confidence interval obtained in Question 4 does not include 1, the odds ratio of 3.5 is statistically significant at the 5% significance level. Consequently, smoking is associated with lung cancer.

However, as pointed in Question 2, the risk for developing lung cancer from smoking cannot be estimated in a case-control study, and thus the odds ratio of 3.5 should not be interpreted as a risk ratio of 3.5. It is also incorrect to look at the two-by-two table by row and understand that 28 of 40 smokers developed lung cancer, thereby estimating that the incidence of lung cancer from smoking is 70% (= 28/40). Where the prevalence is low, however, the odds ratio is approximated to the risk ratio.

Since modeling in economic evaluations generally uses approaches such as decision trees and Markov models, which are used for analysis in prospective studies, it is not appropriate, in principle, to use evidence from case-control studies.

5.1.3 Sample Size Calculation (1)

Example
The average monthly cost per patient for the treatment of disease X is known to be JPY 1M in the standard treatment group. You wish to demonstrate that the average monthly cost of JPY 1.1M or more per patient receiving a new treatment is statistically significantly higher.

Question 1. Give reasons why sample size determination is required.
Question 2. Is it possible to calculate the needed sample size?
Question 3. What additional information is required to determine the required sample size?
Question 4. Based on the answer for Question 3, calculate the required sample size.

Solutions
Question 1. Reasons may include the following: to minimize the number of subjects, minimize the cost required for the study, increase the feasibility of the study, determine the sufficient level of statistical significance (for the evaluation of both effectiveness and cost), and design a subgroup analysis.
Question 2. Not possible.
Question 3. The following four factors need to be considered:

- What is the probability of type I error, α (significance level)?
- What is the statistical power $(1 - \beta)$?

- What is the difference in means between the two groups ($\mu_1 - \mu_0$)?
- What is the standard deviation σ of the population?

As the two means are already given, information on the standard deviation, significance level, and statistical power is additionally required. For instance, a question such as the following would allow for the calculation of sample size: "The average monthly cost per patient for the treatment of disease X is known to be JPY 1M in the standard treatment group, and *the standard deviation, JPY 0.24M.* You wish to demonstrate that the average monthly cost of JPY 1.1M or more per patient receiving a new treatment is statistically significantly higher. Given *the significance level of 5%* and *the power of 90%*, what is the sample size needed?"

Question 4. By substituting the values, $\mu_0 = 1M$, $\sigma = 0.24M$, $\mu_1 = 1.1M$,

$\alpha = 0.05 \rightarrow Z_\alpha = 1.96$,
$1 - \beta = 0.90 \rightarrow \beta = 10\% \rightarrow Z_\beta = -1.28$,

into the formula for sample size calculation:

$$n = \left(\frac{\left(Z_\alpha - Z_\beta \right)\sigma}{\mu_1 - \mu_0} \right)^2 ,$$

$$n = \left(\frac{(1.96 + 1.28)(0.24)}{1.1 - 1} \right)^2 = \left(\frac{0.7776}{0.1} \right)^2 = 60.47.$$

Therefore, the sample size is 61.

5.1.4   Sample Size Calculation (2)

Example
You wish to compare the standard treatment group for a disease with that of another group treated with a new drug X in a randomized clinical trial cost-effectiveness analysis. Given that the difference in average monthly cost of treatment per patient between the two groups is considered statistically significant if the difference is JPY 50K or greater, what is the sample size needed for a statistical test?

Question 1. Is it possible to calculate the sample size needed?

Question 2. Given the standard deviation of JPY 120K for both groups, significance level of 5%, and power of 80%, what is the needed sample size?

Solutions
Question 1. As in Question 2, Sect. 5.1.3, the sample size cannot be calculated without information regarding the standard deviation, significance level, and statistical power.

Question 2. The following formula can be used to determine the total sample size n needed for the two groups, based on the distribution of the difference in mean between the two groups (Δ):

$$n = 2\left(\frac{\left(z_\alpha - z_\beta\right)\sigma}{\Delta}\right)^2.$$

By substituting the values, $\Delta = 50{,}000$, $\sigma = 120{,}000$, the statistical power of 80% $\rightarrow Z_\beta = -0.84$, and the significance level of 0.05 $\rightarrow Z_\alpha = 1.96$ into the above formula:

$$n = 2\left(\frac{(1.96 + 0.84)(120{,}000)}{50{,}000}\right)^2 = 2\left(\frac{33.6}{5}\right)^2 = 90.3.$$

Therefore, the sample size is 91.

5.1.5   Diagnostic Tests and Decision Tree for Lung Cancer

Example
Assume that 18 of the 20 individuals suspected of lung cancer based on a computed tomography (CT) turned out to truly have lung cancer as a result of pathological examination, whereas the 2000 individuals diagnosed as free of lung cancer based on the same CT scan included four overlooked patients that had lung cancer. Given this, answer the following questions:

Question 1. Draw a two-by-two table based on the two factors, test results, and presence or absence of lung cancer.

Question 2. What are the sensitivity and the specificity of this CT scan?

Question 3. What are the positive and negative predictive values?

Question 4. If you were to integrate this CT scan into the analytical modeling in an economic evaluation using a decision tree, what would the tree look like?

Table 5.1 Two by two table for lung cancer test

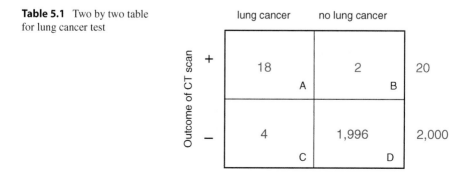

Solutions

  Question 1. See Table 5.1.

  Question 2. Sensitivity = probability of a positive test given that the patient has lung cancer = 18/(18 + 4) = 82%.

  Specificity = probability of a negative test given that the patient is free of lung cancer = 1996/(2 + 1996) = 99.9%.

  Sensitivity and specificity are key test characteristics in laboratory medicine.

  Question 3. Positive predictive value = probability that the patient truly has lung cancer given a positive test = 18/20 = 90%.

  Negative predictive value = probability that the patient is truly free of lung cancer given a negative test = 1996/2000 = 99.8%.

  Positive and negative predictive values are key test characteristics in medical diagnosis.

  Question 4. See Fig. 5.1. Positive and negative predictive values are assigned to the respective chance nodes following the bifurcation into positive and negative tests, as per Fig. 5.1. One should be careful not to assign sensitivity and specificity here.

5.1.6   Number Needed to Treat (NNT)

Example
The results of a clinical trial indicated efficacy rates of 60% and 55% for a new drug and a control drug, respectively. Given this, answer the following questions:

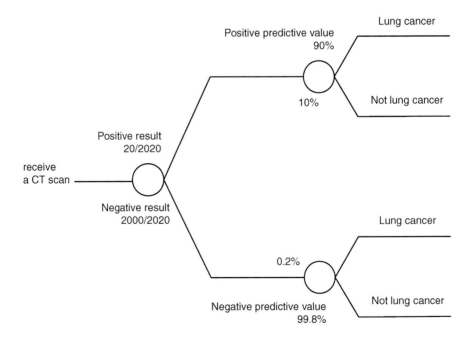

Fig. 5.1   The decision tree of lung cancer test

Question 1. What is the number needed to treat (NNT), and what does it indicate?

Question 2. Does the NNT obtained in Question 1 have any clinical significance?

Question 3. Give one example of where the NNT would take the same value as the one obtained in Question 1.

Question 4. Given that the sample size is 1000 for both groups, what is the 95% confidence interval of the NNT?

Question 5. What would the 95% confidence interval be if the sample size were 100 for both groups?

Question 6. Given that the treatment cost per patient is JPY 400K and 300K for the new and control drugs, respectively, what is the average treatment cost per patient for whom the treatment is effective in the two groups?

Question 7. Based on the treatment costs given in the previous question, what is the incremental cost-effectiveness ratio (ICER)?

Question 8. What is the relationship between the ICER and NNT?

Solutions

Question 1. The number needed to treat (NNT) is defined as the reciprocal of the difference in efficacy between the two groups. Thus, $1/(0.60 - 0.55) = 20$.

This value indicates that, on average, 1 out of 20 patients will benefit from switching to the new drug. Of course, whether a drug is effective in 1 patient is a stochastic phenomenon, and cases where the drug is effective in all or none of the 20 patients are also possible in reality. Therefore, NNT expresses the difference in the efficacy rate of 5% as an outcome measure of switching in terms of the number of patients. Since a difference in efficacy of 10% gives an NNT of 10, the difference needs to be above 10% to obtain a single-digit NNT.

NNT can also be explained in terms of probability. The phenomenon of a drug being effective or not is generally modeled on the "heads or tails" outcome of tossing a coin. The binomial distribution $B(n, p)$ is a typical probability distribution, in which the average number of heads that appear in n number of tosses can be obtained by $n \times p$, where p is the probability of obtaining head on a given trial. Based on this binomial distribution, the average number of patients that will benefit from switching to the new drug $= n \times p$

$$= \text{NNT} \times (1/\text{NNT})$$
$$= 1,$$

where p is the probability of the patient benefiting from switching to the new drug from the control drug and NNT the number of patients switching to the new drug.

Question 2. The smaller the NNT, the more effective the drug is compared to the control drug, although there is no absolute clinical standard for how small the NNT should be. An NNT of 30 or lower is considered "small" enough in some cases, in which the NNT of 20 for the new drug is a reasonable value. However, patients always expect the ideal NNT of 1 and may misunderstand the drug as having little effect when given a rough explanation such as "only 1 out of 20 patients treated with the new drug benefits from it." David Sackett and colleagues, who advocated evidence-based medicine, suggested that the NNT in terms of number of patients is a better measure compared with the probability of patients understanding the benefit of switching treatments. However, it should be noted that a simple conversion of efficacy to the number of patients without the underlying concept of probability could cause confusion.

Question 3. Different pairs of efficacy rates with the same difference between the respective two groups would give the same NNT. As an example of lower efficacy rates, a new and control drug with efficacy rates of only 15% and 10%, respectively, would also give an NNT of $1/(0.15 - 0.10) = 20$. In other words, the NNT has a limitation in that it does not reflect the baseline efficacy rate of treatment.

Question 4. To find the 95% confidence interval of the NNT, we first calculate the 95% confidence interval of the difference in efficacy between the two groups using the following formula:

$$\text{the 95\% confidence interval of the difference in efficacy}$$
$$\text{between the two groups} = \left(p_1 - p_2 \right) \pm 1.96\sqrt{V},$$

where $V = p_1(1 - p_1)/n + p_2(1 - p_2)/m$. Here, p_1 efficacy of the new drug, p_2 efficacy of the control drug, n number of patients in the new drug group, and m number of patients in the control drug group. Thus,

$V = 0.6 \times 0.4 / 1000 + 0.55 \times 0.45 / 1000 = 0.0004875;$

95% confidence interval of the difference in efficacy between the two groups

$= \left(0.60 - 0.55 \right) \pm 1.96\sqrt{0.0004875}$

$= \left(0.00672, 0.0933 \right)$

By taking the reciprocal of the upper and lower limits, the 95% confidence interval of the NNT is calculated to be $(1/0.0933, 1/0.00672) = (11 \text{ patients}, 148 \text{ patients})$.

Question 5. Similar to the previous question, $V = (0.6 \times 0.4/100) + (0.55 \times 0.45/100) = 0.004875$

Thus,

$$95\% \text{ confidence interval} = 0.05 \pm 1.96\sqrt{0.004875} = \left(-0.0868, 0.187 \right).$$

In this case, the 95% confidence interval of the difference in efficacy between the two groups includes zero, meaning there is no statistically significant difference between the two groups. Therefore, there is no clinical significance in obtaining a 95% confidence interval of the NNT that includes negative values.

Question 6. Given a sample size of 1000 for both groups, the new drug group requires JPY 400K × 1000 for 600 patients to benefit from the treatment, and the control drug group requires JPY 300K× 1000 for 550 patients to benefit. Thus, the average treatment cost per patient is

400,000K/600 = JPY 667K for the new drug group and
300,000K/550 = JPY 545K for the control drug group.

Question 7. ICER = difference in cost between the two groups/difference between the two groups in the number of patients for whom the respective treatments were effective

= (400,000K − 300,000K)/(600 − 550)
= JPY 2M per patient for whom the treatment is effective.

Question 8. The ICER in Question 7

= (400,000K − 300,000K)/(600 − 550)
= (400,000 − 300,000) × { 1/(0.6 − 0.55)}
= difference in treatment cost per patient between the two groups × NNT.

That is, the ICER is the product of the incremental cost per patient and NNT.

5.2   Methods for Economic Evaluation

5.2.1   Discounting

Example
Consider two 5-year healthcare programs, A and B, with annual costs as per Table 5.2. The outcomes of these programs are expected to be 25 QALYs from program A and 30 QALYs from program B. Consequently, calculate Questions 1–7.
  Question 1. The average cost-effectiveness ratio of programs A and B without adjustment for inflation and discounting.
  Question 2. The incremental cost-effectiveness ratio of program B to A without adjustment for inflation and discounting.
  Question 3. The average cost-effectiveness ratio of program A and B at a discount rate of 3%.
  Question 4. The incremental cost-effectiveness ratio of program B to A at a discount rate of 3%.
  Question 5. The average cost-effectiveness ratio of programs A and B at a discount rate of 3% and inflation rate of 2%.
  Question 6. The incremental cost-effectiveness ratio of program B to A at a discount rate of 3% and inflation rate of 2%.
  Question 7. What would the answers to Questions 1 through 6 be if the QALYs were adjusted for discount at a rate of 3%?

Table 5.2 Cost of two medical programs

Programs	A	B
First year	JPY300,000	JPY800,000
Second year	400,000	600,000
Third year	800,000	300,000
Fourth year	500,000	300,000
Fifth year	200,000	200,000
Total	2,200,000	2,200,000

Solutions

Question 1. The average cost-effectiveness ratio of programs A and B without adjustment for inflation and discounting

$CER_A = 2,200,000/25 = 88,000$ JPY/QALY
$CER_B = 2,200,000/30 = 73,333$ JPY/QALY

Question 2. The incremental cost-effectiveness ratio of program B to A without adjustment for inflation and discounting

$ICER = (2,200,000 - 2,200,000)/(30 - 25) = 0$

Question 3. The average cost-effectiveness ratio of programs A and B at a discount rate of 3% (Table 5.3, with the cost for year one also discounted)

$CER_A = 2,017,179/25 = 80,687$ JPY/QALY
$CER_B = 2,055,867/30 = 68,529$ JPY/QALY

Question 4. The incremental cost-effectiveness ratio of program B to A at a discount rate of 3%

$ICER = (2,055,867 - 2,017,179)/(30 - 25)$
$\qquad = 7,738$ JPY/QALY

Question 5. The average cost-effectiveness ratio of programs A and B at a discount rate of 3% and inflation rate of 2% (Table 5.4, with the cost for year 1 also discounted)

$CER_A = 1,904,506/25 = 76,180$ JPY/QALY
$CER_B = 1,966,279/30 = 65,543$ JPY/QALY

Question 6. The incremental cost-effectiveness ratio of program B to A at a discount rate of 3% and inflation rate of 2%

$ICER = (1,966,279 - 1,904,506)/(30 - 25) = 12,355$ JPY/QALY

Table 5.3 Setting a discount rate of 3%

Programs	A	B
First year	291,262	776,699
Second year	377,038	565,558
Third year	732,113	274,542
Fourth year	444,244	266,546
Fifth year	172,522	172,522
Total	2,017,179	2,055,867

$$\text{Cost for 5 years} = \frac{C_1}{(1.03)^1} + \frac{C_2}{(1.03)^2} + \frac{C_3}{(1.03)^3} + \frac{C_4}{(1.03)^4} + \frac{C_5}{(1.03)^5}$$

Table 5.4 Setting a discount rate of 3% and inflation with 2%

Programs	A	B
First year	285,551	761,470
Second year	362,398	543,596
Third year	689,887	258,708
Fourth year	410,412	246,247
Fifth year	156,258	156,258
Total	1,904,506	1,966,279

$$\text{Cost for 5 years} = \frac{C_1}{(1.03)^1 \cdot (1.02)^1} + \frac{C_2}{(1.03)^2 \cdot (1.02)^2} + \frac{C_3}{(1.03)^3 \cdot (1.02)^3} + \frac{C_4}{(1.03)^4 \cdot (1.02)^4} + \frac{C_5}{(1.03)^5 \cdot (1.02)^5}$$

Table 5.5 Discount of QALYs with 3%

$$\text{Discounted QALYs} = \frac{\text{Gross QALYs for 5 years}}{(1.03)^5}$$

$$\text{A:} \quad \frac{25}{(1.03)^5} = 21.6 \,\text{QALYs}$$

$$\text{B:} \quad \frac{30}{(1.03)^5} = 25.9 \,\text{QALYs}$$

Question 7. Since the QALYs are given as the outcomes of the entire 5-year programs, the discount is applied to the QALYs in the 5th year (Table 5.5). Question 1′

$CER_A = 2,200,000/21.6 = 101,851$ JPY/QALY
$CER_B = 2,200,000/25.9 = 84,942$ JPY/QALY

Question 2′

$ICER = (2,200,000 - 2,200,000)/(25.9 - 21.6) = 0$ JPY/QALY

Question 3′

$CER_A = 2,017,179/21.6 = 93,388$ JPY/QALY
$CER_B = 2,055,867/25.9 = 79,377$ JPY/QALY

Question 4′

ICER = (2,055,867 − 2,017,179)/(25.9 − 21.6)
     = 8,997 JPY/QALY gained

Question 5′

CER_A = 1,904,506/21.6 = 88,314 JPY/QALY
CER_B = 1,966,279/25.9 = 75,918 JPY/QALY

Question 6′

ICER = (1,966,279 − 1,904,506)/(25.9 − 21.6)
     = 14,366 JPY/QALY

Although, in these solutions, discounts were applied from year 1, another approach may be that values are not discounted in the first year, as shown in the alternative solutions (Table 5.6).

The MHLW Guidelines do not require discounting for study periods of 1 year or shorter or for periods short enough that the impact of time preference can be ignored. If, for instance, the cost for year n occurs early in the nth year, discounts may only be applied to the cost for a period of $n − 1$ years. That is, the cost for year 1 would

be $\dfrac{c_1}{(1.03)^{1-1}} = \dfrac{c_1}{(1.03)^0} = C_1$. The glossary of MHLW Guidelines uses the approach

in which discounts are not applied at year 1. Although, in this exercise, we used a discount rate of 3% for both costs and QALYs, the MHLW Guidelines specify that a rate of 2% be used for both costs and outcomes.

Table 5.6 An alternative answer for discounting

• Assuming the cost of the n-th year occur at early stage of the n-th year, discounting may be calculated as below.
<setting a discount rate at 3%>
$\text{Cost for 5 years} = C_1 + \dfrac{C_2}{(1.03)^1} + \dfrac{C_3}{(1.03)^2} + \dfrac{C_4}{(1.03)^3} + \dfrac{C_5}{(1.03)^4}$
<setting a discount rate at 3% and inflation with 2%>
$\text{Cost for 5 years} = C_1 + \dfrac{C_2}{(1.03)^1.(1.02)^1} + \dfrac{C_3}{(1.03)^2.(1.02)^2} + \dfrac{C_4}{(1.03)^3.(1.02)^3} + \dfrac{C_5}{(1.03)^4.(1.02)^4}$

5.2.2 Standard Gamble Method

Example
Assume that you were diagnosed with gastric cancer and were given 20 years to live with the standard treatment. Given this, answer the following questions:

Question 1. A witch appears with a treasure box and offers you a gamble to opening the box. By opening the box, you will be restored to perfect health with a probability of 10%, which is accompanied by the risk of immediate death with a probability of 90%. Would you open the treasure box?

Question 2. If you chose not to open the box in Question 1, consider increasing the probability of returning to perfect health from 10% to 20%, 30%, and so on until you find a specific probability of returning to perfect health (or a risk of death) you think is reasonable for you to open the box. If you chose to open the box, consider instead decreasing the probability of returning to perfect health until you find a specific probability of returning to perfect health (or a risk of death above 90%) that will stop you from opening the box.

Question 3. Draw a decision tree for the choice of opening or not opening the treasure box (with a utility of gastric cancer of u and a risk of immediate death of p).

Question 4. Based on the von Neumann-Morgenstern utility theorem, find the equation to obtain the utility.

Question 5. What is the estimated utility of your gastric cancer?

Solutions
Question 1. The answer will vary according to individual preferences. Assume, for instance, that you find the 90% probability of death too high, and thus choose not to open the box.

Question 2. After choosing not to open the box, assume that you find the probability of returning to perfect health of 95% (or the 5% probability of death) reasonable for you to open the box.

Question 3. See Fig. 5.2.

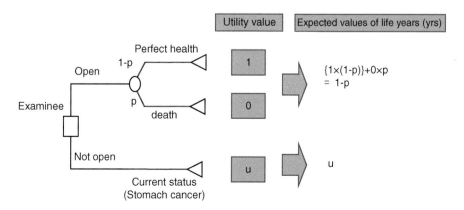

Fig. 5.2 Standard gamble method

Question 4. Based on the von Neumann-Morgenstern utility theorem, the expected utilities of opening and not opening the box will be $1 - p$ and u (the current state of gastric cancer is maintained), respectively, as shown in Fig. 5.2. The fact that the decision of whether to open the box is not easy suggests an equal expected utility for the two outcomes. Thus, the equation of $u = 1 - p$ is derived.

Question 5. By plugging in 0.05 for p from Question 2, $u = 1 - 0.05 = 0.95$.

5.2.3   Time Trade-Off Method

Example
Assume you were diagnosed with gastric cancer and were given 20 years to live with the standard treatment. Given this, answer the following questions:

Question 1. A witch appears and offers you a trade-off for life. By accepting the trade-off, you will immediately be restored to perfect health while, at the same time, required to give up 1 year of your life (that is, you will now have 19 years to live). Would you accept the trade-off?

Question 2. If you chose to accept the trade-off in Question 1, consider increasing the number of life years to give up until you find the maximum number of years you are willing to give up (or the minimum number of years you wish to keep). If you chose not to accept the trade-off, consider decreasing the length of life to give up until you find the maximum length of life that you are willing to give up (e.g., 2 months). You may also consider this as the maximum length of life you wish to maintain (e.g., 19 years and 6 months).

Question 3. Let u be the utility of gastric cancer and t the maximum length of life to keep. Graphically illustrate the two scenarios of accepting the trade-off (alternative 1) and not accepting the trade-off and remaining in the current state (alternative 2), with time on the x-axis and utility on the y-axis. Assume that utility remains constant throughout the entire time until death.

Question 4. Given that the trade-off is accepted, find the equation to obtain the utility.

Question 5. What is the estimated utility of your gastric cancer?

Question 6. Is the value of utility the same as the one obtained using the standard gamble method?

Solutions
Question 1. The answer will vary according to individual preferences. Assume, for instance, that you find the period of 1 life year too long to give up and thus choose not to accept the trade-off.

Question 2. After choosing not to accept the trade-off, assume that you find the period of 19 years and 6 months in perfect health (or 6 months of life to give up) reasonable to accept.

Question 3. See Fig. 5.3.

Fig. 5.3 Time trade-off method

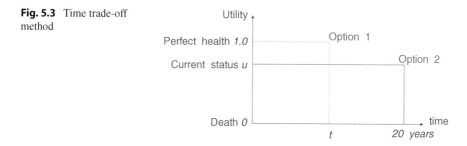

Question 4. Given that the trade-off is accepted, the areas of alternative 1 and 2 are considered equal. Therefore, $1 \times t = u \times 20$, from which the equation $u = t/20$ is derived.

Question 5. By plugging in 19.5 for t from Question 2, $u = 19.5/20 = 0.975$.

Question 6. As shown in Question 5, the utility takes a different value. This indicates the utility of a certain health state may not necessarily be the same when estimated using different methods.

5.2.4   CEA for Colon Polypectomy

Example

A 50-year-old patient A underwent a comprehensive medical examination, during which a colon polyp of 8 mm in diameter was found. According to his physician, the polyp is likely benign with a probability of 80%, although a 20% chance remains that the polyp is malignant. The patient's life expectancy will be 30 years if the polyp turns out to be benign and 2 years if malignant. The physician thus recommended a colonoscopic polypectomy for the patient.

Colonoscopic polypectomies have a success rate of 99.9%, although a risk of failure (e.g., perforation) also exists due to the wall of the large intestine being thin. If the procedure fails, there is a 1% risk that it will result in death in the worst-case scenario. Even if the failure is not life threatening, it may result in reducing life expectancy to around 1 year if the polyp is malignant (if benign, life expectancy will be reduced by around 5 years). At the same time, there is also a 30% chance of recurrence even if the procedure is successfully completed. If there is no recurrence, the patient's life expectancy will be 30 years, as in the case of the benign polyp. A recurrent polyp will have a risk of being malignant that equals the current risk and is estimated to reduce life expectancy to around 1 year if malignant (if benign, life expectancy will be reduced by around 5 years).

If the polyp is left untreated, there will be no cost incurred if the polyp turns out to be benign, while it may cost the patient in the future JPY 5M at present value if the polyp turns out to be malignant and ultimately progresses to colon cancer. If the patient decides to receive a polypectomy, a direct cost of JPY 1M will be incurred. If the polypectomy fails, it will cost the patient an additional treatment cost of JPY 2M if the patient survives and JPY 3M if the patient dies.

Consider if, after all, patient A should receive the polypectomy and how the cost-effectiveness of receiving the procedure compares to that of leaving the condition untreated.

Given the above case, answer Questions 1–6 below:

Question 1. Draw a decision tree of the polypectomy, and calculate and compare the life expectancy if the patient decides to receive or not the procedure.

Question 2. Using the decision tree in Question 1, similarly calculate and compare the expected cost.

Question 3. Based on the results obtained for Questions 1 and 2, find the ICER of the colonoscopic polypectomy by drawing a cost-effectiveness table.

Question 4. If we were to assign a utility of 0 to a malignant polyp, 0.88 to a benign polyp left untreated, and 0.8 to a recurrent benign polyp, to perform a decision analysis based on the QALYs, what would the answers to Questions 1–3 be? Additionally, evaluate the obtained ICER.

Question 5. Let x be the probability of the polyp being malignant, and recalculate the results obtained above. Additionally, present graphically a one-way sensitivity analysis of the expected cost with respect to changes in x. Find the probability of the polyp being malignant, at which the cost incurred will be the same regardless of the patient choosing the polypectomy or not. Overall, what is the best alternative in terms of expected cost?

Question 6. Let y be the probability of an unsuccessful polypectomy, and formulate the sensitivity analysis. Find the probability of the unsuccessful polypectomy at which the life expectancy will be the same regardless of the patient choosing the procedure or not.

Question 7. What would the results of a two-way sensitivity analysis with respect to x and y be, in which Questions 5 and 6 are simultaneously considered?

Solutions

Question 1. Figure 5.4 shows the decision tree. Life expectancies at nodes 1–4 in the figure are calculated as follows:

Node 1: $25 \times 0.8 + 1 \times 0.2 = 20.2$
Node 2: $25 \times 0.8 + 1 \times 0.2 = 20.2$
Node 3: $30 \times 0.7 + 20.2 \times 0.3 = 27.06$
Node 4: $20.2 \times 0.99 + 0 \times 0.01 = 19.998$

From above, the life expectancy will be

$27.06 \times 0.999 + 19.998 \times 0.001 = 27.05$ years when choosing polypectomy (node 5) and
$30 \times 0.8 + 2 \times 0.2 = 24.4$ years when choosing no polypectomy (node 6).

Therefore, the life expectancy will be longer when choosing the polypectomy.

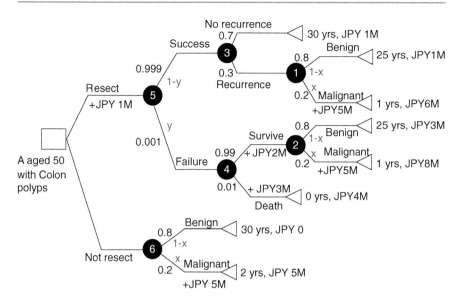

Fig. 5.4 The decision tree of polypectomy for colon polyps

Table 5.7 Cost effectiveness table

Intervention	Cost (JPY M)	Effectiveness (Life years)	Average cost effectiveness ratio (JPY K/year)	Incremental cost (JPY K)	Incremental effectiveness	ICER (JPY K/year)
Resect	1.3027	27.05	48.2	302.7	2.65	114
Not resect	1.00	24.4	41.0	–	–	–

Question 2. Similarly, the expected costs (in million JPY) at nodes 1–4 in Fig. 5.4 are calculated as follows:

Node 1: $1 \times 0.8 + 6 \times 0.2 = 2$
Node 2: $3 \times 0.8 + 8 \times 0.2 = 4$
Node 3: $1 \times 0.7 + 2 \times 0.3 = 1.3$
Node 4: $4 \times 0.99 + 4 \times 0.01 = 4$

From above, the expected cost will be

$1.3 \times 0.999 + 4 \times 0.001 = $ JPY 1.3M when choosing polypectomy (node 5) and $0 \times 0.8 + 5 \times 0.2 = $ JPY 1M when choosing no polypectomy (node 6).

Therefore, the expected cost will be lower when not choosing the polypectomy.
Question 3. See Table 5.7. The ICER is JPY114K/year.

Question 4. As in Question 1, life expectancies at nodes 1–4 in Fig. 5.4 are calculated as follows:

Node 1: $25 \times 0.8 \times 0.8 + 1 \times 0 \times 0.2 = 16$
Node 2: $25 \times 0.8 \times 0.8 + 1 \times 0 \times 0.2 = 16$
Node 3: $30 \times 0.8 \times 0.7 + 16 \times 0.3 = 21.6$
Node 4: $16 \times 0.99 + 0 \times 0.01 = 15.84$

From above, the life expectancy will be

$21.6 \times 0.999 + 15.84 \times 0.001 = 21.59$ QALYs when choosing polypectomy (node 5) and
$30 \times 0.88 \times 0.8 + 2 \times 0 \times 0.2 = 21.12$ QALYs when choosing no polypectomy (node 6).

Therefore, the life expectancy will also be longer when choosing the polypectomy based on QALYs. The incremental QALY is 0.47 years, from which the ICER is calculated as 0.3027M/0.47 = JPY0.644M/QALY gained. This value differs by one order of magnitude from the common cost-effectiveness standard of JPY5 – 6M/QALY, clearly indicating that the procedure is "cost-effective."

Question 5

(i) Expected benefit (life expectancy)

Node 1: $25 \times (1 - x) + 1 \times x = 25 - 24x$
Node 2: $25 \times (1 - x) + 1 \times x = 25 - 24x$
Node 3: $30 \times 0.7 + (25 - 24x) \times 0.3 = 28.5 - 7.2x$
Node 4: $(25 - 24x) \times 0.99 + 0 \times 0.01 = 24.75 - 23.76x$
Node 5: $(28.5 - 7.2x) \times 0.999 + (24.75 - 23.76x) \times 0.001 = 28.49625 - 7.21656x$
Node 6: $30 \times (1 - x) + 2 \times x = 30 - 28x$

(ii) Expected cost (JPY in million)

Node 1: $1 \times (1 - x) + 6 \times x = 1 + 5x$
Node 2: $3 \times (1 - x) + 8 \times x = 3 + 5x$
Node 3: $1 \times 0.7 + (1 + 5x) \times 0.3 = 1 + 1.5x$
Node 4: $(3 + 5x) \times 0.99 + 4 \times 0.01 = 3.01 + 4.95x$
Node 5: $(1 + 1.5x) \times 0.999 + (3.01 + 4.95x) \times 0.001$
$= 1.00201 + 1.50345x$
$\approx 1 + 1.5x$
Node 6: $0 \times (1 - x) + 5 \times x = 5x$

(iii) Cost-effectiveness analysis

ICER $= \{(1.00201M + 1.50345M\ x) - 5M\ x\}/\{(28.496 - 7.212x) - (30 - 28x)\}$
$= (1.00201M - 3.49655M\ x)/(-1.504 + 20.783x)$

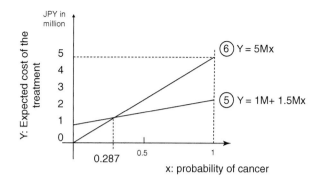

Fig. 5.5 One-way sensitivity analysis

Figure 5.5 shows the results of a sensitivity analysis with respect to x. The point in which the two lines intersect in Fig. 5.5 represents the probability x at which the cost of the polytectomy equals to that of no polytectomy. That is, line 5 = line 6, i.e., $1M + 1.5M x = 5M x$, which gives $x = 28.6\%$. Therefore, the cost will be lower with polypectomy if the probability of cancer is above 28.6% and with no polypectomy if the probability of cancer is below 28.6%.

Question 6

(i) Expected benefit (life expectancy)

Node 1: $25 \times 0.8 + 1 \times 0.2 = 20.2$
Node 2: $25 \times 0.8 + 1 \times 0.2 = 20.2$
Node 3: $30 \times 0.7 + 20.2 \times 0.3 = 27.06$
Node 4: $20.2 \times 0.99 + 0 \times 0.01 = 19.998$
Node 5: $27.06 \times (1 - y) + 19.998 \times y = 27.06 - 7.062y$
Node 6: $30 \times 0.8 + 2 \times 0.2 = 24.4$

(ii) Expected cost (JPY in million)

Node 1: $1 \times 0.8 + 6 \times 0.2 = 2$
Node 2: $3 \times 0.8 + 8 \times 0.2 = 4$
Node 3: $1 \times 0.7 + 2 \times 0.3 = 1.3$
Node 4: $4 \times 0.99 + 4 \times 0.01 = 4$
Node 5: $1.3 \times (1 - y) + 4 \times y = 1.3 + 2.7 y$
Node 6: $0 \times 0.8 + 5 \times 0.2 = 1$

(iii) Cost-effectiveness analysis

$\text{ICER} = \{(1.3M + 2.7M\ y) - 1M\}/\{(27.06 - 7.062y) - 24.4\}$
$= (0.3M + 2.7M\ y)/(2.66 - 7.062y)$

The life expectancy with polypectomy equals that with no polypectomy when the equation for Node 5 = Node 6 in (i) above holds true, i.e., $27.06 - 7.062y = 24.4$, which gives $y = 37.7\%$.

Question 7

(i) Expected benefit (life expectancy)

Node 1: $25 \times (1 - x) + 1 \times x = 25 - 24x$
Node 2: $25 \times (1 - x) + 1 \times x = 25 - 24x$
Node 3: $30 \times 0.7 + (25 - 24x) \times 0.3 = 28.5 - 7.2x$
Node 4: $(25 - 24x) \times 0.99 + 0 \times 0.01 = 24.75 - 23.76x$
Node 5: $(28.5 - 7.2x) \times (1 - y) + (24.75 - 23.76x) \times y$
$= 28.5 - 28.5y - 7.2x + 7.2xy + 24.75y - 23.76xy$
$= 28.5 - 7.2x - 3.75y - 16.56xy$
Node 6: $30 \times (1 - x) + 2 \times x = 30 - 28x$

(ii) Expected cost (JPY in million)

Node 1: $1 \times (1 - x) + 6 \times x = 1 + 5x$
Node 2: $3 \times (1 - x) + 8 \times x = 3 + 5x$
Node 3: $1 \times 0.7 + (1 + 5x) \times 0.3 = 1 + 1.5x$
Node 4: $(3 + 5x) \times 0.99 + 4 \times 0.01 = 3.01 + 4.95x$
Node 5: $(1 + 1.5x) \times (1 - y) + (3.01 + 4.95x) \times y$
$= 1 - 1y + 1.5x - 1.5xy + 3.01y + 4.95xy$
$= 1 + 1.5x + 2.01y + 3.45xy$
Node 6: $0 \times (1 - x) + 5 \times x = 5x$

(iii) Cost-effectiveness analysis

ICER $= \{(1M + 1.5Mx + 2.01My + 3.45Mxy) - 5Mx\}/$
$\{(28.5 - 7.2x - 3.75y - 16.56xy) - (30 - 28x)\}$
$= (1M - 3.5Mx + 2.01My + 3.45Mxy)/(-1.5 + 20.8x - 3.75y - 16.56xy)$

To graphically present the results of a two-way sensitivity analysis, the values need to be considered in terms of three coordinates. For instance, the expected benefits (life expectancies) in the following equations represent three-dimensional surface z, which corresponds to the depth when the xy plane (both x and y take values between 0 and 1) is considered as $z = 0$.

Life expectancy with polypectomy: $z_1 = 28.5 - 7.2x - 3.75y - 16.56xy$
Life expectancy with no polypectomy: $z_2 = 30 - 28x$

Therefore, the relationship between x and y on the xy plane can be determined by assigning the value 0 to z.

That is,

Life expectancy with polypectomy : $0 = 28.5 - 7.2x - 3.75y - 16.56xy$ (5.1)

$$\text{Life expectancy with no polypectomy}: 0 = 30 - 28x \qquad (5.2)$$

From the above, Eq. (5.1) can be written as $y = (28.5 - 7.2x)/(3.75 + 16.56x)$ to determine the relationship between x and y on a two-dimensional plane. Equation (5.2) will be $x = 30/28 > 1$, on which the value of y has no impact (as y is the probability of an unsuccessful polypectomy, it is obvious that y has no impact when no polypectomy is chosen).

5.2.5   Markov Model for Metabolic Syndrome

Example

To model the changes in the health state of a 40-year-old male patient diagnosed with metabolic syndrome from the current condition to diabetes, consider a Markov chain consisting of four clinical states: metabolic syndrome, borderline diabetes, diabetes, and dead. This patient has a 10% probability of progressing to borderline diabetes or developing diabetes and a 0.01% probability of dying after 1 year. Patients with borderline diabetes generally have a 10% probability of returning to the original metabolic syndrome state after 1 year but also have a roughly 20% probability of progressing to diabetes and a risk of around 0.1% of dying. Patients with diabetes still have an around 10% probability of returning to borderline diabetes after 1 year but little chance of returning to the original state of metabolic syndrome with no glucose metabolism disorders. Patients with diabetes also have a 1% risk of dying.

Given this, answer Questions 1–5 below:

Question 1. Draw a state transition diagram with transition probabilities assigned to the respective states.

Question 2. Assume a cohort of 10,000 patients, and draw a state transition table for the 2nd and 3rd years.

Question 3. Assume the utilities of the four states, metabolic syndrome, borderline diabetes, diabetes, and dead, are 0.9, 0.8, 0.6, and 0, respectively. Assign these utilities to the respective states in the state transition table, and find the cumulative utility.

Question 4. Assuming the annual costs incurred in the four states are JPY 2, 5, 100 (respectively, × 10K), and 0, find the cumulative cost.

Question 5. Consider a new drug, Metabo Clear, indications for which include a wide range of conditions from metabolic syndrome to diabetes. Although the drug does not directly reduce the risk of death, it is known to prevent disease progression by 2% or increase the chance of returning to the previous state by 2%. The annual cost of Metabo Clear is JPY 50K per patient. Given this, calculate the ICER of Metabo Clear per 1 QALY gained in the first 3 years of treatment.

Solutions

Question 1. See Fig. 5.6 and Table 5.8.

Question 2. See Table 5.9 (based on matrix calculations in Excel).
Question 3. 25,860 QALYs, as shown in Table 5.10.
Question 4. JPY 3,509,790,000, as shown in Table 5.11.

Fig. 5.6 State transition diagram of Markov model

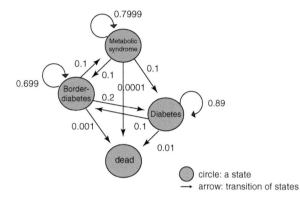

circle: a state
→ arrow: transition of states

Table 5.8 State transition probability (untreated group) and utility values/cost

After transition	Before transition					
	Metabolic syndrome	Borderline	Diabetic	Dead	Utility value	Cost (JPY 10K)
Metabolic syndrome	0.7999	0.1	0.1	0.0001	0.9	2
Borderline	0.1	0.699	0.2	0.001	0.8	5
Diabetic	0	0.1	0.89	0.01	0.6	100
Dead	0	0	0	1	0	0

Table 5.9 State transition table (untreated group)

	First year	Second year	Third year	
Metabolic syndrome	10,000	7,999	6,498.4001	
Borderline	0	1,000	1,598.9	
Diabetic	0	1,000	1,889.9	
Dead	0	1	12.7999	
Total	10,000	9,999	9,987.2001	Total number of people = 29,986.2001

Table 5.10 Utility values (untreated group)

	First year	Second year	Third year	Total
Metabolic syndrome	9,000	7,199.1	5,848.56009	22,047.66009
Borderline	0	800	1,279.12	2,079.12
Diabetic	0	600	1,133.94	1,733.94
Dead	0	0	0	0

Table 5.11   Cost [JPY × 10K] (untreated group)

	First year	Second year	Third year	Total
Metabolic syndrome	20,000	15,998	12,996.8002	48,994.8002
Borderline	0	5,000	7,994.5	12,994.5
Diabetic	0	100,000	188,990	288,990
Dead	0	0	0	0

Table 5.12   State transition probability (metabolic clearance treatment group) and utility values/ cost

After transition	Before transition						
	Metabolic syndrome	Borderline	Diabetic	Dead	Utility value	Cost (JPY 10K)	Improvement rate
Metabolic syndrome	0.8399	0.12	0	0	0.9	7	0.02
Borderline	0.08	0.699	0.12	0	0.8	10	
Diabetic	0.08	0.18	0.87	0	0.6	105	
Dead	0.0001	0.001	0.01	1	0	0	

Table 5.13   State transition table (metabolic clearance treatment group)

	First year	Second year	Third year	
Metabolic syndrome	10,000	8,399	7,150.3201	
Borderline	0	800	1,327.12	
Diabetic	0	800	1,511.92	
Dead	0	1	10.6399	
Total	10,000	9,999	9,989.3601	Total number of people = 29,988.3601

Table 5.14   Utility values (metabolic clearance treatment group)

	First year	Second year	Third year	Total
Metabolic syndrome	9,000	7,559.1	6,435.28809	22,994.39
Borderline	0	640	1,061.696	1,701.696
Diabetic	0	480	907.152	1,387.152
Dead	0	0	0	0
				Full total = 26,083.23609

Question 5. First, we determine the state transition probabilities that consider the effects of Metabo Clear, as well as the costs incurred in the respective states, as shown in Table 5.12. Based on this, a state transition table is obtained (Table 5.13). The cumulative QALY and cost are presented in Tables 5.14 and 5.15, respectively. Table 5.16 summarizes the cumulative number of patients, as well as the cumulative QALY and cost (in JPY × 10K) for the first 3 years, for which the QALYs gained and cost incurred per patient are calculated as per Table 5.17. Overall, the incremental

Table 5.15 Cost [JPY × 10K] (metabolic clearance treatment group)

	First year	Second year	Third year	Total
Metabolic syndrome	70,000	58,793	50,052.2407	178,845.2407
Borderline	0	8,000	13,271.2	21,271.2
Diabetic	0	84,000	158,751.6	242,751.6
Dead	0	0	0	0
				Full total = 442,868.0407

Table 5.16 Summary of the outcomes in two groups

	Total number of people	Accumulative utility	Cost [JPY × 10K]
Untreated	29,986.2001	25,860.72009	350,979.3002
Treated	29,988.3601	26,083.23609	442,868.0407

Table 5.17 QALY and cost per patient

	QALY per patient	Cost per patient [JPY × 10K]
Untreated	0.862420714	11.70469413
Treated	0.869778674	14.76799796

Table 5.18 The estimate of ICER

	Incremental cost [JPY × 10K]	Incremental effectiveness [QALY]	ICER [JPY × 10K/ QALY]
Untreated	–	–	
Treated	3.06330383	0.007357961	416

cost and effect are calculated to be JPY 30,633 and 0.007358 QALYs, respectively, as shown in Table 5.18, which gives the following:

ICER = 30,633 JPY/0.007358 QALYs = 416 × 10KJPY/QALY gained.

5.2.6 Scatter Plot

Example
Figure 5.7 shows a scatter plot obtained from the results of a randomized controlled trial cost-effectiveness analysis. The values inside the ellipse indicate the number of points in each area. Given this, answer the following questions:

Question 1. What is the probability of the intervention dominating by simple dominance?

Question 2. Find the percentage for the following combined cases: cases where the intervention is more effective but also costlier with an ICER of within 30K USD/QALY and cases where the intervention dominates by simple dominance.

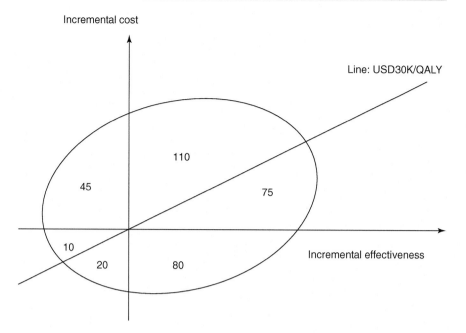

Incremental cost

Line: USD30K/QALY

110

45   75

10

20   80

Incremental effectiveness

Fig. 5.7 Example of a scatter plot

Question 3. What is the difference between the percentage obtained in Question 2 and the percentage of cases where the intervention is evaluated as being cost-effective based on the threshold of 30K USD/QALY?

Solutions

Question 1. The total number of points on the scatter plot is

$$80 + 75 + 110 + 45 + 10 + 20 = 340.$$

The number of cases where the intervention dominates by simple dominance (more effective and less costly) is 80, and thus,

$$80/340 = 23.5\%.$$

Question 2. The scatter plot shows that 75 of the points have an ICER that ranges from 0 to 30K USD/QALY. Therefore,

$$(75 + 80)/340 = 45.6\%.$$

Question 3. An intervention is evaluated as being cost-effective when the ICER falls in the area under the threshold of USD 30K. In the scatter plot, there are 20 + 80 + 75 = 175 such points. Therefore, the percentage of cases where the intervention is evaluated as being cost-effective is

175/340 = 51.5%.

This percentage includes the 20 points where the intervention is less costly but also less effective and thus overestimates the cost-effectiveness of intervention compared with the percentage for the cases where the intervention is more effective and also more cost-effective (ideal in practice).

5.2.7 Cost-Effectiveness Acceptability Curve (CEAC) (1)

Example
Figure 5.8 shows a cost-effectiveness acceptability curve (CEAC) obtained from the results of a probabilistic sensitivity analysis performed in a cost-effectiveness analysis. Given this, answer the following questions:

Question 1. What is the probability that the intervention has a positive net monetary benefit (NMB) at the threshold of 50K USD/QALY?

Question 2. In which cases does the NMB take positive values?

Question 3. The plot shows a probability of 9% at the threshold λ of 0. What does this indicate?

Question 4. Is the threshold of 50K USD/QALY appropriate in this case?

Solutions
Question 1. By looking at Fig. 5.8, 60%.

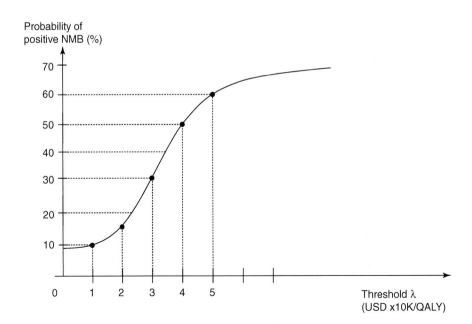

Fig. 5.8 Example of cost-effectiveness acceptability curve

Question 2. The NMB takes a positive value when the point representing the cost and effect of intervention falls below the threshold line on the incremental cost-effectiveness plane.

Question 3. The threshold λ of 0 indicates that the threshold line overlaps the x-axis. Thus, 9% of the points on the incremental cost-effectiveness plane fall below the x-axis.

Question 4. Whether the threshold is appropriate cannot be determined by looking at the CEAC, as there is no absolute standard for the threshold. However, the threshold of 50K USD/QALY has traditionally been adopted by US researchers as a guide and the curve in Fig. 5.8 plateaus as λ increases above 50K USD/QALY, suggesting that increases in probability cannot be expected at thresholds above 50K USD/QALY. From the above, the threshold of 50K USD/QALY may be interpreted as a valid criterion.

5.2.8   Cost-Effectiveness Acceptability Curve (CEAC) (2)

Example

The distribution by quadrant was examined in a scatter plot obtained from the results of a cost-effectiveness analysis, and the results were presented as the two subgroup curves represented with dotted lines in Fig. 5.9.

In Fig. 5.9, what does area A indicate, and why is the subgroup curve drawn as a straight line?

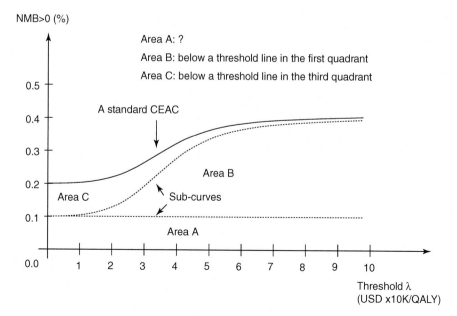

Fig. 5.9 Example of sub-analysis of CEAC

Solutions
In the scatter plot drawn on the cost-effectiveness plane, the area under the threshold line includes three quadrants: first (NE; North-East), third (SW), and fourth (SE). Areas B and C in Fig. 5.9 represent the areas under the threshold line in the first and third quadrants, respectively, and thus the remaining area A corresponds to the area in the fourth quadrant. In the fourth quadrant, the new intervention is more effective and less costly (simple dominance), suggesting that area A is where the intervention is dominant by simple dominance. When drawing a CEAC, the threshold line is rotated from the slope of 0 (corresponds to the *x*-axis) to infinity (corresponds to the *y*-axis), during which the fourth quadrant always falls under the threshold line. Therefore, the proportion of area A remains constant, and the curve representing this proportion will naturally be a straight line.

The area under the CEAC represents the case where the intervention is evaluated as being cost-effective based on a given threshold. However, area C is not necessarily favorable, as it represents the case where the intervention is less effective. Thus, it is important to examine the subgroup curve that represents areas A and B together, but excludes area C, in fully interpreting the CEAC.

5.2.9   Cost-Effectiveness Acceptability Curve (CEAC) (3)

Example
Figure 5.10 shows a scatter plot obtained from the results of a cost-effectiveness analysis. Given this, graphically illustrate the CEAC expected from this plot.

Solutions
In this case, the scatter plot falls mainly in the third quadrant. This suggests that most of the points will fall below the threshold line at the start of the rotation (at the slope of 0) of the line over the plot. By contrast, the proportion of points that fall

Fig. 5.10 Example of a scatter plot

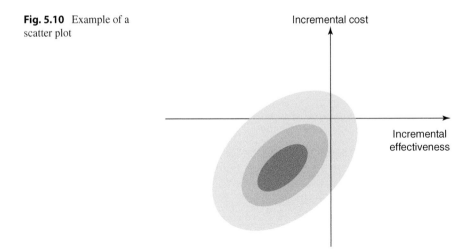

Incremental cost

Incremental effectiveness

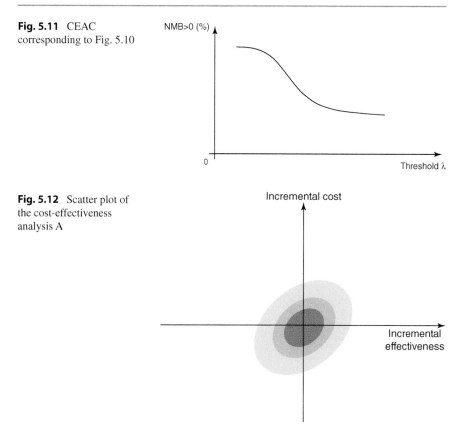

Fig. 5.11 CEAC corresponding to Fig. 5.10

Fig. 5.12 Scatter plot of the cost-effectiveness analysis A

right of the *y*-axis will be small at the end of the rotation (at the slope of infinity). Therefore, the curve will not be a typical CEAC that traces a positively sloped, s-shaped curve originating at around 0% on the vertical axis but is expected to trace a completely inverted, negatively sloped curve originating at around 100%, as shown in Fig. 5.11. One should note that CEACs are not always positively sloped as seen in this example and that they may trace a curve that looks very different from a typical CEAC, depending on the distribution and shape of the scatter plot.

5.2.10 Cost-Effectiveness Acceptability Curve (CEAC) (4)

Example
Figure 5.12 shows a scatter plot obtained from the results of a cost-effectiveness analysis A. From the results of another cost-effectiveness analysis B, the scatter plot shown in Fig. 5.13 was obtained, with a similar shape but scattered over a larger area compared to Fig. 5.12. How would the CEACs obtained from Figs. 5.12 and 5.13 could be compared?

Fig. 5.13 Scatter plot of
the cost-effectiveness
analysis B

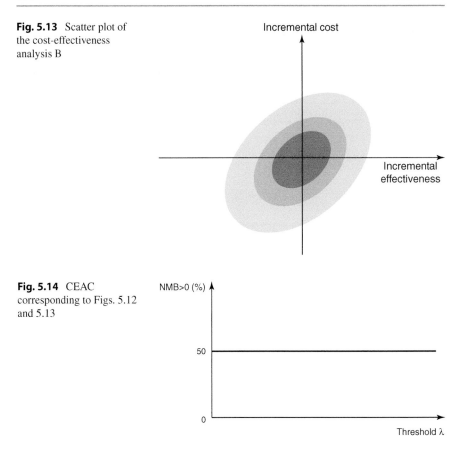

Fig. 5.14 CEAC
corresponding to Figs. 5.12
and 5.13

Solutions

First, the scatter plot in Fig. 5.12 takes the shape of an ellipse that is centered near
the origin, suggesting that the proportion of points that fall under the threshold line
remains constant at around 50%, regardless of what values threshold λ takes. This
can be illustrated as a horizontal line at around 50%, as shown in Fig. 5.14.

Similarly, the scatter plot in Fig. 5.13 takes a shape similar to that in Fig. 5.12,
suggesting that, despite the absolute values of cost and effect being greater, the
proportion of points that fall under the threshold line remains constant at an almost
equal percentage as for the scatter plot in Fig. 5.12. Therefore, the CEACs obtained
from Figs. 5.12 and 5.13 will be equivalent. Alternatively, the shape of the corresponding scatter plot cannot be uniquely determined given a CEAC. This should
also be noted when interpreting a CEAC.

5.2.11   Budget Impact Analysis (BIA)

Example

Assume a region subject to treatment for disease X has a population of 1M. According
to an epidemiological survey, the prevalence of disease X in this region is 10%.

The current standard treatment A for disease X costs JPY 10K per patient, with an additional JPY 2000 per patient for the treatment of side effects. On the other hand, the new treatment B costs JPY 30K per patient but is expected to have clinical benefits that will result in saving JPY 10K per patient. Given this, answer the following questions:

Question 1. Assuming that 10% of subjects switch to the new treatment B, perform a budget impact analysis (BIA). What is the expected budget impact in terms of total cost?

Question 2. What would be the results of the BIA in Question 1, if the rate of switching were 90%?

Question 3. Let x be the rate of switching and formulate the BIA.

Question 4. Using the formula obtained in Question 3, graphically present the results of a sensitivity analysis in terms of the rate of switching x.

Solutions

Question 1. First, we estimate the number of subjects as follows:

$$1M \times \text{prevalence} = 1M \times 0.1$$
$$= 100K \text{ subjects.}$$

Multiplying this by the sum of the cost of JPY 10K for standard treatment A and JPY 2K for side effects,

$$(\text{JPY } 10K + \text{JPY } 2K) \times 100K \text{ subjects} = \text{JPY } 1200M.$$

Since 90% of the subjects will continue to receive treatment A, its cost after the adoption of treatment B is calculated as follows:

$$\text{JPY } 1200M \times 0.9 = \text{JPY } 1080M.$$

At the same time, 10% of the 100K patients will switch to receiving treatment B, which equals 10K patients, whose treatment will cost

$(\text{JPY } 30K - \text{JPY } 10K) \times 10K \text{ patients} = \text{JPY } 200M.$ When combined, treatments A and B will cost

$\text{JPY } 1080M + \text{JPY } 200M = \text{JPY } 1280M.$ Therefore, the total cost is expected to increase by JPY 80M (= JPY 1280M − JPY 1200M).

Question 2. As in Question 1, the cost of treatment A will be

$$\text{JPY } 1200M \times 0.1 = \text{JPY } 120M,$$

and the cost of treatment B for 90K patients will be

$$(\text{JPY } 30K - \text{JPY } 10K) \times 90K \text{ patients} = \text{JPY } 1800M.$$

Thus, the cost of treatments A and B combined will be

JPY 120M + JPY 1800M = JPY 1920M,

and the increase in cost will be

JPY 1920M – JPY 1200M = JPY 720M.

Question 3. Given the rate of switching x, the cost of treatment A can be expressed as JPY 1200M$(1 - x)$.

The number of patients receiving treatment B will be 100K x, with which the cost of treatment B can be expressed as

(JPY 30K – JPY 10K) × 100K x.

The total cost of treatments A and B will thus be

$1200M(1 - x) + 20K \times 100K\ x$
$= 1200M + 800M\ x$,

and the increase in cost will be

$(1200M + 800M\ x) - 1200M$
$= 800M\ x$.

That is, the increase in cost estimated in the BIA can be formulated as follows:

Increase in cost JPY= 800M x.

Using this formula, the answers to Questions 1 and 2 can be confirmed by plugging in 0.1 and 0.9 for x. Such a formula also allows for a sensitivity analysis by varying the value of x.

Question 4. The following formulae were obtained in Question 3:

1. Total cost of treatments A and B = JPY 1200M + JPY 800M x (where A = 1200M $(1 - x)$ and B = 2000M x)
2. Total cost with treatment A only = JPY 1200M

This can be presented as the graph in Fig. 5.15, with the rate of switching x on the horizontal axis and the cost on the vertical axis.

5.2.12   Budget Constraint and ICER

Example
The ICER of a new drug X to standard drug S_0 was found to be JPY 3M/QALY (= JPY 0.3M/0.1 QALY). The number of patients with indications for new drug X is

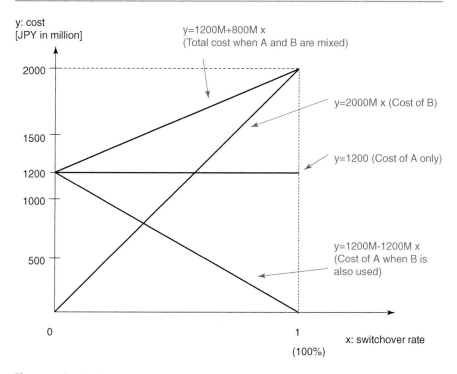

y: cost
[JPY in million]

y=1200M+800M x
(Total cost when A and B are mixed)

2000

y=2000M x (Cost of B)

1500

y=1200 (Cost of A only)

1200

1000

y=1200M-1200M x
(Cost of A when B is
also used)

500

0   1

(100%)

x: switchover rate

Fig. 5.15 Sensitivity analysis by switchover rate

estimated to be 100K. At the same time, another new drug Y was also found to have an ICER of JPY 3M/QALY (= JPY0.3M/0.1 QALY) to standard drug S_1, with the number of patients estimated at 300K. The government has specified JPY 30 billion as the maximum allowable increase in cost with the adoption of new drugs X or Y. Given this, answer the following questions:

Question 1. Based on the ICERs, are new drugs X and Y considered cost-effective?

Question 2. What is the estimated increase in cost with the adoption of new drug X? Is the increase within the budget specified by the government?

Question 3. Answer Question 2 for new drug Y.

Question 4. If the costs of new drugs exceed the government-specified budget, what does it indicate in terms of the ICER?

Question 5. What would happen if the ICER of new drug Y were JPY 30K/0.01 QALY?

Solutions
Although the relationship between the ICER and the budget is not always simple, this exercise assumes the simplest case, as per Fig. 5.16, where the incremental cost is inversely proportional to the number of patients under a specific budget limitation (here, by definition, the incremental cost is determined by ICER × incremental effect).

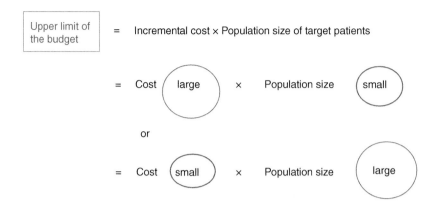

Fig. 5.16 Incremental cost and the population size of target patients

Question 1. Although there is no absolute standard, an ICER of JPY 3M (about USD 30K)/QALY would be considered cost-effective by standards in developed countries.

Question 2. From ICER = JPY 3M/QALY = 0.3M/0.1, the incremental cost is JPY 0.3M. The expected increase in cost will thus be JPY 0.3M × 100K patients = JPY 30 billion. This falls within the budget specified by the government.

Question 3. For new drug Y, the incremental cost will be the same, but the number of patients will be three times larger. Therefore,

JPY 0.3M × 300K patients = JPY 90 billion.

This far exceeds the government budget.

Question 4. Given the number of patients of 300K and the incremental cost x,

x × 300K patients ≤ JPY 30 billion,

and thus, x ≤ JPY 0.1M. The incremental cost must therefore be JPY 0.1M or smaller for new drug Y, indicating that an ICER of JPY 1M/ QALY (= JPY 0.1M/0.1) should be adopted as a threshold.

Question 5. If new drug Y had an incremental cost of JPY 30K, the total cost increase will be

JPY 30K × 300K patients = JPY 9 billion

and will fall within the budget.

As shown above, the issue of ICER and budget limitations needs to be examined in terms of the original incremental cost and effect data from which the ICER was derived, even in the simplest case scenario. Refer to Sect. 7.6 for more detailed formulations.

5.3   Business Strategy

5.3.1   Hurdle or Opportunity?

Example
The discipline of *iyaku keizaigaku* in Japanese, which corresponds to pharmaco-economics and the economics of medical devices in English, has yet to be well recognized in Japan. It may be considered as a sub-discipline of *iryo keizaigaku* (health economics), although there are likely not many healthcare professionals able to illustrate the difference between health and pharmacoeconomics. Recently, the concept of pharmacoeconomics has been widely introduced in business in the USA and Europe, whereas in Japan, economic evaluation remains to be not so much embraced by healthcare businesses. With this in mind, answer the following questions:

Question 1. Why is pharmacoeconomics not as widely recognized in Japan?

Question 2. What is the policy of the Ministry of Health, Labour and Welfare (MHLW)?

Question 3. What are the possible barriers for companies to adopt the concept of pharmacoeconomics?

Question 4. What are the reasons to believe there are no advantages to adopting pharmacoeconomics in business?

Question 5. By contrast, what are the factors in considering the adoption of pharmacoeconomics as an opportunity in business?

Question 6. What is essential in taking advantage of the opportunity for success?

Points to Consider
Question 1. It is likely due to a combination of factors, including the following: (1) success of universal healthcare system resulting in a mental block with respect to reform, (2) tradition to disregard clinical outcomes research, (3) illusion that HTA can be a drag on promoting clinical trials, (4) vertically segmented administrative system with the MHLW as the governing authority, (5) complex and isolated "Galapagos" drug pricing system, (6) delay by the MHLW in officially adopting cost-effectiveness evaluations until April 2016, (7) submission of new economic evidence being a negative corporate incentive, (8) lack of vision in the previous administrations to focus on HTA as a national strategy until the second Abe cabinet, (9) shortage of experts in the field of pharmacoeconomics, and (10) limited accessibility to epidemiological and cost data.

Question 2. According to the handouts at the meeting of the Special Committee on Cost-Effectiveness at Chuikyo on December 16, 2015 (underlined by the author), "The need for cost-effectiveness evaluation was recognized *in light of concerns over the impacts of costlier and more advanced health technologies for health and insurance funding, and is accounted for by the lack of consideration for cost-effectiveness in listing and reimbursement decisions, which led to the launch of the Special*

Committee on Cost-Effectiveness in May 2012 and subsequent discussions. The 'Preliminary Summary of the Outcome of Discussion' was released in November 2013, following which the meeting focused on the 'examination of specific cases' from April 2014 to May 2015 to extract challenges to be addressed for designing a new system, and published the 'Interim Report of the Outcome of Discussion on the Preliminary Implementation' on August 26, 2015." This ultimately led to the preliminary implementation of cost-effectiveness evaluations in April 2016 and full-scale implementation in April 2019.

Question 3. Possible barriers include (1) added expense, (2) lack of experts and specialized departments within the company, and (3) limited availability of epidemiological and cost data.

Question 4. The reasons may include that (1) Japan has established its own pricing system that has been functioning reasonably well, (2) the implementation of economic evaluation may lead to issues such as drug lag and limited patient accessibility, and (3) confusions may be caused due to a lack of understanding of economic evaluation by the respective concerned parties.

Question 5. The factors may include (1) strategic use of economic evaluation data under MHLW's new pricing system, (2) possibility of receiving high premiums, (3) new system allowing for negotiation over pricing decisions, (4) environment to value innovations, (5) use of cost-effectiveness evidence in clinical practice, and (6) application to the existing cost calculation method.

Question 6. Necessary actions include (1) launching a project within the company to promote the strategic use of economic evaluation and (2) designing the project.

5.3.2   Moving from Multidisciplinary to Interdisciplinary Approach

Example

Health technology assessment (HTA) is considered a practice based on learning that requires interdisciplinary knowledge and experience. What does interdisciplinarity refer to here? Answer the following questions:

Question 1. What is the concept of interdiscipline (interdisciplinary/interdisciplinarity)?

Question 2. Why does HTA require interdisciplinarity?

Question 3. What are the experiences and knowledge required for HTA experts?

Question 4. What are the ways to acquire interdisciplinary knowledge and experience?

Question 5. Which is required in developing and marketing pharmaceuticals, interdisciplinarity or expertise?

Points to Consider

Question 1. Interdisciplinarity involves the combining of experience, knowledge, and skills from two or more disciplines to address common issues. The term interdisciplinary is most common in English, although terms such as cross-disciplinary, multidisciplinary, and transdisciplinary are also used.

The differences between these terms are defined as follows by the US National Cancer Institute Transdisciplinary Research on Energetics and Cancer (TREC) initiative in collaboration with the Fred Hutchinson Cancer Research Center and the research centers at four US universities (http://www.obesity-cancer.wustl.edu/About/What-Is-Transdisciplinary-Research):

- Transdisciplinary research: "Collaboration in which exchanging information, altering discipline-specific approaches, sharing resources and integrating disciplines achieves a common scientific goal."
- Multidisciplinary research: "Researchers from a variety of disciplines work together at some point during a project, but have separate questions, separate conclusions, and disseminate in different journals."
- Interdisciplinary research: "Researchers interact with the goal of transferring knowledge from one discipline to another. Allows researchers to inform each other's work and compare individual findings."

Based on these definitions, the interdisciplinarity in economic evaluation studies requires a basis of transdisciplinarity, implies primarily interdisciplinary, and involves multidisciplinary collaborations.

Question 2. HTA is defined as a multidisciplinary process of analyzing, summarizing, and interpreting information about the medical, social, economic, and ethical issues related to the use of a health technology, using the scientific method and thus involving multiple disciplines in its efforts.

Question 3. Required experiences and knowledge, so-called HTA literacy, may include (1) knowledge of pharmaceuticals, (2) knowledge of and experience in clinical trials, (3) knowledge of strategic planning and market access, (4) knowledge of clinical trials and drug pricing (including application for manufacturing approval), (5) knowledge of statistical analysis, (6) knowledge in epidemiology and evidence-based medicine, (7) knowledge in health economics/pharmacoeconomics, (8) knowledge of healthcare system/application for listing, and (9) computer literacy.

Question 4. Possible means include (1) interest in multiple disciplines and determination to actively collect information, (2) to be assigned to the project team full time, (3) taking advantage of on-the-job training opportunities (participation in conferences and meetings, including those of the ISPOR and HTAi), (4) enrollment in graduate training programs (overseas and domestic study programs and certification programs), (5) networking with universities and researchers, (6) networking with hospitals and clinicians (especially those that are able to take part in clinical outcomes research), and (7) collaborating in clinical trials.

Question 5. The project team should ideally consist of both types of members, with expertise and interdisciplinarity.

5.3.3 Use of Pharmacoeconomics to Support Manufacturer Internal Decision-Making

Example
Adoption of pharmacoeconomics in business requires the launching of a project within the company, whose success depends on the team and the vision.

If you were to be appointed as the project leader, how would you answer the following questions?

Question 1. What is the process required for the proposal and approval of an in-house project?

Question 2. What consists an ideal team of when launching a project from scratch, and what are the recruitment strategies?

Question 3. What are the points to be discussed for launching the project?

Question 4. What are the possible plans and visions for the project?

Question 5. What are the appropriate duration of a project and the appropriate means to evaluate its outcomes?

Points to Consider

Question 1. See Fig. 5.17. The process here refers not to the rules of launching an in-house project but to the process of realizing the hierarchical picture of a new business model. Particularly, the vision of company's leader (including a CEO) is essential.

Question 2. The project team should consist of members with the knowledge and experience discussed in Sect. 5.3.2, Question 4. The recruitment category should be extended to include candidates who have received professional training in pharmacoeconomics at universities outside Japan.

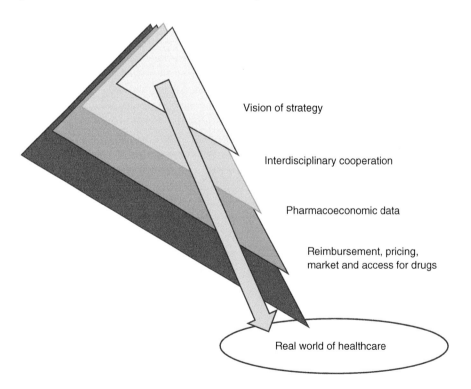

Fig. 5.17 Hierarchical concept of new business models in healthcare

Question 3.

1. Launching of an in-house project to promote the strategic use of economic evaluation topics may include methodology, validity, feasibility, discussion among concerned parties, and human resources/departments/budget.
2. Designing of project topics may include change of perspective from "passive" to "aggressive," attitude in negotiating drug prices, focus of negotiation, decision of whether to pursue cost reduction, development of sophisticated strategy in drug price calculations, securing support from the CEO, training of staff, building of networks with universities and experts, and outsourcing of analyses.

Question 4. Similar to the outcomes research required in clinical research and development, projects must be planned in line with the phases of development, as follows:

1. Business as usual
   Training of staff, data collection, organization building, networking with external and international experts, and development of infrastructure and awareness building for patient participation, for the purpose of economic evaluation and outcomes assessment.
2. Preclinical phase
   Assessment of the future value of the new drug (value positioning), including the expected benefits, ICER, sales volume, and financial impacts.
3. Clinical phase
   Collection and analysis of cost data and cost-effectiveness analysis alongside clinical trials (piggyback studies).
4. Application for insurance coverage
   Preparation of value data (the results of economic evaluation in particular). Under the preliminary implementation in FY2016, submission of cost-effectiveness evidence is required by Chuikyo for new drugs that satisfy specific criteria, and cost-effectiveness evidence will be considered in pricing decisions for existing drugs that satisfy specific criteria.
5. Post-marketing surveillance phase
   Writing and publishing the outcomes (may be required prior to application for insurance coverage), collection and analysis of real-world data, submission of required value data (the results of economic evaluation in particular) (designing and performing CEAs to generate cost-effectiveness evidence for repricing decisions), and communicating the value proposition to the society (clinicians and patient associations) in accordance with the product's marketing strategy.

Additionally, the project may adopt visions related to the company's management strategy (including benchmarking of the "performance" of the company's products in terms of cost-effectiveness and collaborating internationally in the development, application, and marketing of new products) that are independent of the phases of clinical development.

Question 5. There is no absolute standard for the duration of a project, and so the duration has to be decided on a project-by-project basis. It will be based on the duration of clinical development in cases where the project proceeds along the phases of clinical development; otherwise the period is between 6 months to a year, where 6 months is the standard length for short-term projects with a single objective.

5.3.4 External Consulting

Example
Adoption of HTA in business may require external consultation in addition to launching in-house projects. As a project leader, how would you answer the following questions?

Question 1. In what cases is external consultation required?

Question 2. What are the expected outputs of consultation?

Question 3. Who will be responsible for reading and reporting the outcomes of consultation?

Points to Consider

Question 1. The need for external consultation is evaluated in terms of six factors that correspond to 5W1H, that is, "who," "what," "when," "where," "why," and "how," as well as the seventh factor of "to whom."

The individual factors consider the following key points:

Who: at the level of chief manager, project manager, or expert member of the team

What: a pilot survey, collection of analysis data, a CEA, or a broader analysis

When: preclinical or clinical phases, prior to application for insurance coverage, or post-marketing

Where: whether the places of data collection and discussion vary for desk analysis, clinical trials, and modeling

Why: financial reasons, lack of internal personnel, limited data availability, or strategic requirement

How: consultation fees, timetables, outputs, frequency and time of meetings, and follow-ups

To whom: consultants from academia or analysis/consulting firms or a combination of both

Question 2. Outputs correspond to "what" and relate to "to whom" in Question 1.

Where scholarly articles are preferred as the form of output, the inclusion of qualified researchers from academia as external consultants is recommended. Where CEAs are to be conducted, clinical experts in the area of analysis are generally included, in addition to experts in economic evaluation. As the scientific integrity of output depends on "to whom" the consultation is committed, prior examination of consultants' experience, credibility, academic ability, and performance is required for any outputs to be received.

Question 3. Who in the company assumes the role of liaison with external consultants is the key to successful consultation. Lack of (sub)specialists in HTA within the company may result in the company's inability to appreciate the outcomes of consultation as reported by external consultants. To avoid this, it is essential to have in-house (sub)specialists, who are able to accurately interpret the reports and communicate them to the rest of the company, instead of leaving all the decision-making to external consultants.

5.3.5 Dissemination of Information on Results

Example

What would be the approach taken when disseminating the results of in-house HTA projects? As a project leader, how would you answer the following questions?

Question 1. Who and what type of organizations are the target audiences?

Question 2. What are the formats of dissemination?

Question 3. What are the possible means of disseminating the results?

Question 4. What are the means to evaluate the impact of the results being disseminated?

Points to Consider

Question 1. The audience for the outcomes may include the MHLW, clinicians, health managers, patients and patient associations, analysts, the general public, or their combinations.

Question 2. The formats may include documents submitted to the MHLW, poster presentations, reports, newsletters, and scholarly articles (in magazines, peer reviewed journals, Japanese or English publications, general medical journals such as the New England Journal of Medicine and the Lancet, and major specialized journals).

Question 3. At the same time, means of communication other than paper-based publications need to be considered. Electronic journals are increasing in numbers in recent years, and electronic means may be more efficient and have greater influence compared with printed media. Communication of information through web pages is thus recommended, which involves not simply releasing of information but also provides a platform for interaction if technologically feasible. It is also essential to communicate such information as part of the traditional duties of a medical representative at clinical practice sites, including hospitals. You may also consider providing venues such as seminars for direct communication to both clinicians and patients.

Results need to be communicated not only externally but also internally. Departments and project teams related to HTA may not be fully recognized within the company, thus requiring active in-house publicity, particularly directly reporting to executives, including the CEO, and gaining their understanding.

Question 4. Indirect measures of impact include the number of presentations at conferences, the number of times cited, impact factors, the number of reports distributed, and comments and feedback by academic societies and experts. The impact can also be measured indirectly by electronic means, such as online votes. Where an online platform for interactive information communication is available, the number of visits can be counted and feedback from visitors collected.

Direct measures of impact include the price assigned to the technology and its sales, although these measures may not always reflect the cost-effectiveness of the technology due to external factors. Where direct measures indicate unfavorable outcomes, possible causes need to be identified for future improvement.

5.3.6   Pricing and Premium Rate in Japan

Example
The following data were obtained for a new drug A in development:
    Price and dosage

- New drug A: price to be determined, two tablets daily
- Analogous drug B: JPY 500 per tablet, three tablets daily

Expected incremental effect (for 300 days): 0.01 QALYs
Relevant non-pharmaceutical cost (total cost for 300 days)

- New drug A: JPY 1.4M
- Analogous drug B: JPY 1.5M

Willingness-to-pay threshold: JPY 5M/QALY
Based on the data obtained in the 300-day treatment, you wish to determine the pharmacoeconomically appropriate rate of an additional premium to be given to new drug A according to the similar efficacy comparison method. The above pharmaceutical and non-pharmaceutical costs will be the only costs considered. Given this, answer the following questions:

Question 1. According to the traditional similar efficacy comparison method, what is the basic price for new drug A without an additional premium?

Question 2. What is the cost of treatment with analogous drug B for 300 days?

Question 3. If we let x be the price for new drug A, what is the cost of treatment with new drug A for 300 days?

Question 4. Based on the willingness-to-pay threshold, what is the maximum value x can take?

Question 5. According to the traditional similar efficacy comparison method, what is the rate of additional premium given to new drug A in Question 4?

Question 6. Perform a sensitivity analysis by varying the willingness-to-pay threshold from JPY 2 to 10M in increments of JPY 1M, and find the values for price x and premium rate at each threshold.

Solutions

   Question 1. We assume that the daily cost is the same for new drug A and analogous drug B. The daily cost of drug B is $500 \times 3 = $ JPY 1500.

   Thus, the cost of drug A per tablet will be JPY 1500/2 = JPY 750.

   Question 2. JPY 1500 per day $\times$ 300 days = JPY 450K.

   Question 3. The daily cost will be JPY $2x$ for two tablets daily. Multiplying this by 300 days, the cost will be JPY $600x$.

   Question 4. By substituting the costs (including the non-pharmaceutical cost) for 300 days, $\Delta E = 0.01$ and $\lambda = $ JPY 5M/QALY into the ICER formula of $C_1 = C_0 + \Delta E \times \lambda$,

$$600x + \text{JPY } 1.4\text{M} = (\text{JPY } 0.45\text{M} + \text{JPY } 1.5\text{M}) + (\text{JPY } 5\text{M} \times 0.01),$$

which gives $x = (\text{JPY } 1.95\text{M} - \text{JPY } 1.4\text{M} + \text{JPY } 0.05\text{M})/600$

$$= \text{JPY } 1000.$$

   This can also be expressed as follows according to the definition of ICER ($\lambda = \Delta C/\Delta E$):

$$\text{JPY } 5\text{M/ QALY} = \{(600x + \text{JPY } 1.4\text{M}) - (\text{JPY } 0.45\text{M} + \text{JPY } 1.5\text{M})\}/0.01.$$

   The above calculation indicates the traditional empirical pricing method used in Japan with consideration for additional premiums can be formulated using the ICER formula, according to which the additional cost can be expressed as the product of clinical benefit (ΔE) and willingness to pay (λ), which translates to the greater the clinical benefit and the willingness to pay, the greater the additional cost is. It is of note that such a value-based pricing method has developed empirically in Japan.

   Although in this example the clinical benefit is measured by QALYs and the willingness to pay is expressed in JPY/QALY, the advantage of using the ICER formula for the premium calculation is that the measures of clinical benefit and willingness to pay need not necessarily be based on QALYs, as the units of these two measures cancel out in the calculation, regardless of with what units (other than QALYs) the clinical benefit and willingness to pay are measured in.

   This can be expressed as (preferred unit) $\times$ (JPY/preferred unit) = JPY, which may be used as a rationale for allowing the use of the preferred (or arbitrary) measure of clinical benefit when considering cost-effectiveness evidence in price calculations.

   Question 5. As the price of JPY 750 was evaluated as JPY 1000 per tablet with the premium, the rate of additional premium will be $(1000 - 750)/750 = 33\%$.

   Question 6. The values can be determined by repeating the calculations in Questions 4 and 5 with $\lambda = $ JPY 2 to 10M in 1M increments. The results are shown in Table 5.19.

Table 5.19 Sensitivity analysis of pricing and premium rate over the change of a threshold

Standard threshold (JPY 1M/QALY)	New pricing (JPY/tablet)	Premium rate (%)
2	950	26
3	966	28
4	983	31
5	1000	33
6	1016	35
7	1033	37
8	1050	40
9	1066	42
10	1083	44

Intermediate Level Methods

6.1 Clinical Diagnosis and Decision Analysis

6.1.1 Key Points

- In a decision analysis involving diagnostic testing, the integration of the test into a decision tree and the assigning of probabilities require careful attention.
- A diagnostic test has four characteristics that measure its performance in identifying a given condition: (1) sensitivity, (2) a false-positive rate, (3) a false-negative rate, and (4) specificity.
- A posttest probability obtained using Bayes' formula is assigned for estimating the probability of a condition, given the results of a diagnostic test.

6.1.2 Essential Knowledge

When performing a decision analysis that involves diagnostic testing, the approach used to illustrate the test in a decision tree and to assign probabilities requires special attention. To better understand this, we first need to understand the characteristics of a diagnostic test. A diagnostic test has the following four characteristics that measure its performance in identifying the condition of interest: (1) sensitivity (or the true-positive rate, i.e., the probability of a positive test given that the patient has the condition), (2) a false-positive rate (i.e., the probability of a positive test given that the patient is free of the condition), (3) a false-negative rate (i.e., the probability of a negative test, given that the patient has the condition), and (4) specificity (or the true-negative rate, i.e., the probability of a negative test given that the patient is free of the condition).

The relationships among these characteristics can be defined using a two-by-two table as shown in Fig. 6.1. Here, given a group with M cases that have a condition and N cases that are free of the condition, and a out of M cases and b out of N cases test positive, then the value of each characteristic 1–4 above can be calculated as a/M, b/N, c/M, and d/N, respectively (where $c = M - a$, and $d = N - b$).

© Springer Nature Singapore Pte Ltd. 2019
I. Kamae, *Health Technology Assessment in Japan*,
https://doi.org/10.1007/978-981-13-5793-0_6

Fig. 6.1 Four characteristics of a diagnostic test

Fig. 6.2 A decision-tree scheme for four characteristics of diagnostic testing

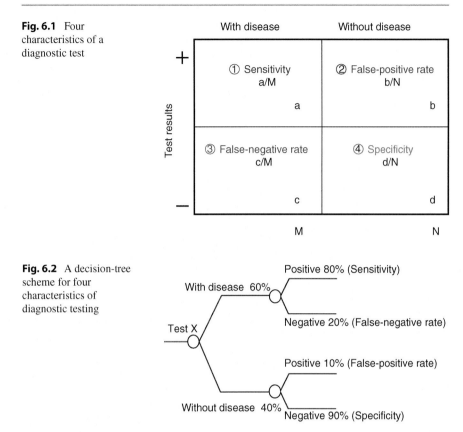

Assuming, for instance, that a diagnostic test with a sensitivity of 80% and a specificity of 90% is performed in a group of $M = 60$ and $N = 40$ subjects (the prevalence is $M/(M + N) = 60\%$), the possible scenarios in terms of test results can be illustrated in a decision tree as shown in Fig. 6.2. The four terminal branches in the decision tree correspond to the four cells of the two-by-two table in Fig. 6.1. However, the prevalence in a given subject group is not always known at the time of testing, so it is sometimes necessary to enter the test results into a decision tree beforehand and then add branches to show the presence or absence of the condition afterward.

Figure 6.3 shows a common mistake made in such cases. From Fig. 6.2, the probabilities of positive and negative tests are calculated to be 52% ($=(60\% \times 80\%) + (40\% \times 10\%)$) and 48% ($=(60\% \times 20\%) + (40\% \times 90\%)$), respectively, so 52% and 48% are assigned to the first level of branches extending from the decision tree. Although this is correct, it would be a mistake to subsequently assign the probabilities of 60% for the condition being present and 40% for it being absent to the second level of branches as was done in Fig. 6.2. Instead, the four terminal branches in Fig. 6.3 must be assigned the posttest probabilities of the presence or absence of the condition after the test results are known. For example, the posttest probability of the condition being present when a positive test result is obtained is written as a conditional probability Pr(disease present | test positive).

This posttest probability is calculated using Bayes' formula. Figure 6.4 shows the formula for the posttest probability Pr(disease present | test positive), which is

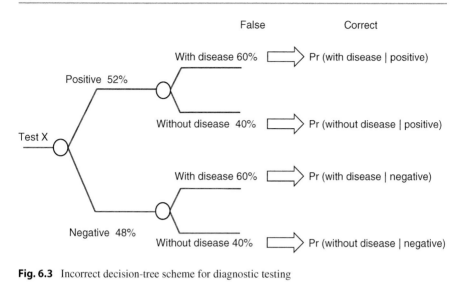

Fig. 6.3   Incorrect decision-tree scheme for diagnostic testing

Pr (*with disease / test positive*)

$$= \frac{Pretest\ probability \times sensitivity}{Pretest\ probability \times sensitivity + (1 - Pretest\ probability) \times False\ positive\ rate}$$

Fig. 6.4   Bayes' formula for Post-test probability

calculated by dividing the product of the pretest probability and sensitivity in the numerator by the sum of the product of pretest probability and sensitivity and the product of (1 − pretest probability) and the false-positive rate in the denominator. Since the pretest probability is unknown, the prevalence is used as the initial value.

For the case shown in Fig. 6.2, the prevalence is 60% so by entering that together with a test sensitivity of 80% and a false-positive rate of 10% into the formula shown in Fig. 6.4, then the posttest probability is calculated as:

$$Pr\left(disease\ present \mid test\ positive\right) = (0.6 \times 0.8) / \left((0.6 \times 0.8) + (0.4 \times 0.1)\right) \approx 0.923.$$

That is, the probability of the patient truly having the condition given a positive test result is 92.3%. This indicates that the estimate of the probability of the condition being present improved from 60% to 92.3% by the use of the diagnostic test. Therefore, the benefit of a diagnostic test can be quantitatively evaluated using Bayes' formula. The posttest probability Pr(disease present I test positive) is also referred to as the positive predictive value (PPV).

6.1.3   Self-Check!

1. What is the false-positive rate of a diagnostic test given a specificity of 85%?
2. Calculate the posttest probability Pr(disease presentItest positive) for the example in the text using the two-by-two table.
3. Using Bayes' formula, find the equation to calculate Pr(disease absent I test negative).

6.2   Calculation of QALYs and Related Issues

6.2.1   Key Points

- The UK's NICE has adopted QALY and pound sterling/QALY thresholds.
- Germany is against the use of QALY, while the US PCORI is against the use of USD/QALY thresholds.
- Different methods of estimation will yield different values of utility.
- The combined use of different estimation methods may yield inconsistent results.
- Attention should be paid to differences in cultural values among countries and populations.

6.2.2   Essential Knowledge

The US Patient-Centered Outcomes Research Institute (PCORI) drew attention to the use of QALYs. PCORI announced that it would not allow the use of USD-per-QALY thresholds in developing cost-effectiveness league tables and reimbursement decisions and implementing incentive programs (the 2010 Patient Protection and Affordable Care Act), which caused controversy among international experts. One of the factors behind this policy may be an ethical concern within the country about economic disparities which may arise when adopting such thresholds. However, there are a number of issues that can easily lead to a misunderstanding in the interpretation of cost-per-QALY estimates.

For instance, assume that a new drug X has an ICER of USD15K/QALY relative to the standard of care and that an existing drug Y also has the same ICER relative to the standard of care. In this case, is it appropriate to assume that new drug X and existing drug Y are equivalent in terms of cost-effectiveness? Although the ICERs indicate equal values for the two drugs, their financial impacts may not necessarily be equivalent. For example, if the original cost and effectiveness data from which the ICERs were derived indicated USD45K/3 QALYs and USD4.5/0.3 QALYs for drugs X and Y, respectively, drug X would cost ten times more than drug Y, suggesting a larger financial impact for drug Y compared to drug X. In this case, it would not be appropriate to consider drugs X and Y as equal.

When carefully analyzed, PCORI is not against the use of ICER itself, and thus does not disapprove of using QALYs in economic evaluation studies. Nevertheless, the policy of PCORI has undeniably had a substantial negative impact on the use of QALY in the USA (at least in comparative efficacy studies). Similarly, in Germany, the concept of QALY is recently being considered as a violation of the Constitution, effectively making the use of QALY in Germany difficult.

The major problem with the calculation of a QALY is in its validity as an interval scale. That is, a given condition will typically have different values of utility, depending on the method of estimation (EQ-5D and the standard gamble, for instance (see Sect. 5.2.2)).

Assume that the utilities of stages I and II of a condition were estimated to be 0.8 and 0.6, respectively, using the EQ-5D scale and 0.8 and 0.7 using the standard

gamble method. Here, estimates by EQ-5D indicate decreases in utility in increments of 0.2 with the progression of the condition from perfect health to stages I
and II. That is, the ratio of stage I to stage II in terms of utility reduction is
0.2:0.2 = 1:1. On the other hand, estimates by the standard gamble method indicate
decreases in utility of 0.2 and 0.1 for stages I and II, respectively, giving the ratio
of 2:1. The question is whether the fact that EQ-5D is accepted as a valid interval
scale should make us question the validity of the standard gamble method as an
interval scale?

This illustrates that the use of utility estimates obtained together by different
methods in an analysis may yield inconsistent results. Assume, for instance, that we
are to compare treatments A and B in terms of QALYs. Using utility estimates
obtained by the time trade-off method (see Sect. 5.2.3), the QALYs for treatments A
and B are calculated as follows:

- Treatment A: 4 years × 0.78 = 3.12 QALYs.
- Treatment B: 5 years × 0.61 = 3.05 QALYs.

In this case, treatment A provides a greater benefit in terms of QALYs.

On the other hand, assume that QALYs are calculated as follows using utility
estimates obtained by EQ-5D. While treatments A and B are ranked the same in
order of utility, their utility values differ slightly from those obtained through the
time trade-off method:

- Treatment A: 4 years × 0.734 = 2.936 QALYs.
- Treatment B: 5 years × 0.608 = 3.04 QALYs.

In this case, treatment B provides a greater benefit in terms of QALYs. If a study
were to recommend treatment A based solely on an evaluation using the time trade-
off method, then those conclusions would differ from an analysis using EQ-5D, and
if an analysis using EQ-5D is not also conducted, then the inconsistency in the findings may go unnoticed. Therefore, when different methods are used to calculate
QALY, then comparability is no long maintained, which threatens the comparability
characteristic of QALY.

Another issue with the use of QALYs is that the assumption that the product of
utilities and years of life will be equal does not always hold true. Evidently, the
expression, "1 QALY = 1 QALY," always holds true and so does the relation,
"1 year × 1.0 = 1 year × 1.0." However, would it be true to assume that the product,
"1 year × 1.0," is equal to the product, "4 years × 0.25"? Although, arithmetically,
both products equal "one," and it thus holds true, what if the equation is interpreted
as the following statement?

"One year of life lived in perfect health is worth the same as 4 years of life lived
with severe angina (assuming a utility of 0.25)."

Individuals may have different opinions on this statement. Of course, an analysis involving QALY calculations is based on averages and thus allows for individual differences in utility. However, even if individual preferences and the
population average are appropriately distinguished, when it comes to comparing
analyses by country the above assumption about the equivalence of benefits may

not always be possible due to differences in cultural values. Therefore, one should use caution when interpreting the results of international comparative research using QALYs.

6.2.3 Self-Check!

1. New drug X has an ICER of USD50K/QALY relative to a comparator, and another drug Y also has an ICER of USD50K/QALY using the same comparator. Are drugs X and Y considered equivalent?
2. Assume that the utilities of 0.43 and 0.38 were obtained using the standard gamble method for treatments A and B, respectively, as in the example in the text comparing treatment A and B. How would the results compare with those obtained using other methods?

6.3   Incremental Net Benefit (INB) and the Cost-Effectiveness Acceptability Frontier (CEAF)

6.3.1   Key Points

- Incremental net benefit may be used as an alternative measure of cost-effectiveness to the ICER.
- Incremental net benefit can be classified into net monetary and net health benefits.
- Incremental net benefit can be used to draw the cost-effectiveness acceptability curve.
- The cost-effectiveness acceptability frontier is not used much, but a useful approach, which complements the cost-effectiveness acceptability curve.

6.3.2   Essential Knowledge

6.3.2.1 Incremental Net Benefit
A commonly used alternative measure of cost-effectiveness to the ICER is the concept of incremental net benefit (INB), which can be classified into net monetary benefit (NMB) and net health benefit (NHB) depending on whether the benefit is measured in terms of cost or effectiveness.

Figure 6.5 shows how NMB and NHB are presented on the cost-effectiveness plane. When a given point X representing the ICER of new technology X (ΔE, ΔC) (where ΔE = incremental effect and ΔC = incremental cost) falls below the straight line representing the threshold λ_0, there will be a certain distance from point X to the threshold line. Here, the vertical distance from point X to the line is defined as NMB and the horizontal one as NHB. Given that threshold λ_0 represents the slope of the straight line, this line can be expressed as $C = \lambda_0 E$, and NMB can be formulated as the difference between two costs, $\lambda_0 \cdot \Delta E$ and ΔC, as follows:

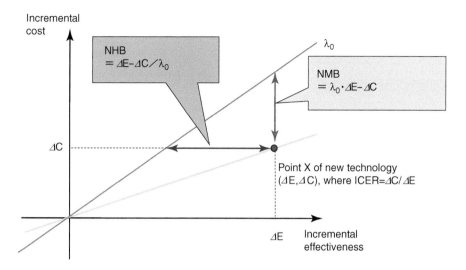

Fig. 6.5 ICER and incremental net benefit (INB)

$$\text{NMB} = (\lambda_0 \cdot \Delta E) - \Delta C.$$

Similarly, NHB can be obtained as the difference between two effects, ΔE and $\Delta C/\lambda_0$, as follows:

$$\text{NHB} = \Delta E - (\Delta C / \lambda_0).$$

Accordingly, NMB and NHM will both take negative values when point X falls above the λ_0 threshold line. Therefore, the position of point X above or below the λ_0 threshold line can be determined by identifying whether NMB and NHM take positive or negative values. These characteristics can be utilized when drawing a cost-effectiveness acceptability curve.

From the definitions, by taking λ_0 as the variable, NMB is a linear function of λ_0, and NHB is a linear function of the reciprocal of λ_0. Figure 6.6 shows the linear relationship between NMB and the threshold. Since cost and effect variables are generally associated in one way or another, the variance of NMB can be determined by the equation in Fig. 6.6 by assigning the covariance $\text{cov}\left(\Delta \bar{E}, \Delta \bar{C}\right)$ of cost and effect (where $\Delta \bar{E}$ = mean incremental effect and $\Delta \bar{C}$ = mean incremental cost) [1]. Consequently, the 95% confidence interval of NMB can also be calculated as shown in Fig. 6.6, which indicates that the width of the 95% confidence interval increases with increases in threshold λ as a variable. Similarly, Fig. 6.7 shows the graph of NHB, which is not a straight line, as NHM is not a linear function of λ. In this respect, NHB cannot be handled as easily as NMB.

As an application of NMB, the expected value of perfect information (EVPI) can be calculated (see Sect. 6.5).

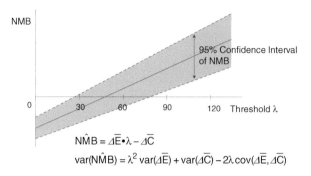

Fig. 6.6 Net monetary benefit (NMB) and threshold

Fig. 6.7 Net health benefit
(NHB) and threshold

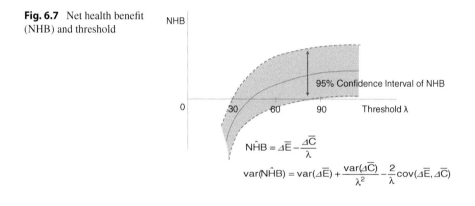

6.3.2.2 Cost-Effectiveness Acceptability Frontier (CEAF)

NMB and NHB can be used to draw the cost-effectiveness acceptability curve (CEAC) and to calculate the EVPI as discussed above. Recently, an approach called the cost-effectiveness acceptability frontier (CEAF) has been increasingly adopted, in addition to the CEAC and EVPI [2].

The CEAC is used to illustrate the relationship between the accepted threshold level and the probability that the ICER of a new technology falls below the threshold and is characteristic in that it shows the probability that the technology being evaluated (e.g., a new drug) is cost-effective relative to a standard drug at a given maximum acceptable threshold (see Sect. 3.14). However, when the decision-maker has a certain range that is considered an acceptable threshold, the standard CEAC has a limitation in that it cannot always present a clear answer to the question of whether the adoption of a new standard drug is more cost-effective within that threshold range. The CEAF can be used to address this problem. Table 6.1 shows the concept of what is required to draw the CEAF, which is similar in principle to the approach of drawing the CEAC.

Table 6.1 Concept of cost-effectiveness acceptability frontier (CEAF)

	Treatment A	Treatment B	INB (A–B)	Recommended treatment (with larger NMB)
Trial 1	NMB_{1A}	NMB_{1B}	INB_1	e.g. A
Trial 2	NMB_{2A}	NMB_{2B}	INB_2	e.g. B
:	:	:	:	:
:	:	:	:	:
Trial k	NMBkA	NMBkB	INBk	e.g. A
				⇩
				Count the frequency of A.

The probability of treatment A, $P_A(\lambda)$, for a threshold λ is defined as "Frequency of A divided by k", while the probability of B is $1 - P_A(\lambda)$. The CERF is depicted by plotting the pair of λ and $P_A(\lambda)$

First, assume two alternatives, treatment A (a new drug) and treatment B (the standard of care). For each treatment, the NMB at threshold λ_0 can be expressed as follows:

$$NMB_A = \lambda_0 \times (\text{effect of A}) - (\text{cost of A}).$$

$$NMB_B = \lambda_0 \times (\text{effect of B}) - (\text{cost of B}).$$

The incremental net benefit (INB) can, in turn, be obtained as the difference between the above two equations:

$$INB = NMB_A - NMB_B.$$

By running a probabilistic sensitivity analysis, with the calculations repeated for a k number of trials, k sets of data consisting of NMB_A, NMB_B, and INB are obtained, as shown in Table 6.1. From these results, we can identify the treatment with the greater net benefit in each trial and enter it in the rightmost column. Alternatively, we can select A for positive INB values and B for negative INB values. Once either of the two treatments has been selected in all k trials, we can count the number of times A was selected and divide this by k to obtain the probability treatment A is recommended, $P_A(\lambda_0)$. The results can be plotted as points with λ_0 as the x-axis coordinate and $P_A(\lambda_0)$ as the y-axis coordinate. The CEAC is the curve obtained by repeating the above procedure for different thresholds λ.

To obtain the CEAF, we also need to count the number of times B was selected in Table 6.1 and find the probability that treatment B is recommended, $P_B(\lambda_0)$. As with treatment A, the CEAC for treatment B is drawn by plotting the points with λ_0 as the x-axis coordinate and $P_B(\lambda_0)$ as the y-axis coordinate. Since the frequency of B being selected is equal to k minus the frequency of A being selected, the

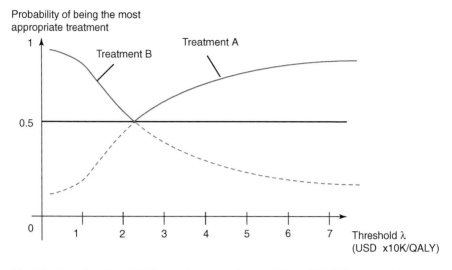

Fig. 6.8 Example of the CEAF for two treatments. The solid line is CEAF. Treatment A is recommended if the threshold is over USD 22K/QALY, otherwise B is recommended

probabilities of A and B are obviously complementary, where $P_B(\lambda_0) = 1 - P_A(\lambda_0)$ holds true. Accordingly, the CEACs for A and B are drawn as reflections of the horizontal line through the point 0.5 (50%) on the y-axis, as shown in Fig. 6.8, for example. Here, the CEAF is represented as the curve that takes a greater y value at any given threshold. The CEAF is referred to as a frontier, as it defines the uppermost border of multiple CEACs. The CEAF is associated with the EVPI (see Sect. 6.5), and clarifying the relationship between CEAF and EVPI is also a useful approach for evaluating uncertainty.

When there are three or more possible alternative treatments, the CEAF can similarly be obtained by selecting the treatment with the greatest net benefit and connecting the uppermost borders of the multiple CEACs, just as in the case with two alternative treatments. Figure 6.9 shows a hypothetical example with three alternative treatments, A, B, and C. As the figure indicates, the advantage of CEAF is that it shows the best treatment alternative for a given range of the threshold, along with the probability that the alternative is cost-effective.

It should be noted, however, that only when the INB is distributed symmetrically can the CEAF be drawn as the reflection of each of the two alternative treatments with a switch between the two curves at a probability of 50%. The CEAF will switch to a level below 50% when the distribution of INB is skewed to the right (positively skewed) and above 50% when the distribution is skewed to the left (negatively skewed) [2]. Table 6.2 shows a hypothetical example where the distribution of INB is positively skewed. In this case, treatment A with a greater expected net benefit is selected only twice out of five trials, indicating a decrease in $P_A(\lambda_0)$, the probability that A is selected.

The practical significance of CEAF owes to its adoption by the UK's NICE in its April 2013 Guidance [3]. Among the items in a sensitivity analysis, NICE requires a representation and explanation of CEAF when presenting CEACs. In Japan, under

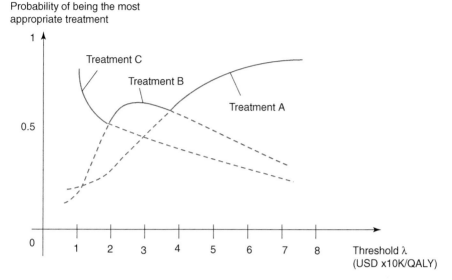

Fig. 6.9 Example of the CEAF for three treatments. The solid line is CEAF. A recommended treatment varies from C, B and A according to two thresholds of USD 20K or 38K /QALY

Table 6.2 Expected net benefit and the probability of selected treatment

	Treatment A	Treatment B	INB (A–B)	Selected treatment
Trial 1	23	17	+6	A
Trial 2	18	19	−1	B
Trial 3	21	14	+7	A
Trial 4	14	15	−1	B
Trial 5	19	20	−1	B
Expected net benefit	19	17	+2	A: twice, B: three times

$P_A(\lambda)$ decreases if the distribution of INB is skewed to the right (positive)

the provisional implementation of cost-effectiveness evaluation implemented in April 2016, item 14.5 of the MHLW Guidelines recommended that CEACs be presented, while there is no mention of CEAF. Although the approach to be taken in adopting thresholds has yet to be thoroughly discussed in Japan, the use of CEAF should also be considered in the system, as evaluations using it are expected to provide useful information.

6.3.3   Self-Check!

1. List two measures that constitute the INB.
2. For what reason is NMB easier to handle compared with NHB?
3. What does CEAF stand for?
4. What is the advantage of CEAF?

6.4   Efficiency Frontier and Innovation[1]

6.4.1   Key Points

- The efficiency frontier is an approach to economic evaluation proposed by the German IQWiG.
- It visualizes the level and stage of development for healthcare innovations and evaluates cost-effectiveness on a graph.
- Unlike the approach adopted by the UK's NICE, it does not necessarily require QALY estimation, and it allows for analysis using any clinical outcome measures.
- The efficiency frontier can also be used in pricing decisions.

6.4.2   Essential Knowledge

The Institute for Quality and Efficiency in Healthcare (IQWiG), a German agency for health technology assessment, proposed the efficiency frontier approach to visualize the level and stage of development for healthcare innovations, which may play an important role in considering a successor model for Japanese quasi-VBP in the future.

The "efficiency frontier" is obtained by presenting the cost-effectiveness of a given set of health technologies (e.g., different drug therapies for diabetes) on a two-dimensional cost-effectiveness plane and refers to the boundary of areas where interventions are either cost-effective or not. For instance, assume that the cost and effectiveness of seven healthcare technologies (e.g., pharmaceuticals), A through G, are given as per Fig. 6.10. Illustration of cost and effectiveness pairs on a two-dimensional plane in such a way allows for multiple interpretations in terms of cost-effectiveness. For example, since products F, D, and E are almost equivalent in terms of cost, the product that falls above the other product is considered to have a greater clinical benefit. Moreover, since products B and E are equivalent in terms of clinical benefit, product B, which falls to the left of product E, is clearly more cost-effective. In other words, health technologies that fall to the upper left-hand side of the plane are more cost-effective and those that fall to the lower right are less cost-effective. Therefore, by identifying the product with the greatest clinical benefit along the horizontal axis of cost, a line graph can be obtained that connects the origin and products A, C, F, and G, which represents the cost-effectiveness boundary. This boundary is referred to as the efficiency frontier for the cost-effectiveness of the seven products A through G. The area under this line represents reduced cost-effectiveness (contains products B, D, and E), whereas the area above the line represents improved cost-effectiveness. Additionally, the slope of the line connecting any two products represents the ICER. For example, the slope of segment CF equals the reciprocal of the ICER for products F to C. Figure 6.10 presents the cost on the

---

[1]This section is a revised version of the following original article: *Kamae I. Perspective on pharmacoeconomic approaches to health technology assessment (5): innovation assessment using efficiency frontier.* Pharmaceutical and Medical Device Regulatory Science 2012; 43(11):1005–1009.

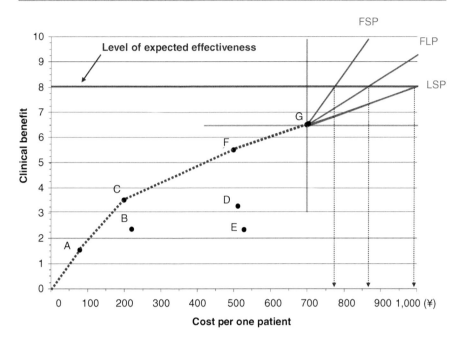

Fig. 6.10 Efficiency Frontier Curve and a method of pricing

horizontal axis and the clinical benefit on the vertical axis, but if the efficiency frontier were drawn instead by placing the clinical benefit on the horizontal axis and the
cost on the vertical axis, the slope of a segment would equal the ICER between the
two technologies comprising the two ends of the segment. The trend in which the
slope of the line connecting products A to C, F, and G becomes increasingly smaller
in the horizontal direction indicates that advances in technology generally lead to
reduced cost-effectiveness. Although it is preferred that a breakthrough innovation
is achieved to significantly improve cost-effectiveness, the efficiency frontier
implies that cost-effectiveness reduction is impossible with a level of innovation
that does not go beyond standard technological improvement.

IQWiG, the German agency for health technology assessment, has proposed the
efficiency frontier approach to calculate the maximum appropriate reimbursement.
This requires an extension of the existing efficiency frontier curve. In Fig. 6.10, this
equates to the question of what is the appropriate extension line to be drawn from
product G to the right of the plane. For instance, the IQWiG Guidelines consider the
following three approaches: LSP (simple extension of segment FG, the rightmost
segment of the efficiency frontier), FLP (extension of the line connecting the origin
and the rightmost product G), and FSP (extension of the line that has the same slope
as segment 0A (the line connecting the point zero and A), the leftmost segment of
the efficiency frontier). Where the expected level of clinical benefit is known for a
new drug (at the benefit level of 8 in Fig. 6.10), the points on the *x*-axis that correspond to the intersections between the horizontal line of expected benefit level and

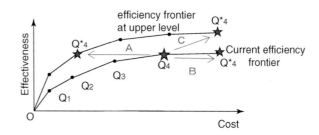

Fig. 6.11 Innovation defined by Efficiency Frontier
Three types of innovation, developing technology Q*4 from Q4:
• Type A: Improving efficiency by cost-reduction
• Type B: Moving on the EF curve
• Type C: Jumping onto the upper EF curve

the three extension lines represent the maximum costs at the respective effect levels. It is clear that cost is highest when the LSP approach with the smallest slope is adopted, and it is lowest when the FSP approach is adopted. No criteria have been established for determining which of the three approaches to extending the efficiency frontier is most favorable. It should also be noted that this approach assumes the equivalence of the cost presented on the horizontal axis and the price of product. Since the price of a given product and the cost incurred for the technology are generally not the same, a more detailed discussion is needed distinguishing between price and cost. Nevertheless, Fig. 6.10 facilitates the basic understanding of how the efficiency frontier analysis is applied to pricing decisions.

Another advantage of the efficiency frontier approach is that it allows for the visualization of the level and direction of innovation. For instance, Fig. 6.11 shows two efficiency frontier curves, from which the upper line is clearly more cost-effective. If we assume that an existing health technology is represented by point X on the lower curve, there are the following three possible patterns of innovation that are expected in the future:

1. Type A (reduction in cost)
2. Type B (extension of the efficiency frontier curve)
3. Type C (jump to the upper curve)

Type A represents a new technology that allows for a cost reduction while maintaining the same level of clinical benefit. The usual cost minimization efforts are considered a strategy that follows this pattern. The second pattern, type B, represents a new technology developed as a natural extension of the existing efficiency frontier curve. Many new technologies follow this pattern in their development, with cost-effectiveness diminishing with the curve extension. For example, the process of development from product A to products C, F, and G in Fig. 6.10 follows this type B pattern. The ICER of product F compared to product C is larger than that of product C to product A. The cost-effectiveness of product G relative to product F will further diminish. In other words, the incremental cost per one unit of benefit increases for products A, C, F, and G in this order. The third pattern, type C, represents a breakthrough innovation. Assuming two different efficiency frontier curves, such innovation is represented as jumping from a point on the lower curve to one on the upper curve. Such innovation is obviously expected to dramatically improve cost-effectiveness. In addition to analysis based on these patterns, the efficiency frontier curve allows for the determination of whether a given ICER is acceptable considering multiple ICERs that correspond to the slopes of multiple segments on the curve. ICER calculation generally requires the comparison of old and new technologies, which has given rise to the issue of selecting an appropriate old (or standard) technology as a comparator when establishing guidelines for economic evaluation. However, an efficiency frontier analysis assumes that multiple ICERs are given, thus eliminating the issue of selecting an appropriate comparator. Such characteristics of the efficiency frontier analysis have the potential to offer a superior approach to determining acceptability compared with the approach adopted by the UK's NICE, which is based on a single ICER threshold. However, despite IQWiG completing a pilot study on the efficiency frontier approach in Germany, the approach has yet to be widely adopted. Assuming that it has a potential for development in Japan, it is worth examining the methodological conditions for adapting it to the Japanese system and its validity based on specific examples.

6.4.3   Self-Check!

1. What do the slopes of segments that constitute the efficiency frontier in Fig. 6.10 correspond to in a cost-effectiveness analysis?
2. The strategy to pursue efficiency through "reduction in cost" is considered as what type of innovation in Fig. 6.11?

6.5   Expected Value of Perfect Information (EVPI)

6.5.1   Key Points

- Economic evaluations in recent years have adopted EVPI in their analyses.
- EVPI is calculated by using NMB in economic evaluations.
- EVPI represents the additional value expected to be obtained given perfect information.

6.5.2   Essential Knowledge

The expected value of perfect information (EVPI) is an approach used in recent economic evaluations to measure the degree of uncertainty surrounding information [4].

It is generally defined by using NMB (see Sect. 6.3). As shown in Table 6.3, NMB_A, obtained from treatment with drug A, and NMB_B, obtained from treatment with drug B, are calculated in each repeated measurement by the bootstrap method. For each repetition, the values of NMB_A and NMB_B are compared to indicate the

Table 6.3 EVPI and NMB

Bootstrapping	NMB$_A$ of the treatment by drug A	NMB$_B$ of the treatment by drug B	Larger NMB
Repeated computation 1	NMB$_{A1}$	NMB$_{B1}$	max$_1$(NMB$_{A1}$, NMB$_{B1}$)
" 2	NMB$_{A2}$	NMB$_{B2}$	max$_2$(NMB$_{A2}$, NMB$_{B2}$)
⋮	⋮	⋮	⋮
" n	NMB$_{An}$	NMB$_{Bn}$	max$_n$(NMB$_{An}$, NMB$_{Bn}$)
Total	ΣNMB$_A$	ΣNMB$_B$	Σmax(NMB$_A$, NMB$_B$)

Select larger one
max(ΣNMB$_A$, ΣNMB$_B$)

greater NMB as max(NMB$_A$, NMB$_B$), following which the sum of max(NMB$_A$, NMB$_B$) obtained for all repetitions, Σmax(NMB$_A$, NMB$_B$), is calculated. At the same time, the sum of NMB obtained in all repetitions is calculated for both treatments A and B. That is, ΣNMB$_A$ and ΣNMB$_B$ (Σ refers to the sum) are calculated to identify the one with a greater value, indicated as max(ΣNMB$_A$, ΣNMB$_B$). Given this, the EVPI is defined by the following equation:

$$EVPI = \Sigma \max \left(NMB_A, NMB_B \right) - \max \left(\Sigma NMB_A, \Sigma NMB_B \right).$$

The first term of this equation represents the sum of the greater NMBs from all repetitions and can thus be calculated only when the treatment providing a greater NMB can be perfectly estimated. In other words, it is an estimate when perfect information is obtained.

However, where it cannot be determined which treatment provides the greater benefit due to incomplete information, the values of both ΣNMB$_A$ and ΣNMB$_B$ will be smaller than Σmax(NMB$_A$, NMB$_B$), whether A or B is chosen. Therefore, by subtracting from the first term whichever is greater between ΣNMB$_A$ and ΣNMB$_B$ as the second term, one can determine how much larger an NMB can be achieved given perfect information. The EVPI is thus a quantitative measure of expected value.

The EVPI can also be obtained using outcome measures others than NMB. For instance, Table 6.4 shows two treatments, A and B, along with the relationship between the benefits of the two treatments. Assume that the values in the two-by-two table represent life expectancies. According to the definition, the EVPI is expressed as follows:

$$EVPI = \Sigma \max \left(\text{benefit of A, benefit of B} \right) - \max \left(\text{sum of benefits of A, sum of benefits of B} \right).$$

The largest values of life expectancy are 20 and 10 years for when treatment is effective and not effective, respectively, which gives 20 + 10 for the first term

Table 6.4 Example of treatments and the effectiveness

	Treatment A	Treatment B	Maximum
Effective	20	10	20 yrs
Ineffective	8	10	10 yrs
Total	28	20	30

of the above equation. Moreover, the sum of estimates of life expectancy is 28 (=20 + 8) for treatment A and 20 (=10 + 10) for treatment B, which gives the following:

$$\text{EVPI} = (20 + 10) - (\text{whichever is greater between } 28 \text{ and } 20, \text{ that is, } 28)$$
$$= 2 \text{ years.}$$

This indicates that one can expect to obtain an additional 2 years of life expectancy given perfect information.

The example in Fig. 6.12 only assumes cases where the treatment is either effective or not effective and does not consider the probability that it is effective. However, the EVPI can also be calculated with consideration for the efficacy. Assume an efficacy of p, as shown in Fig. 6.12, in which case the probability that treatment is not effective will be $1 - p$. Here, the life expectancies in the two-by-two table are weighted by their probabilities p (or $1 - p$), as shown in Table 6.5. Consequently, the EVPI with consideration for the efficacy p is expressed as follows:

$$\text{EVPI} = (10p + 10) - \{\text{whichever is greater between } (12p + 8) \text{ and } 10\}.$$

The probability at which $12p + 8$ equals 10 is 0.167 by the following calculation:

$$12p + 8 = 10$$
$$\text{Hence, } p = (10 - 8) / 12$$
$$= 0.167.$$

Fig. 6.12 Decision tree considering efficacy

Expected life years

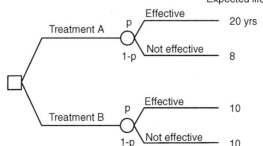

Table 6.5 Contingency table considering efficacy

	Treatment A	Treatment B	Maximum
Effective (p)	$20p$	$10p$	$20p$
Ineffective ($1 - p$)	$8(1 - p)$	$10(1 - p)$	$10(1 - p)$
Total	$12p + 8$	10	$10p + 10$

Fig. 6.13 Expected life years of each treatment and EVPI, considering efficacy

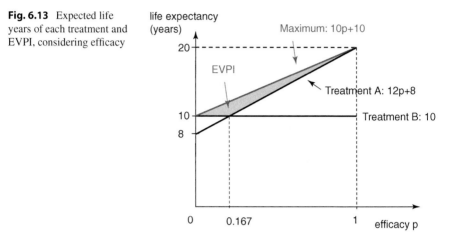

The relationship between $12p + 8$ and 10 can be graphically illustrated as in Fig. 6.13. Consequently, the following conclusions can be obtained with respect to the value of EVPI:

1. At an efficacy of 0.167 or greater,

$$EVPI = 2 - 2p;$$

2. At an efficacy of 0.167 or smaller,

$$EVPI = 10p.$$

The above conclusions can be graphically presented as in Fig. 6.14. At $p = 0.167$ (efficacy of 16.7%), the maximum EVPI of 1.67 years is obtained.

Fig. 6.14 Graph of EVPI according to the change of efficacy

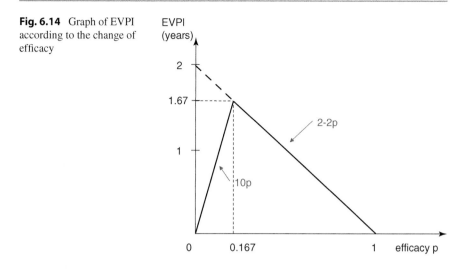

6.5.3   Self-Check!

1. Assume that the life expectancies of five patients are estimated as in the table below for the cases in which patients receive treatments A and B. What is the EVPI in this case?

	Treatment A	Treatment B
Patient 1	20 years	10 years
Patient 2	8	10
Patient 3	15	8
Patient 4	10	12
Patient 5	12	11

6.6   Logistic Regression and Risk Estimation

6.6.1   Key Points

- Logistic regression analysis is a statistical method that considers multiple variables.
- It is used to estimate risk and analyze risk factors.
- The coefficients of the explanatory variables are related to the odds ratio.
- It allows for the systematic examination of confounding effects.

6.6.2   Essential Knowledge

Logistic regression analysis is a method of statistical analysis that allows for the estimation of risk and analysis of risk factors for a response variable based on multiple explanatory variables. In the economic evaluation of healthcare, logistic regression analysis is used to identify the risk factors of studied patients and to estimate the probabilities to be incorporated into a model.

Logistic regression can be defined as a regression model by the following equation, which considers the natural log of odds (i.e., the ratio of the probability p of an event occurring to the probability $1 - p$ of the event not occurring), with the explanatory variables (also called covariates) expressed as $x_1, x_2, \ldots, x_m$, the constant term β_0, and respective coefficients $\beta_1, \beta_2, \ldots, \beta_m$:

$$\log\left(\frac{p}{1-p}\right) = \beta_0 + \beta_1 x_1 + \beta_2 x_2 + \beta_3 x_3 + \ldots + \beta_m x_m.$$

By modifying the equation as follows, we can obtain the odds:

$$\frac{p}{1-p} = e^{\beta_0 + \beta_1 x_1 + \beta_2 x_2 + \beta_3 x_3 + \ldots + \beta_m x_m}.$$

The equation can be further modified to give probability p as follows:

$$p = \frac{e^{\beta_0 + \beta_1 x_1 + \beta_2 x_2 + \beta_3 x_3 + \ldots + \beta_m x_m}}{1 + e^{\beta_0 + \beta_1 x_1 + \beta_2 x_2 + \beta_3 x_3 + \ldots + \beta_m x_m}} = \frac{1}{1 + e^{-(\beta_0 + \beta_1 x_1 + \beta_2 x_2 + \beta_3 x_3 + \ldots + \beta_m x_m)}}$$

which can be used to estimate the probability that the event being studied occurs (e.g., prevalence of a disease). Here, the explanatory variable data must be obtained from prospective studies (e.g., cohort studies and randomized controlled trials).

Logistic regression is used to identify risk factors on the theoretical basis that the odds ratio of explanatory variable x_i can be obtained from its coefficient β_i. Let us consider a simple logistic regression model with the presence (+) or absence (−) of a disease (lung cancer) as the response variable and the exposure (+) or no exposure (−) to cigarette smoke (below "smoking") as the explanatory variable. That is, where

$$y = \begin{cases} 1 : \text{lung cancer} (+) \\ 0 : \text{lung cancer} (-) \end{cases} \quad yx = \begin{cases} 1 : \text{smoking} (+) \\ 0 : \text{smoking} (-) \end{cases},$$

the model can be expressed by the following equation:

$$\log\left(\frac{p}{1-p}\right) = \beta_0 + \beta_1 x.$$

If we let p_1 be the probability of developing lung cancer in the group of smoking (+), and p_0 be the probability of that in the group of smoking (−), then,

$$\log\left(\frac{p_1}{1-p_1}\right) = \beta_0 + \beta_1 (1) = \beta_0 + \beta_1,$$

$$\log\left(\frac{p_0}{1-p_0}\right) = \beta_0 + \beta_1 (0) = \beta_0.$$

If we take the difference between the above two equations then,

$$\log\left(\frac{p_1}{1-p_1}\right) - \log\left(\frac{p_0}{1-p_0}\right) = \beta_0 + \beta_1 - \beta_0 = \beta_1,$$

which gives

$$\log\frac{\left(\dfrac{p_1}{1-p_1}\right)}{\left(\dfrac{p_0}{1-p_0}\right)} = \beta_1, \text{ that is, } \log\left(\text{odds ratio}\right) = \beta_1.$$

This ultimately gives the relationship of odds ratio $= e^{\beta_1}$, indicating that the odds ratio can be calculated given β_1. This is considered an advantage of logistic regression.

Let us look at the odds ratio for a more specific example given the data in Table 6.6. Analysis using a classical two-by-two table gives the odds ratio in all subjects (see Table 6.6c) calculated as follows:

$$\text{odds ratio} = \frac{33 \times 240}{182 \times 30} = 1.45.$$

The obtained odds ratio is above 1, which suggests an association between lung cancer and alcohol. However, analysis using Table 6.6a, b for subjects stratified by smoking status gives the odds ratios of 1.073 and 0.968, respectively, which nearly equal 1. Therefore, the odds ratios that exclude the effect of smoking indicate no association between lung cancer and alcohol drinking. That is, smoking is shown to confound the association between lung cancer and alcohol.

Logistic regression provides us with a systematic approach to performing such stratified analysis with classical two-by-two tables using a mathematical model. For instance, supposing that

Table 6.6 Example of stratified analysis by smoking

	Lung cancer+	Lung cancer-			Lung cancer+	Lung cancer-			Lung cancer+	Lung cancer-	
drinking +	22	82	104	drinking +	11	100	111	drinking +	33	182	215
drinking -	5	20	25	drinking -	25	220	245	drinking -	30	240	270
	27	102	129		36	320	356		63	422	485

Table a: stratified by smoking (+)   Table b: stratified by smoking (-)   Table c: crude

The 2 by 2 tables, a and b, indicate a relation between drinking and lung cancer, stratified by smoking. Table c is a crude one without any stratification

$$y = \begin{cases} 1: \text{lung cancer}\,(+) \\ 0: \text{lung cancer}\,(-) \end{cases} \quad x_1 = \begin{cases} 1: \text{drinking}\,(+) \\ 0: \text{drinking}\,(-) \end{cases} \quad x_2 = \begin{cases} 1: \text{smoking}\,(+) \\ 0: \text{smoking}\,(-) \end{cases},$$

consider the following three logistic regression models.

1.

$$\log\left(\frac{p}{1-p}\right) = \beta_0 + \beta_1 x_1,$$

2.

$$\log\left(\frac{p}{1-p}\right) = \beta_0 + \beta_2 x_2,$$

3.

$$\log\left(\frac{p}{1-p}\right) = \beta_0 + \beta_1 x_1 + \beta_2 x_2.$$

If we perform a logistic regression using statistical software based on these models, we obtain, for example, the results in Table 6.7 for model (3) above. Based on these results, the odds ratio (OR) for lung cancer associated with alcohol drinking, which excludes the effect of smoking is obtained as follows:

$$OR = e^{\beta_1} = e^{0.00038} = 1.0004.$$

Here, the 95% confidence interval of the odds ratio is calculated as $e^{0.00038 \pm 1.96 \times 0.15595} = 0.74$ to 1.36, which includes 1, indicating no significant difference.

Similarly, the odds ratio for lung cancer associated with smoking that excludes the effect of drinking is obtained as follows:

$$OR = e^{\beta_2} = e^{0.42765} = 1.53,$$

with the 95% confidence interval of $e^{0.42765 \pm 1.96 \times 0.15931} = 1.12$ to 2.10. In this case, the 95% confidence interval does not include 1, indicating a significant difference.

The odds ratio and its 95% confidence interval can be similarly obtained for models (1) and (2).

Table 6.8 summarizes the odds ratio and the 95% confidence interval obtained for each of the three models. The fact that the odds ratio associated with drinking varies for different models implies confounding. In other words, smoking is a

Table 6.7 Example of the results by logistic regression analysis

	Estimate	Standard error	Chi-square	P-value
β_0	1.75701	0.14063	156.11	<0.0001
β_1	0.00038	0.15595	0.00	0.9980
β_2	0.42765	0.15931	7.21	0.0073

Table 6.8 Change of odds ratio by models

variables	Model (1)	Model (2)	Model (3)
X_1:drinking	0.92~1.57 1.20	change	0.74~1.36 1.0004
X_2:smoking		1.17~2.02 1.53	1.12~2.10 1.53
		stable	

Upper: 95%CI of OR,
Lower: Point estimate of OR

Upper: 95%CI of OR, Lower: Point estimate of OR

confounding factor for the association between lung cancer and drinking. On the other hand, the association between lung cancer and smoking is not affected by confounding. We therefore identify smoking as a key risk factor for lung cancer. The odd ratios obtained for models (1) and (2) are referred to as an "unadjusted odds ratio," whereas the odds ratio obtained for model (3) is an "adjusted odds ratio." As seen in this example, the values of the odds ratio obtained by logistic regression vary depending on the choice of the covariates used in modeling. We therefore must remember to consider confounding in evaluating risks and risk factors.

6.6.3 Self-Check!

1. What are the characteristics of logistic regression?
2. Data from a case-control study were used for probability estimation. Is this appropriate?
3. What does an adjusted odds ratio refer to?

6.7 Meta-analysis and Indirect Treatment Comparisons

6.7.1 Key Points

- Meta-analysis is a systematic approach to collecting and combining previously reported evidence.
- When a meta-analysis is conducted, the method used, evaluation of heterogeneity, forest plotting, pooled estimates, and their confidence intervals must be reported.
- Three models are used in quantitative synthesis: fixed effects, random effects, and Bayesian.
- Sensitivity analysis and additional statistical analyses (such as meta-regression analysis) may also be performed.

- Indirect comparison is used when evidence from head-to-head clinical trials is not available.
- There are two approaches to indirect comparison: with and without adjustment.
- A challenge inherent to indirect comparison is how to adjust for heterogeneity.
- Multiple treatment comparison is also used for indirect comparisons.

6.7.2   Essential Knowledge

6.7.2.1 Meta-analysis

Meta-analysis is formed from the prefix "meta (transcending/higher/comprehensive)" and the term "analysis." It may be referred to as transcendent analysis (or comprehensive analysis), although the term meta-analysis is generally used. As defined in the glossary of the MHLW Guidelines (see Glossary: Meta-analysis), meta-analysis refers to a method to systematically collect evidence from previously reported research outcomes and synthesize them quantitatively using statistical methods [5].

In economic evaluation studies, meta-analysis is needed when combining evidence from multiple studies reported in literature to be used for analysis. Item 5.2.6 of the MHLW Guidelines Ver. 2.0 recommends that meta-analysis be performed "if deemed appropriate," in which case the statistical method used, evaluation of heterogeneity, forest plotting, pooled estimates, and their confidence intervals must be presented.

Since a meta-analysis is conducted on evidence reported in the literature and not on individual patient data, it may be considered as an analysis of the results of individual randomized controlled trials at a "higher level," and thus the term "meta" is used (see Fig. 6.15).

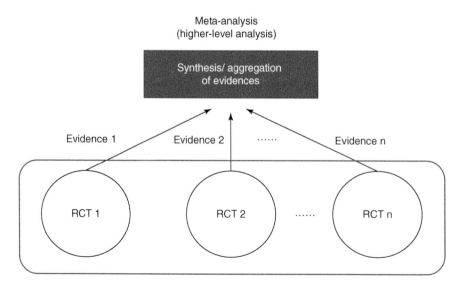

Fig. 6.15 Concept of meta-analysis

Table 6.9 Fundamental steps for meta-analysis

Step 1 Preparation	
(a)	Organize a study group
(b)	Develop a study plan (protocol)
Step 2 Data collection	
(a)	Survey literature
(b)	Choose target studies
(c)	Extract and record the data
Step 3 Evaluation/analysis	
(a)	Evaluate the quality of analyses
(b)	Synthesize evidences
(c)	Additional analyses including sensitivity analyses
Step 4 Report	

Table 6.9 shows the basic steps of a meta-analysis. The first step is to make sufficient preparations for the subsequent steps. A key to performing a meta-analysis is to minimize bias and, for this reason, a study group consisting of multiple researchers is formed, rather than a single researcher only, which can be more prone to personal bias. It is also essential to take enough time to develop a protocol for the analysis. The working hypotheses must be defined first, and the subsequent steps should be specified in advance along a deductive process of collecting and analyzing data.

The second step is to collect the data. Journals and references must be extensively searched, including online databases. As necessary, contacting of the original authors may be preferred, although this may be difficult for practical reasons. The fundamental problem in data collection is the presence of publication bias, due to the fact that studies that show statistically insignificant results are generally less likely to be reported. This is particularly relevant when significant results are obtained in a meta-analysis. When only evidence that is statistically significant is collected due to publication bias, it is difficult to avoid bias, even if the results are statistically significant. To address this, approaches such as a funnel plot and fail-safe number may be used for the assessment of publication bias. Generally, the smaller the sample size, the greater the variability of the results and vice versa. A funnel plot can be drawn by plotting studies on a plane with the sample size on the vertical axis and the effect size on the horizontal axis. The presence or absence of bias can be determined by assessing whether or not the distribution of studies is funnel-shaped (see Fig. 6.16). As shown in Fig. 6.16, a blank space in the funnel indicates bias. The fail-safe number is a measure that represents the number of additional studies with negative results needed for the results of the meta-analysis to be insignificant. It is considered that the larger the fail-safe number, the more robust the results of the meta-analysis are. However, several limitations have been pointed out with respect to this approach and the Cochrane Collaboration does not recommend its use.

The selection of studies in Step 2b involves determining whether the selected studies are eligible for inclusion based on the inclusion criteria specified in the protocol. A record of studies that are excluded should also be kept for future reference.

Sample size

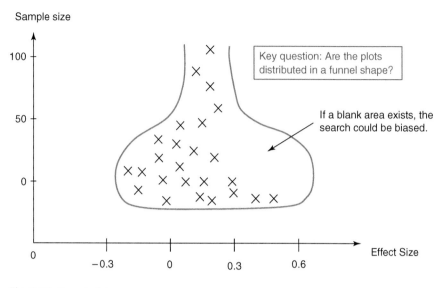

Fig. 6.16 Funnel plot

For abstraction of data in Step 2c, identifiers such as names of authors and affiliated institutions are masked to eliminate bias, and any one study is to be reviewed by more than one researcher. Any conflicts due to inconsistencies among reviewers in the data extracted from one study are to be resolved through discussions. This may require contacting the original authors for any questions. Reviewers should use a common format for data abstraction and recording to avoid variations in the methods used.

The third step is the evaluation and analysis of data. While this step consists mainly of statistical analysis, Step 3a requires the assessment of the quality of studies prior to performing a quantitative synthesis of evidence. Classical approaches include the scale for the quality assessment of randomized controlled trials (RCTs) by Chalmers et al. [6] and the standards by DerSimonian et al. [7] The CONSORT Statement [8] is often used by clinicians as a set of standards for the critical appraisal of RCTs. The MHLW Guidelines Ver. 2.0 (item 5.2.4) recommend that the PRISMA Statement [9] be followed in the reporting of systematic reviews. Studies that are insufficient in quality may be excluded from the subsequent quantitative synthesis.

Once the set of studies to be included is determined in the process up to Step 3a, a quantitative synthesis of the evidence is performed. The following three models are used to synthesize evidence on treatment effects:

1. Fixed effects model [10]: assumes only within-study effect variability
2. Random effects model [11]: assumes both within-study and between-study effect variability
3. Bayesian model [12]: an approach based on Bayesian statistics

Table 6.10 Inverse variance-weighted method

Step 1.	For each study, find the variance of difference D_i between the experimental group and the control group. (Provided that the sample size of each group is n_i, and the standard deviations are S_{i1}, S_{i0}.) $$\mathrm{SE}_i^2 = \left(S_{i1}^2 + S_{i0}^2 \right) / n_i$$
Step 2.	Calculate the weight w_i for each study. $$w_i = 1 / \mathrm{SE}_i^2$$
Step 3.	Find the estimate of the difference D_{meta} of the two groups integrated for k studies. $$D_{\mathrm{meta}} = \sum_{}^{k} \left(w_i^* D_i \right) / \sum_{}^{k} w_i$$
Step 4.	Find the 95% confidence interval of the difference D_{meta} of the two groups. $$95\% \text{confidence interval} = D_{\mathrm{meta}} \pm 1.96 \sqrt{1 / \left(\sum_{}^{k} w_i \right)}$$

Although there are no criteria in deciding whether to use a fixed or random effects model, a random effects model generally gives more "conservative" results and a wider confidence interval compared to a fixed effects model.

Different statistical methods are used depending on the model chosen, but the fundamental approach to quantitative synthesis is to weigh the study estimates by the inverse of the estimates' variance (weight = 1/variance). For example, Table 6.10 shows the steps in the classical inverse-variance-weighted method.

More practical approaches include the Mantel-Haenszel method [10], based on a fixed effects model, and the DerSimonian-Laird method [11], based on a random effects model. Table 6.11 shows the formulae for computing the summary odds and risk ratios using the Mantel-Haenszel method.

In Table 6.11, the odds ratio OR_i and the variance are $(a_i d_i)/(b_i c_i)$ and $n_i/(b_i c_i)$, respectively, which gives the numerator and denominator of the summary odds ratio as follows:

Numerator: $\dfrac{a_i d_i}{n_i} = \dfrac{\left(b_i c_i \right) \mathrm{OR}_i}{n_i} = \left(\text{inverse of variance of the } i\text{th study} \right) \times \mathrm{OR}_i,$

Denominator: $\dfrac{b_i c_i}{n_i} = \text{inverse of variance of the } i\text{th study}.$

From above, the summary odds ratio is calculated as

$$\mathrm{OR}_{\mathrm{MH}} = \left(\sum_{}^{k} \left(\text{inverse of variance of the } i\text{th study} \right) \times \mathrm{OR}_i \right) / \left(\sum_{}^{k} \left(\text{inverse of variance of the } i\text{th study} \right) \right),$$

indicating it is based on the concept of inverse variance weighing.

Table 6.11 Synthesis by Mantel-Haenszel method

Contingency table for the i-th study			
	Number of responders	Number of non-responders	Total
Experimental group	a_i	b_i	
Control group	c_i	d_i	
			n_i
• Summary odds ratio	$$\mathrm{OR}_{\mathrm{MH}} = \left(\sum^{k} \frac{a_i d_i}{n_i} \right) \Big/ \left(\sum^{k} \frac{b_i c_i}{n_i} \right)$$		
• Summary risk ratio	$$\mathrm{RR}_{\mathrm{MH}} = \left(\sum^{k} \frac{a_i (c_i + d_i)}{n_i} \right) \Big/ \left(\sum^{k} \frac{c_i (a_i + b_i)}{n_i} \right)$$		

When conducting a quantitative synthesis, studies must be tested for homogeneity (or heterogeneity). A test for homogeneity, for example, in the inverse variance-weighted method, assumes that

$$Q = \sum^{k} w_i \left(D_i - D_{\mathrm{meta}} \right)^2 ,$$

in the case of inverse variance-weighted method, and

$$Q = \sum^{k} \left\{ \frac{b_i c_i}{n_i} \times \left(\ln \mathrm{OR}_{\mathrm{MH}} - \ln \mathrm{OR}_i \right)^2 \right\},$$

in the case of odds ratio follows a chi-square distribution with $k - 1$ degrees of freedom (k = number of studies). When the null hypothesis that the odds ratios of all studies are equal is rejected, the synthesis must be terminated and reasons for heterogeneity investigated. Even when the null hypothesis is not rejected, it requires a careful consideration of the possibility that it cannot be rejected due to low statistical power.

Once the results of the quantitative synthesis are obtained, Step 3c is to perform, as needed based on the study protocol, a sensitivity analysis and additional statistical analyses (e.g., a cumulative meta-analysis [analysis in chronological order] and a meta-regression analysis [applies logistic regression]).

The last step is the reporting of results. Forms of presentation include reports and scholarly articles, which generally use a forest plot (see Fig. 6.17).

A forest plot indicates the mean measure of effect and its confidence interval for each study along the vertical axis, illustrating the relative distance from the vertical line drawn at the reference effect measure (0 in the case of difference in risk and 1 in the case of odds ratio and risk ratio). Where the odds ratio or risk ratio is used as the effect measure on the horizontal axis, the reference point will be at 1, about which the horizontal axis will represent a symmetrical log scale. The mean measure of effect reported in each study is represented as a square, whose size is proportional

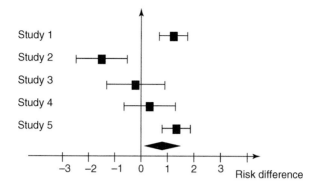

Fig. 6.17 Forest plot
■: mean reported in each study
├─┤ : confidence interval
◆: synthesized estimate and its confidence interval

to its weight (squares may also take equal sizes), with the horizontal lines emerging from the square, ■, indicating the width of the associated confidence interval. The summary measure is indicated as the center of a diamond, ◆, with the width of the diamond representing the confidence interval. Whether or not the individual or summary estimates are statistically significant can be determined based on whether or not the confidence interval line intersects the vertical axis.

6.7.2.2 Indirect Treatment Comparisons

Item 5 of the MHLW Guidelines Ver. 2.0 presents its policy on additional benefits, and items 5.5 and 5.5.1 of the guidelines state that indirect treatment comparisons (see Glossary: Indirect comparison) may be used in analysis.

Here, let us consider again what is being compared in an indirect treatment comparison. First, we need to start by clarifying the difference between effectiveness and additional benefit in terms of effectiveness. Generally, what is referred to as efficacy or effectiveness (or broadly benefit) is measured as the clinical benefit of a new technology relative to a placebo or no treatment. In contrast, additional or relative benefit refers to the additional clinical benefit of a new technology relative to the standard of care or an existing technology as a comparator.

Therefore, when evidence available for drug A includes the results of direct comparisons with placebo *P* and drugs C, D, and E and evidence available for drug B includes the results of direct comparisons with placebo *P* and drugs C, E, and F (see Fig. 6.18), the summary of clinical benefit can be calculated for both drugs A and B as an indirect comparison. This is referred to as an unadjusted indirect comparison. Although it has the advantage of being a simple and convenient approach that allows for the inclusion of studies other than randomized controlled trials, it does not distinguish between benefit and additional benefit and may be strongly biased as in the case of a simple observational study [13].

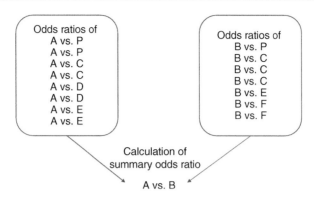

Fig. 6.18 Unadjusted indirect comparison

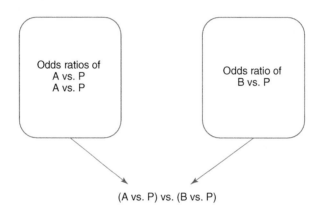

Fig. 6.19 Adjusted indirect comparison

Hence, an indirect comparison is preferably conducted between the results of direct comparison with a common comparator, which is referred to as an adjusted indirect comparison (see Fig. 6.19). However, even in an adjusted indirect comparison, between-study variability such as in subject characteristics and dosage may still be present. A classical approach to adjusted indirect comparison is meta-regression. This approach allows controlling for confounding factors and the adjustment to reduce heterogeneity, but a minimum of ten studies are said to be required. Additionally, as this is a regression analysis, potential bias due to unknown confounding factors cannot be eliminated.

How to adjust for heterogeneity is a key issue in indirect comparison. This suggests that indirect comparison and meta-analysis share common methodological challenges. Recently, an approach called mixed treatment comparison meta-analysis or multiple treatment comparison meta-analysis is being adopted, both of which are abbreviated as MTC and are also referred to as network meta-analysis.

The basic concept of the MTC meta-analysis approach to evidence synthesis is the inverse variance-weighted method. That is, given the evidence of direct comparison (log odds), $d_{AB(direct)}$ and $d_{AC(direct)}$ between treatments A and B and between treatments A and C, respectively, the evidence of indirect comparison, $d_{BC(indirect)}$, between treatments B and C is expressed as follows:

$$d_{BC(indirect)} = d_{AC(direct)} - d_{AB(direct)},$$

where the evidence of direct comparison, $d_{BC(direct)}$, is also available, the pooled log odds ratio between treatments B and C, $d_{BC(pooled)}$, can be calculated as follows:

$$d_{BC(pooled)} = \frac{w_{direct} \times d_{BC(direct)} + w_{indirect} \times d_{BC(indirect)}}{w_{direct} + w_{indirect}},$$

where

$$w_{(direct)} = 1 / \operatorname{Var}\left(d_{BC(direct)}\right),$$

$$w_{(indirect)} = 1 / \operatorname{Var}\left(d_{BC(indirect)}\right)$$

$$= 1 / \left\{ \operatorname{Var}\left(d_{AC(direct)}\right) + \operatorname{Var}\left(d_{AB(direct)}\right) \right\}.$$

In any case, MTC allows us to maintain the advantage of randomization by including evidence from available randomized controlled trials and to quantify the degree of consistency among multiple treatment groups in the network. While MTC can be applied to a group as small as three studies, it also has the limitation of being a complex approach that lacks the transparency expected by users and consistent validation is difficult. Indirect comparison is therefore only used when evidence based on direct comparison is not available and is not meant to be used in place of direct comparison.

6.7.3 Self-Check!

1. What does "meta" refer to?
2. What is the purpose of using the funnel plot?
3. List the four steps of a meta-analysis.
4. What is the name of the approach fundamental to quantitative synthesis?
5. Assume the pooled summary odds ratio was calculated to be 1.54 (with the 95% confidence interval of 0.83–1.96). How do you interpret this result?
6. Given the following data, answer the following questions based on the inverse variance-weighted method, assuming a fixed effects model (see Table 6.10).

Study	Sample size	Blood triglyceride level	
		Placebo	Actual drug
A	61 per group	180 ± 10	150 ± 12
B	82 per group	168 ± 8	128 ± 10
C	52 per group	176 ± 12	132 ± 8
		(mean ± standard deviation)	

  (a) Find the variance $(SE_i)^2$ of the reduction in blood triglyceride level for each study.

  (b) Find the weight w_i of each study.

  (c) Find the pooled difference D_{meta} between the two groups.

  (d) Find the 95% confidence interval.

7. In a test for homogeneity, what is the action to take when the null hypothesis is rejected?

8. Are indirect comparisons required by the MHLW Guidelines Ver. 2.0?

9. What does MTC stand for?

6.8   Cox Proportional Hazard Models

6.8.1   Key Points

- Survival analysis is often used for risk estimation in prospective studies.
- The simplest model of approximating the survival function is an exponential function that assumes a constant risk of death (hazard).
- The Kaplan-Meier method is a standard nonparametric approach that does not assume a specific hazard.
- The log-rank test is used to compare survival curves for two groups.
- The Cox proportional hazard model further generalizes the assumption of constant hazards.
- In the Cox model, the hazard function is proportional to the baseline hazard.
- The Cox regression coefficient is equal to the log of the hazard ratio.

6.8.2   Essential Knowledge

Prospective studies, such as cohort studies and randomized controlled trials, often use survival analysis to estimate risks. For example, assume that a difference in survival rates was observed between treatment groups A and B, as shown in Fig. 6.20. In that case, the first question is how to express the survival function $S(t)$ of one group quantitatively.

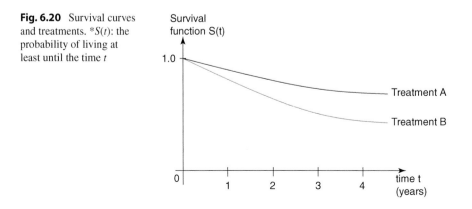

Fig. 6.20 Survival curves and treatments. *$S(t)$: the probability of living at least until the time t

The simplest approach to answering this question is to assume a constant risk of death (referred to as hazard in survival analysis). We let λ denote the hazard and describe the survival function using an exponential function as follows:

$$S(t) = e^{-\lambda t}.$$

In survival analysis, the risk of death is usually expressed by the hazard function $h(t)$, which, under the assumption of constant hazard, will be $h(t) = \lambda$ (a constant). More complex parametric approaches include approximation by using models such as a Gompertz function.

The Kaplan-Meier method is a nonparametric approach used to estimate the survival function $S(t)$ without assuming a specific function for the hazard function $h(t)$. This method allows for the estimation of median survival time and the 95% confidence interval of the probability of survival at the time that an event involving death occurs, through arithmetic computation not based on a specific function.

If survival curves for two treatment groups are given as in Fig. 6.20, another question is how to statistically test for differences between the two curves. Here, a commonly used statistical approach is the log-rank test. This test applies the Mantel-Haenszel test, which evaluates the statistical significance of differences between n estimates of odds ratios obtained from n sets of two-by-two tables and is essentially the same approach as the Mantel-Haenszel test despite being referred to by a different name. The log-rank test is used to test if the null hypothesis, i.e., the hypothesis that the survival functions $S_A(t)$ and $S_B(t)$ (or the hazard functions $h_A(t)$ and $h_B(t)$) for groups A and B are identical holds true. That is, the null hypothesis is stated as follows:

$$\text{Null hypothesis } H_0 = S_A(t) = S_B(t) \text{ or } h_A(t) = h_B(t).$$

Another widely used approach to risk estimation in survival analysis is to generalize the assumption of constant hazards ($h(t) = \lambda$) to assume proportional hazards. This is the Cox proportional hazard model (or the Cox regression model), which assumes the following: [14]

$$h(t|x) = h(t|x_1, x_2, x_3, \ldots, x_n) = h_0(t) e^{\beta_1 x_1 + \beta_2 x_2 + \beta_3 x_3 + \ldots + \beta_n x_n}.$$

Here, $h_0(t)$ is referred to as the baseline hazard, as it denotes the hazard when the covariates in the regression equation $\beta_1 x_1 + \beta_2 x_2 + \beta_3 x_3 + \ldots + \beta_n x_n$ all equal zero. That is,

$$h(t|x_1 = 0, x_2 = 0, x_3 = 0, \ldots, x_n = 0) = h_0(t) e^0 = h_0(t).$$

The ratio between the hazard function $h(t|x)$ and the baseline hazard $h_0(t)$ can then be written as

$$\frac{h(t|x)}{h_0(t)} = e^{\beta_1 x_1 + \beta_2 x_2 + \beta_3 x_3 + \ldots + \beta_n x_n},$$

Fig. 6.21 Image of Cox proportional hazards. *$h_0(t)$: baseline hazards

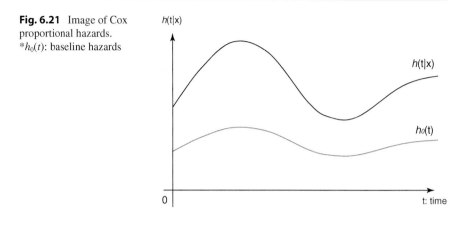

where, at any given time t with known coefficients $\beta_1, \beta_2, \beta_3, \ldots \beta_n$, the ratio between $h(t|x)$ and $h_0(t)$ will be constant according to covariates $x_1, x_2, x_3, \ldots, x_n$ (see Fig. 6.21). In other words, $h(t|x)$ is proportional to $h_0(t)$ independent of changes in time, hence it is called proportional hazards.

Let us now consider the significance of the regression coefficient β. Assume that

$$h(t|x) = h_0(t)e^{\beta_x},$$

where

$$x = \begin{cases} 1 : \text{treatment A} \\ 0 : \text{treatment B} \end{cases}.$$

The equation can be written as

$$h(t|x=1) = h_0(t)e^{\beta \cdot 1} = h_0(t)e^{\beta} \quad \text{for treatment A, and}$$

$$h(t|x=0) = h_0(t)e^{\beta \cdot 0} = h_0(t) \quad \text{for treatment B.}$$

This gives the hazard ratio between treatment groups A and B as follows:

$$\text{Hazard ratio between treatment groups A and B} = \frac{h(t|x=1)}{h(t|x=0)} = \frac{h_0(t)e^{\beta}}{h_0(t)} = e^{\beta}.$$

e^{β} is exactly the odds ratio in the logistic regression (see Sect. 6.6). The coefficient β thus equals the log of the hazard ratio between treatment groups A and B, as follows:

$$\beta = \log(\text{hazard ratio}).$$

The Cox proportional hazard model is thus closely associated with logistic regression.

6.8.3 Self-Check!

1. Write the formula for the survival function using an exponential function. What does it indicate when $t = 0$?
2. The Mantel-Haenszel test, a method of analysis using two-by-two tables in epidemiology, is referred to by what name in survival analysis? State the null hypothesis for this test.
3. Write the formula for the Cox regression model, given two covariates x_1 and x_2.

6.9 Propensity Score Analysis

6.9.1 Key Points

- Propensity score (PS) analysis is based on a prospective model of logistic regression.
- PSs are used to equate two groups being compared based on background factors.
- PS analysis allows one to simulate a randomized clinical trial.

6.9.2 Essential Knowledge

Analysis using propensity scores (PS) [15] is increasingly being adopted in economic evaluations. The basis of this approach is the logistic regression discussed in Sect. 6.6. It would thus be useful to clarify the concept of logistic regression again to understand PS analysis. There were two primary purposes in using logistic regression. That is, based on the regression formula

$$\log\left(\frac{p}{1-p}\right) = \beta_0 + \beta_1 x_1 + \beta_2 x_2 + \ldots + \beta_n x_n,$$

logistic regression can be used to

1. Estimate the probability p that an event, indicated as the response variable ($y = 1$: event, 0: no event), occurs given a set of explanatory variables (covariates) x_1, x_2, ..., x_n.
2. Estimate the odds ratio of covariate x_1 based on the odds ratio being equal to $e^{\beta i}$.

The PS analysis uses the first property of logistic regression, which allows for the estimation of probability p for the matching of each of the distributions of covariates x_1, x_2, ..., x_n given two groups ($y = 1$ or 0). Therefore, in order to make the PS interpreted as probability p which can be done in logistic regression, we need to understand how the regression formula is related to the direction of observation, as shown in Table 6.12.

For instance, if we are to examine the association between smoking and lung cancer, whether a retrospective model or a prospective model is used depends on whether smoking or lung cancer is assigned as the response variable. We should note that, although either model can be selected in theory, whether the data are

Table 6.12 Association between a model and the direction of observation

(1) Retrospective model	(2) Prospective model
$\log\left(\dfrac{\text{prob. of exposure}}{1-\text{prob. of exposure}}\right)$ $= \beta_0 + \beta_1 x_1 + \beta_2 x_2 + \ldots$ $x_1 = 1$: with disease, 0: without disease	$\log\left(\dfrac{\text{prob. of disease}}{1-\text{prob. of disease}}\right)$ $= \beta_0 + \beta_1 x_1 + \beta_2 x_2 + \ldots$ $x_1 = 1$: with exposure, 0: without exposure

Table 6.13 Predictability of probability p

	Case-control data	Cohort data
Retrospective model	× (meaningless)	–
Prospective model	△ (difficult to interpret)	OK

obtained from a retrospective (e.g., case-control) or prospective (e.g., cohort) study affects the interpretation of PS according to the combination shown in Table 6.13. As a general rule, analysis should be based on the prospective model and use data from prospective studies.

A real PS analysis would compare two treatment groups A and B using the formula

$$\log\left(\frac{\text{probability of receiving treatment A}}{\text{probability of receiving treatment B}\left(\text{not receiving treatment A}\right)}\right)$$
$$= \beta_0 + \beta_1 x_1 + \beta_2 x_2 + \ldots + \beta_n x_n,$$

based on the prospective model and including the background factors $x_1, x_2, \ldots, x_n$ as covariates prior to the assignment to treatments A or B. This gives the probability p of being assigned to treatment A, although the estimate p is referred to as a score in this case because it is different in the normal sense of the probability of developing a disease given some contributing factor. Based on this model, with a PS analysis, we first obtain two comparable groups.

Here, comparable groups refer to two groups with identical distributions of all background factors $x_1, x_2, \ldots, x_n$. This requires the following procedures:

1. Calculate the PS for individual patients using the model's formula.
2. Once the distribution of frequencies relative to PSs is obtained for both treatment groups A and B (see Fig. 6.22), the overlapping region (referred to as common support) between the two groups is identified, and patient data that fall outside the region of common support are excluded from the analysis.
3. Each patient in treatment group A is matched with a patient in treatment group B who has an identical PS (or a PS within a specific range).
4. Once matching based on PSs is completed, the distributions of background factors $x_1, x_2, \ldots, x_n$ between the two groups are compared. Since it is not likely that all background factors will align across treatments A and B, priorities should be set when it comes to alignment of background factors, and a model should be used that balances two or three high priority background factors well.

Fig. 6.22 Distribution of PS and the common support

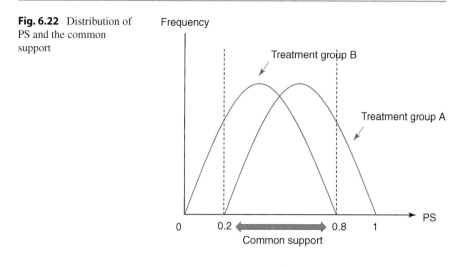

This may require experimenting with the formula by taking the square (x_i^2), cube (x_i^3), or log (log x_i) of the covariates or adding an interaction term ($x_i \times x_j$) before deciding on a model formula.

Once two comparable groups are obtained by the above procedure, the cost and effect are calculated for both groups in an economic evaluation, based on which an ICER can be estimated.

In conclusion, PS analysis allows us to use evidence from databases to simulate a randomized controlled trial without actually conducting one. However, it does require careful attention to eliminating bias. Matching and stratification are generally considered effective at eliminating bias, but the PS matching is basically intended to eliminate bias first. Then additionally, if stratification into around five strata is to be applied, it might be possible to eliminate the majority of bias. PS analysis, however, has limitations in its ability to control for hidden bias due to confounding factors.

6.9.3 Self-Check!

1. What are the two models of analysis used for logistic regression?
2. Write the equation for calculating propensity score p.
3. What does common support refer to?
4. What are the two approaches to eliminating bias?

6.10 Bayesian versus Frequentist Statistics

6.10.1 Key Points

- There are two schools of thought in statistics: Frequentist and Bayesian.
- In the economic analysis of healthcare, Bayesian statistics is used in probability estimation, cost estimation, meta-analysis, and modeling.
- In Bayesian statistics an inference is made based on a subjective prior distribution.

- Posterior distribution of a Bayesian probability is evaluated by the degree of belief and the 95% credibility interval.
- Recent economic evaluations increasingly use Bayesian networks for analyses.

6.10.2 Essential Knowledge

As discussed in Sect. 6.1, Bayes' formula (theorem) is used to quantitatively express the process of updating the probability of a given illness that may change from the point prior to conducting clinical testing to after clinical testing. Bayes' theorem is named after the eighteenth-century English reverend Thomas Bayes and remains referred to by this name today, for this theorem has posthumously formed the basis for a school of thought in probability theory. Recently, Bayesian statistics is increasingly employed in the economic evaluation of healthcare.

Statistics can generally be classified into two schools of thought, Frequentist and Bayesian. The former has been established by Neyman, Pearson, and Fisher, with probability being defined based on the frequency of observational data. By contrast, the latter assumes a prior probability distribution and defines posterior probability based on prior knowledge and observed data by adopting the concept of conditional probability. We have seen the Bayesian approach expressed in Fig. 6.4 in Sect. 6.1 in the context of diagnostic testing although, more generally, the theorem is stated as per the equation in Fig. 6.23. In the case of a binary diagnostic test where the results are given as either + or −, denominator Pr(x) can be expressed as follows to indicate the probability of a positive test:

$$\Pr(+) = \text{pretest probability} \times \text{sensitivity} + \left((1 - \text{pretest probability}) \times (\text{false positive rate}) \right).$$

In addition to the interpretation of clinical test results, Bayes' theorem, as shown in Fig. 6.23, can also be applied in the context of clinical trials, such as the Bayesian model—an approach to performing meta-analysis of randomized controlled trials. An advantage of Bayesian statistics is that it allows one to insert in the analysis information newly acquired during the phases of a clinical trial in a more timely manner than is possible with Frequentist statistics and to perform a phased meta-analysis when new findings from published reports become available.

Fig. 6.23 Bayes theorem

$$\Pr(p|x) = \frac{\Pr(x \mid p) * \Pr(p)}{\Pr(x)}$$

Pr (p|x) = Conditional probability of p given x

Pr (x|p) = Conditional probability of x given p

Pr (p) = prior probability of p

Pr (x) = probability to observing x

where   p, x: independent

x: observation data

In the context of a clinical trial, the Bayesian approach to interpreting its results can be expressed as per the following formula, where D denotes the truth and T the evidence acquired from the trial:

$$\Pr\left(D|T\right) = \frac{\Pr\left(T|D\right) \times \Pr\left(D\right)}{\Pr\left(T\right)}.$$

The probability distribution prior to a clinical trial $\Pr(p)$ is revised to the posttrial distribution $\Pr(p|x)$, based on evidence x from the trial. Figure 6.24 illustrates this process of probability revision as a change in the probability distribution. Analogous to the 95% confidence interval in Frequentist statistics, a 95% credibility interval can be determined for the posttrial probability distribution (see Fig. 6.25). In Bayesian statistics, prior probability is considered to be subjective. Accordingly, the posttrial probability, based on new findings, is similarly considered to be subjective; hence it is referred to as the degree of belief and estimated as the area under the distribution curve. Therefore, the term credibility interval is used instead of confidence interval.

Unlike in traditional Frequentist statistics, interpretation of clinical trial results is slightly more complex with the Bayesian approach. In Frequentist statistics, the mean efficacies p_0 and p_1 obtained for the treatment and control groups, respectively, are statistically tested. Conversely, Bayesian statistics assumes two distributions of mean efficacies, p_0' and p_1', for the treatment and control groups prior to the clinical trial, respectively, and two posttrial distributions with means p_0'' and p_1'' are obtained relative to their respective prior distributions (see Fig. 6.26).

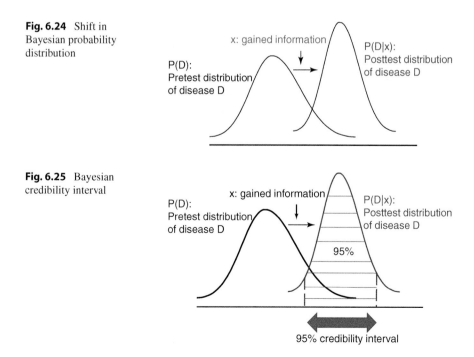

Fig. 6.24 Shift in Bayesian probability distribution

P(D): Pretest distribution of disease D

x: gained information

P(D|x): Posttest distribution of disease D

Fig. 6.25 Bayesian credibility interval

P(D): Pretest distribution of disease D

x: gained information

P(D|x): Posttest distribution of disease D

95%

95% credibility interval

Frequentist

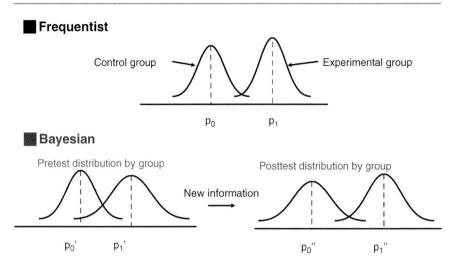

Bayesian

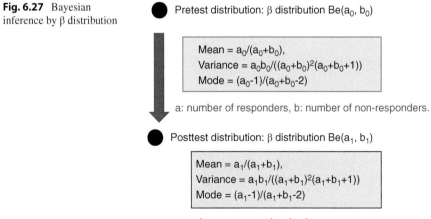

Fig. 6.26 Difference between Frequentist and Bayesian approaches

Fig. 6.27 Bayesian inference by β distribution

Pretest distribution: β distribution $Be(a_0, b_0)$

Mean = $a_0/(a_0+b_0)$,
Variance = $a_0 b_0/((a_0+b_0)^2(a_0+b_0+1))$
Mode = $(a_0-1)/(a_0+b_0-2)$

a: number of responders, b: number of non-responders.

Posttest distribution: β distribution $Be(a_1, b_1)$

Mean = $a_1/(a_1+b_1)$,
Variance = $a_1 b_1/((a_1+b_1)^2(a_1+b_1+1))$
Mode = $(a_1-1)/(a_1+b_1-2)$

where $a_1= a_0+a$, $b_1= b_0+b$

The assumption of prior distribution is unique to Bayesian inference, although this subjective assumption has been historically controversial.

Specifically, the beta distribution $Be(a_0, b_0)$ is often applied to prior distributions. Here, given the evidence of the number of subjects a and b for which treatment was effective or not effective, respectively, the posterior distribution is known to also have a beta distribution $Be(a_1, b_1)$ (where $a_1 = a_0 + a$, $b_1 = b_0 + b$). Figure 6.27 summarizes the equations for the mean, variance, and mode of the prior and posterior distributions. These equations, based on the beta distribution, allow for the estimation of the efficacy rate in a clinical trial by Bayesian inference. For example, assume the control group in a clinical trial of new drug X has the prior probability $Be(10, 5)$. Here, the mean is calculated as $10/(10 + 5) = 0.67$. That is, the prior estimation of the efficacy rate is 67%. Now assume that, as a result of the clinical trial, treatment was found to be effective in 60 out of 100 subjects in the control group. As such, the posterior distribution is determined as

$$Be(10+60,\ 5+100-60) = Be(70,\ 45).$$

The mean can then be calculated as $70/(70 + 45) = 0.61$, indicating that the posterior estimate of the efficacy rate is reduced to 61%. As shown in this example, Bayesian inference is characteristic here in its quantification of the process of obtaining a revised estimate of 61% by reflecting the new evidence of 60% to the prior estimate of 67%, instead of taking the trial results (60%) as an estimate of the efficacy rate. This allows for repeated revisions of probability by taking the efficacy estimate in Phase 1 as the prior probability and obtaining the posterior probability based on the results of Phase 2, and then taking this latter estimate as the prior efficacy rate and calculating the posterior efficacy rate based on the results of Phase 3, and so on. However, it should be noted that whether modeling based on the beta distribution is appropriate or not should be separately examined on a case-by-case basis.

As shown in Fig. 6.26, in Bayesian statistics two posterior distributions are obtained in a clinical trial: one for the control group and one for the treatment group. Consequently, the question is how to test for the significance of differences between the two groups. To answer this question, let us consider a change of variables for efficacy rates p_0'' and p_1''. That is, if we let a new random variable x denote the difference between the log transformed odds of efficacy rates p_0'' and p_1'' for the two groups, we obtain

$$
\begin{aligned}
x &= \delta_0 - \delta_1 \\
&= \log(\text{odds of } p_0) - \log(\text{odds of } p_1) \\
&= \log(p_0/(1-p_0)) - \log(p_1/(1-p_1)) \\
&= \log\left[\{p_0/(1-p_0)\}/\{p_1/(1-p_1)\}\right] \\
&= \log(\text{odds of } p_0/\text{odds of } p_1),
\end{aligned}
$$

which shows that random variable x indicates the log odds ratio. Here, x is known to follow a normal distribution. By using this property, the difference in the magnitude between efficacy rates p_0'' and p_1'' before transformation can be translated into the difference in magnitude between δ_0 and δ_1, based on difference $\delta_0 - \delta_1$. In other words, the distribution of random variable x can be used to determine the degree of belief, or the 95% credibility interval, of the difference between efficacy rates p_0'' and p_1''. For outcome measures other than the efficacy rate that take real values, such as blood glucose level and cost, different approaches that assume a normal distribution are used (Sect. 7.8).

A Bayesian network is another approach being increasingly adopted in recent years for economic evaluations. This approach illustrates Bayes' theorem as a network of dependencies according to the conditional probabilities among nodes that represent multiple random variables (see Fig. 6.28). If dependency is observed

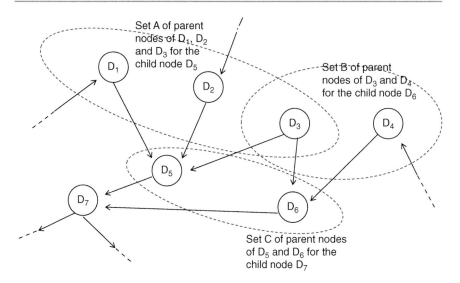

Fig. 6.28 Bayesian network. Node D_i: random variable

Table 6.14 Example of conditional probability table

Four possible states of two parent nodes					
		None	D3 only	D4 only	Both
Discrete states of child node (test results)	+	0.05	0.75	0.65	0.9
	±	0.1	0.1	0.2	0.05
	−	0.85	0.15	0.15	0.05

Assume Set B with parent nodes D_3 and D_4, and the child node D_6 in Fig. 6.28

based on a conditional probability for random variables D_i to D_j, variables D_i and D_j are referred to as parent and child nodes, respectively, and their dependency is represented by an arrow ($\rightarrow$), as shown in the figure. Figure 6.28 presents three parent-child units as follows:

1. Child node D_5 and its parents (D_1, D_2, D_3), represented as group A
2. Child node D_6 and its parents (D_3, D_4), represented as group B
3. Child node D_7 and its parents (D_5, D_6), represented as group C

Given complete information on the conditional dependencies between a child node and all its parent nodes, estimation by Bayesian inference is possible by considering the group of parent nodes as one unit and the child node as another. For example, for the second child-parent unit above, we assume there are four possible statuses for parent group B—(1) neither condition is present, (2) only condition D_3 is present, (3) only condition D_4 is present, and (4) both conditions are present—and three possible dispersion statuses +, ±, and −, for the child node D_6, which represents the results of a clinical test Tx for conditions D_3 and D_4. Table 6.14 shows the conditional probability table for this example.

As a network generally consists of multiple parent-child units as per Fig. 6.28, it is theoretically possible to connect different parent-child units to reach a complex inference based on the entire network. However, it is likely that data on conditional probabilities become less available as the structure of the network becomes more complex. The amount of time required for computation will also increase accordingly and may prevent the analysis from being completed within a realistic time frame.

6.10.3 Self-Check!

1. Name the two schools of thought in statistics.
2. What is the term used to refer to the process of obtaining a posterior distribution from a prior one by Bayesian inference?
3. Given the prior distribution of Be(12, 8) and the results of a clinical trial that treatment was found effective in 70 out of 100 subjects in the new drug group, find the posterior distribution. Additionally, what is the estimate for the efficacy rate?
4. What is the name of the table that specifies the conditional dependencies between a child node and its parent group in a Bayesian network?
5. Describe the advantages and disadvantages of Bayesian statistics.

References

1. Drummond M, McGuire A (eds) (2001) Economic evaluation in health care: merging theory with practice. Oxford University Press, New York, NY
2. Fenwick E, Claxton K, Sculpher M (2001) Representing uncertainty: the role of cost-effectiveness acceptability curves. Health Econ 10(8):779–787
3. National Institute for Health and Care Excellence. Guide to the methods of technology appraisal. 2013. Available at: https://www.nice.org.uk/article/pmg9/resources/non-guidance-guide-to-the-methods-of-technology-appraisal-2013-pdf. Accessed June 1, 2016.
4. Groot Koerkamp B, Myriam Hunink MG, Stijnen T et al (2006) Identifying key parameters in cost-effectiveness analysis using value of information: a comparison of methods. Health Econ 15(4):383–392
5. Sutton AJ, Abrams KR, Jones DR (2001) An illustrated guide to the methods of meta-analysis. J Eval Clin Pract 7(2):135–148
6. Chalmers TC, Smith H Jr, Blackburn B et al (1981) A method for assessing the quality of a randomized control trial. Control Clin Trials 2(1):31–49
7. DerSimonian R, Charette LJ, McPeek B et al (1982) Reporting on methods in clinical trials. N Engl J Med 306(22):1332–1337
8. Consolidated Standards of Reporting Trials. Available at: http://www.consort-statement.org. Accessed June 8, 2016.
9. Preferred Reporting Items for Systematic Reviews and Meta-Analyses. Available at: http://prisma-statement.org. Accessed June 8, 2016.
10. Mantel N, Haenszel W (1959) Statistical aspects of the analysis of data from retrospective studies of disease. J Natl Cancer Inst 22(4):719–748

11. DerSimonian R, Laird N (1986) Meta-analysis in clinical trials. Control Clin Trials 7(3):177–188
12. Smith TC, Spiegelhalter DJ, Thomas A (1995) Bayesian approaches to random-effects meta-analysis: a comparative study. Stat Med 14(24):2685–2699
13. Gartlehner G, Moore CG (2008) Direct versus indirect comparisons: a summary of the evidence. Int J Technol Assess Health Care 24(2):170–177
14. Cox DR (1972) Regression models and life-tables. J R Stat Soc Ser B 34(2):187–220
15. Rosenbaum PR, Rubin DB (1983) The central role of the propensity score in observational studies for causal effects. Biometrika 70(1):41–55

Advanced Research Topics

7.1   Cost-Effectiveness Function and ICER

7.1.1   Key Points

- The relationship between cost and effectiveness is typically expressed by a convex monotonically increasing function.
- Basic models for the cost-effectiveness function include exponential and quadratic functions.
- The incremental cost-effectiveness ratio (ICER) is determined by the slope of the line segment connecting two points for a given cost-effectiveness function.
- Given a cost-effectiveness function, the tangent ICER can be defined.

7.1.2   Essential Knowledge

Generally, the relationship between cost and effectiveness is not proportional: While effectiveness increases with increase in cost, the growth rate gradually diminishes. This relationship is known in economics as the law of diminishing marginal utility. In a two-dimensional graph, if we represent effectiveness on the horizontal axis and cost on the vertical axis as in Fig. 7.1, the cost-effectiveness function is expressed as convex and downward, monotonically increasing from the lower left hand to the upper right hand of the first quadrant.

For this cost-effectiveness function, ICER is represented by the chord (linear segment) that connects two points on the curve. For example in Fig. 7.1, given two points $A(E_1, C_1)$ and $B(E_0, C_0)$ (where the effectiveness and cost of drug A are E_1 and C_1, and of drug B are E_0 and C_0, respectively) the ICER of drug A relative to drug B can be determined by dividing $C_1 - C_0$ by $E_1 - E_0$. This equation represents the slope of segment AB.

Let us now consider that point A moves closer to point B on the cost-effectiveness function. Here, the slope of segment AB (i.e., the ICER of A relative to B) gradually

© Springer Nature Singapore Pte Ltd. 2019
I. Kamae, *Health Technology Assessment in Japan*,
https://doi.org/10.1007/978-981-13-5793-0_7

Fig. 7.1 ICER and
cost-effectiveness curve

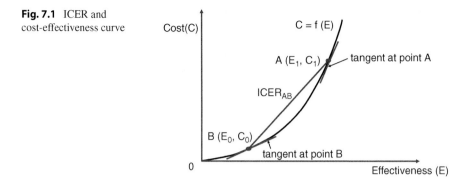

Table 7.1 Function model and tangent ICER

	Analytic function	Tangent (dC/dE)
Exponential	$C = \mathrm{Exp}((E - p)/q)$ $p = (E_1 \log C_0 - E_0 \log C_1)/(\log C_0 - \log C_1)$ $q = (E_1 - E_0)/\log(C_1/C_0)$	$(1/q)\mathrm{Exp}((E - p)/q)$
Quadratic	$C = (1/q)E^2 - p/q$ $p = (C_0(E_1)^2 - C_1(E_0)^2)/(C_0 - C_1)$ $q = ((E_1)^2 - (E_0)^2)/(C_1 - C_0)$	$2E/q$

approaches the slope of the tangent at point B. Therefore, the slope of the tangent at
point B can also be interpreted as the ICER and is the derivative of the cost-
effectiveness function at point B. To express this shift of cost-effectiveness in
another way, it is the infinitesimal change in cost with respect to an infinitesimal
change in effectiveness. This derivation is the rate of change in ICER at point B. Let
us call this rate of change in ICER, the tangent ICER.

The following simple models are possibilities for representing the cost-
effectiveness function in Fig. 7.1:

1. Exponential function (or logarithmic function): $C = \mathrm{Exp}((E - p) / q)$
   (or $E = p + q \log C$).
2. Quadratic function (or irrational function): $C = \left(1/q\right)E^2 - p/q \left(\text{or } E = \sqrt{p + qC}\right)$.

Here, E and C represent effectiveness and cost, respectively.

For instance, for the exponential model, the coordinates of points A and B can be
substituted into the above equation to give the following two equations:

$$E_1 = p + q \log C_1,$$
$$E_0 = p + q \log C_0,$$

where coefficients p and q can be calculated as per Table 7.1. Similarly, the quadratic model can also be formulated as in Table 7.1.

Once the cost-effectiveness function is formulated, the tangent ICER can be
obtained by differentiating the cost-effectiveness function (i.e., dC/dE) as

previously discussed. Therefore, for the exponential function, the tangent ICER can be formulated by differentiating the equation $C = \mathrm{Exp}((E - p)/q)$ with respect to E (Table 7.1): $dC/dE = (1/q)\,\mathrm{Exp}((E - p)/q)$.

The tangent ICER can similarly be obtained by differentiating it for the quadratic model as $2E/q$ (Table 7.1).

7.1.3   Self-Check!

Assume the following two drugs, and answer the questions below.
New drug A: 8.6 QALYs, USD 150K
New drug B: 7.6 QALYs, USD 100K

1. What is the ICER of drug A relative to drug B?
2. Find the tangent ICER for each drug using the exponential model.
3. Repeat the calculations in Question 2 using the quadratic model.

7.2   Interval Estimations Using the Tangent ICER

7.2.1   Key Points

- Once the cost-effectiveness function is formulated, the tangent ICER can be used to estimate the upper and lower limits of ICER (the tangent ICER interval).
- The relationship between the willingness to pay or ICER threshold and the tangent interval can be applied to reimbursement and pricing decisions.

7.2.2   Essential Knowledge

As discussed in Sect. 7.1, once the cost-effectiveness function is formulated by either the exponential model or the quadratic model, it allows us to find the two tangent ICERs.

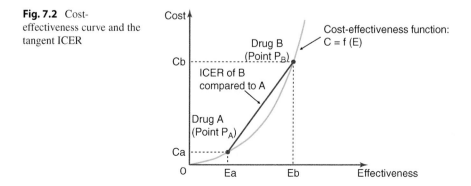

Fig. 7.2 Cost-effectiveness curve and the tangent ICER

Since a cost-effectiveness function is represented by a monotonically increasing curve, as shown in Fig. 7.2, the following relationship holds true in magnitude.

The tangent ICER of A < slope of line segment $P_A P_B$ < tangent ICER of B.

As the slope of segment $P_A P_B$ represents the ICER of the new technology B relative to the previous technology A, the tangent ICERs of B and A can be considered upper and lower limits, respectively, of the ICER of new technology B for the cost-effectiveness function. Let us call this the tangent ICER interval of B, and define it as follows:

Tangent ICER interval of $B = ($tangent ICER of A, tangent ICER of $B)$.

For instance, given the cost-effectiveness function $C = (1/2)E^2$, the interval can be obtained by $dC/dE = E$. That is, given two points $P_A(2, 2)$ and $P_B(4, 8)$, the tangent ICER interval is simply calculated as the values of E, that is, (2, 4). In this example, the ICER of B relative to A is $(8 - 2)/(4 - 2) = 3$, which is within the tangent ICER interval $(2 < 3 < 4)$. Figure 7.3 illustrates these relationships.

The width of the tangent ICER interval offers a measure of the uncertainty of the point estimate of B's ICER. Accordingly, if uncertainty should be minimized, it is important to determine the proportion of the interval width to B's ICER in addition to identifying the interval itself.

In the previous example, the proportion of the interval width is calculated as follows:

$$\text{Width of interval} \div B\text{'s ICER} = (4-2)/3 = 67\%.$$

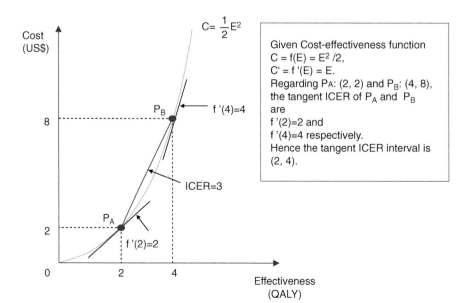

Fig. 7.3 Example of estimating the tangent ICER interval

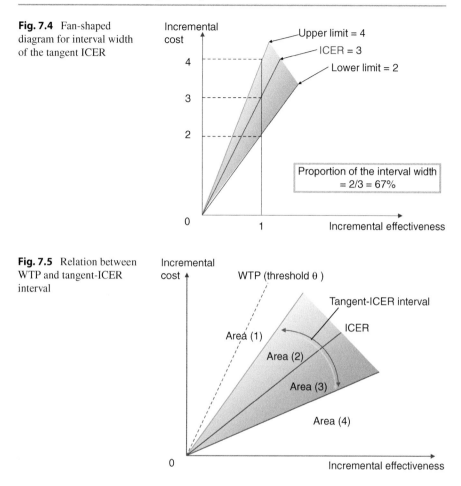

Fig. 7.4 Fan-shaped diagram for interval width of the tangent ICER

Fig. 7.5 Relation between WTP and tangent-ICER interval

Although there is no reference for the proportion, it can be considered that 67% captures a relatively large change. Figure 7.4 illustrates the tangent ICER interval on the incremental cost-effectiveness plane.

Additionally, Fig. 7.5 shows the relationship between the willingness to pay θ (WTP) (or threshold θ) and the tangent ICER interval. The first quadrant can be divided into areas (1)–(4) by the ICER and its upper and lower limits. Here, the area in which the slope of willingness to pay, θ, falls determines whether a given ICER is acceptable. In principle, the following four decisions are possible:

Area (1): ICER is accepted.
Area (2): ICER is accepted as a rule, although it may not be accepted, depending on the value of the upper limit.
Area (3): ICER is not accepted as a rule, although it may be accepted, depending on the value of the lower limit.
Area (4): ICER is not accepted.

7.2.3   Self-Check!

1. Using the example from the self-check questions in Sect. 7.1, confirm the ICER is within the tangent ICER interval for both the quadratic and exponential models.
2. Using the same example, calculate the width of the tangent ICER interval and its proportion for the exponential model.
3. Assuming threshold θ is at USD 60K/QALY, determine whether the ICER for the exponential model in the above example is accepted.
4. Would the decision in Question 3 be different for the quadratic model?

7.3   Which Is Better Index, ICER or Average Cost?

7.3.1   Key Points

- A decision between new and previous technologies can be based on average cost or on ICER.
- The outcome may vary depending on whether average cost or ICER is used.
- The approach using ICER is superior in that it reflects threshold requirements.

7.3.2   Essential Knowledge

In cost-effectiveness analysis (CEA), it is recommended to calculate ICER when comparing new and previous technologies, instead of comparing their average costs. Generally, comparison in terms of average cost is easier to understand than ICER.

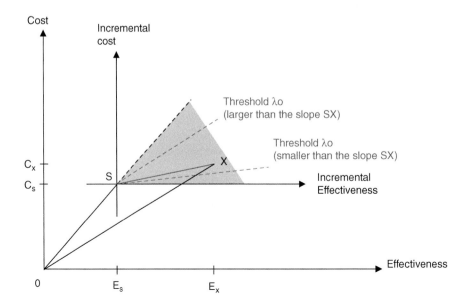

Fig. 7.6 Relation between average cost and ICER: case of extended dominance

As such, let us consider why ICER is preferred over average cost.

As per Fig. 7.6, assume that the effectiveness and cost of a new drug X are given as point (E_X, C_X) and of a comparator S as point (E_S, C_S). Here, drug X shows extended dominance over drug S when it falls in the shaded area.

Let us now consider which drug, S or X, should be adopted. We first examine this in terms of average cost, which can be calculated as follows:

$$\text{Average cost of drug S} = C_S / E_S \, (\text{the slope of line segment OS}),$$
$$\text{Average cost of drug X} = C_X / E_X \, (\text{the slope of line segment OX}).$$

The slope of segment OS is clearly higher than that of segment OX, indicating that the average cost of drug S is higher. Therefore, drug X, with a lower average cost, is adopted.

By contrast, the situation becomes slightly more complicated if calculated by ICER methodology. The ICER of drug X relative to drug S is, by definition, obtained as follows:

$$\text{ICER}_{SX} = (C_X - C_S) / (E_X - E_S).$$

This calculation is equivalent to the slope of segment SX. If the ICER threshold, λ_0, is lower than the slope of segment SX, drug S will be selected over drug X. If threshold λ_0 is higher than the slope of segment SX, drug X will be accepted and adopted. In terms of average cost, drug X was the only option, whereas when ICER is considered, both alternatives X and S are possible, depending on the value of the threshold.

Similarly, as per Fig. 7.7, decisions based on average cost and ICER will not necessarily be consistent when point X falls in the shaded area, where X is dominated by S. Here, in terms of average cost, the slope of segment OS is lower than

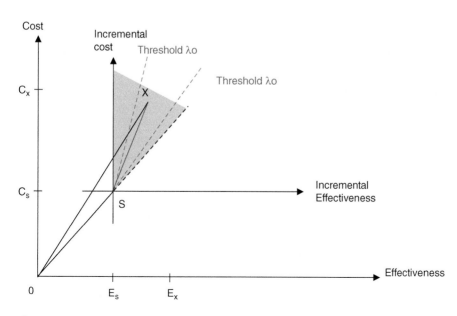

Fig. 7.7 Relation between average cost and ICER: case of being dominated

that of segment OX and, thus, the drug with the lower average cost, S, is adopted. By contrast, when calculated by ICER, a slope of segment SX higher than threshold λ_0 will result in the adoption of drug S, as drug X will not be accepted, and a slope lower than the threshold λ_0 will accept drug X and thus result in the adoption of drug X.

As shown here, when two alternatives S and X are available, a decision based solely on average costs does not reflect the willingness to pay (i.e., the value of threshold λ_0). Consequently, ICER is calculated as the basis of CEA.

7.3.3   Self-Check!

1. The effectiveness and cost of a new drug X and a comparator S are (4.2 QALYs, JPY 22M) and (2.2 QALYs, JPY 12M), respectively. Determine which drug is preferred based on average cost.
2. In the above example, what is the ICER of X relative to S?
3. Given a threshold of JPY 3M/QALY, which of the two drugs, S or X, will be adopted?
4. Given a threshold of JPY 6M/QALY, which of the two drugs, S or X, will be adopted?

7.4   Change of ICER Estimation Due to Comparator Selection

7.4.1   Key Points

- ICER estimates vary depending on comparator choice.
- The decision between standard of care and placebo as comparator depends on whether the new technology is dominant.
- When standard of care is chosen as comparator, ICER is underestimated for the new technology that is dominant by extended dominance.

7.4.2   Essential Knowledge

The estimates of ICER vary depending on comparator choice. Standard of care is generally recommended as the comparator of choice, although the question of whether to choose the next best alternative, (e.g., placebo), may also arise because when placebo is the comparator, it is expected to give a lower ICER estimate. To confirm this assumption, we must understand the theoretical framework for the estimation of ICER for a new therapy relative to each of the possible comparators, standard of care and placebo.

As shown in Fig. 7.8, assume the effectiveness and cost of a new technology X, standard of care S, and placebo P are given by points $X(E_X, C_X)$, $S(E_S, C_S)$, and $P(E_P, C_P)$, respectively. The plane is divided into upper and lower areas by the line that connects points P and S, Fig. 7.8 illustrating the case where the cost C_X of new technology X falls above line PS. Here, the ICER of new technology X relative to

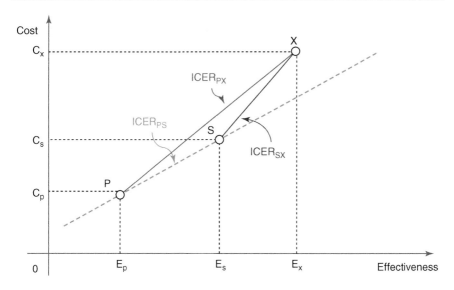

Fig. 7.8 Relevant ICERs in case of being not dominant

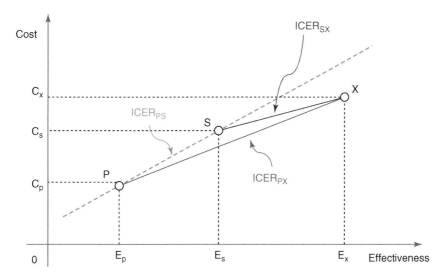

Fig. 7.9 Relevant ICERs in case of extended dominance

placebo P ($ICER_{PX}$) is clearly lower than the ICER of new technology X relative to standard of care S ($ICER_{SX}$). This implies that new technology X is not dominant by the principle of efficiency frontier and, thus, a concave downward cost-effectiveness curve (the efficiency frontier) can be drawn by connecting points P, S, and X. Hence, standard of care S will be the appropriate comparator choice in this case.

On the other hand, Fig. 7.9 illustrates the case where cost C_X falls below line PS. However, it is clear that if cost C_X is lower than the cost of standard of care, C_S, new technology X will dominate by simple dominance and, thus, require no further consideration. We therefore assume the case where C_X is higher than C_S but falls below line PS, in which new technology X is referred to as being dominant over standard of care S by extended dominance. Here, relationship $\text{ICER}_{SX} < \text{ICER}_{PX}$ holds true. However, in this case, point S is excluded by extended dominance by the principle of the efficiency frontier, and points P and X connect to form the efficiency frontier. In this case, placebo P will be the appropriate comparator choice.

On line PS, cost C_{max} associated with effect E_X can be determined analytically by the following equation:

$$C_{max} = \{(C_S - C_P)E_X + (C_P E_S - C_S E_P)\}/(E_S - E_P).$$

This leads to the conclusion that a C_X that is higher than C_{max}, indicating standard of care S as the comparator of choice, and a C_X that is below C_{max} indicates placebo as the comparator of choice. Table 7.2 summarizes these decision rules in four steps.

In Fig. 7.9, as point S is excluded from analysis, as previously discussed, this leaves placebo as the comparator choice, and the estimate of ICER will naturally take a slightly higher value. Here, the difference between ICER_{PX} and ICER_{SX} (i.e., the ICER gap) can be computed analytically by the following equation as a linear function of C_X:

$$\text{ICER gap} (= \text{ICER}_{PX} - \text{ICER}_{SX})$$
$$= \{1/(E_X - E_P) - 1/(E_X - E_S)\} C_X + C_S/(E_X - E_S) - C_P/(E_X - E_P).$$

Figure 7.10 shows the graph of this function for a hypothetical case. Given $P(1.0, 50,000)$, $S(1.1, 55,000)$, and $X(2.0, C_X)$ (where (QALY, USD), respectively), ICER_{PX} and ICER_{SX} are obtained as follows:

$$\text{ICER}_{PX} = C_X - 50,000,$$

$$\text{ICER}_{SX} = 10(C_X - 55,000)/9.$$

Table 7.2 Decision rule for selecting a comparator	*Step 1.* Find a line P-S by the following equation.
	Cost = a (Effectiveness) + b,
	where $a = (C_S - C_P)/(E_S - E_P)$ and $b = (C_P E_S - C_S E_P)/(E_S - E_P)$.
	Step 2. Find C_{max} by plugging in Ex for Effectiveness in the equation of Step 1.
	i.e., $C_{max} = aE_X + b$.
	Step 3. Compare C_X with C_{max}
	if $C_X < C_{max}$, "extended dominance"
	if $C_X > C_{max}$, "not dominant"
	Step 4. Select a comparator according to the judgement at Step 3.
	if "extended dominance", placebo (or suboptimal technology)
	if "not dominant", standard of care (or optimal technology)

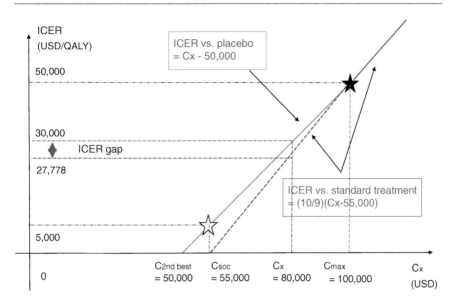

Fig. 7.10 Hypothetical example of estimating the ICER gap

By taking the difference between the two ICERs, the ICER gap can be formulated as $(100,000 - C_X)/9$. As per Fig. 7.10, if we take the cost of new technology C_X on the x-axis, an ICER gap is observed in the expected range of cost, from USD 55K to 100K. For instance, when C_X is USD80K, $ICER_{PX}$ = USD30K/QALY and $ICER_{SX}$ = USD27.778K/QALY, which gives an ICER gap of USD2,222/QALY. This comparative assessment indicates that when standard of care is chosen as the comparator, the ICER of new technology at the expected cost of USD80K is underestimated by a net USD2,222K/QALY.

7.4.3 Self-Check!

1. In what case is standard of care preferred as comparator?
2. In what case does the ICER gap need to be considered?

7.5   Decision Criteria for ICER at the Multiple Levels

7.5.1   Key Points

- Evaluating ICER based on multiple threshold levels is preferable to a single threshold.
- The concept of the tangent ICER allows for the development of multiple quantitative references.
- Evaluation with multiple threshold levels based on the cost-effectiveness function does not require establishing a single threshold.

7.5.2 Essential Knowledge

Once the ICER of a new technology relative to the comparator is estimated, the simplest approach to determining its value is to compare it with a single threshold. For example, when given a threshold of five million JPY/QALY, whether the estimated ICER is higher or lower than five million JPY/QALY determines whether the new technology is "not cost-effective" or "cost-effective." The advantage of this approach is in its straightforwardness, although arguments exist that it may be too simple.

In light of these concerns of oversimplification, let us consider an approach that allows for the evaluation of ICER at multiple levels based on the following two points:

1. To establish multiple threshold levels with justifications
2. To enable the evaluation of cost and effectiveness of a new technology based on the law of diminishing marginal utility

To satisfy these two points, we need to employ the theories of cost-effectiveness function and tangent ICER (see Sect. 7.1).

Assume that the effectiveness and cost of two existing technologies are $P_0(e_0, c_0)$ and $P_1(e_1, c_1)$, based on which the cost-effectiveness function $C = f(E)$ is formulated. Let us also assume that the effectiveness of a new technology P_x is e_x, while its cost is estimated as c_x.

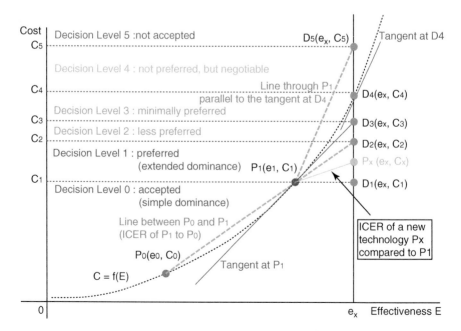

Fig. 7.11 Multiple decision levels for an ICER

Based on these assumptions, as per Fig. 7.11, we can quantitatively identify five reference points on the perpendicular line that passes through point $x = e_x$ on the x-axis of the cost-effectiveness plane. The five reference points are as follows:

1. The point with cost at the c_1 level;
2. The point of intersection between the line extended to the right from segment P_0P_1 (the ICER of P_1 relative to P_0) and perpendicular line $x = e_x$: the level of c_2;
3. The point of intersection between tangent ICER of point P_1 and perpendicular line $x = e_x$: the level of c_3;
4. The point of intersection between the cost-effectiveness function $C = f(E)$ and perpendicular line $x = e_x$: the level of c_4;
5. The point of intersection between the line parallel to tangent ICER of the point of intersection in (4) that also passes through point P_1 and perpendicular line $x = e_x$: the level of c_5.

Based on these reference points, we can establish the following six levels of decision:

1. Level 0: cost is below c_1.
2. Level 1: cost is at c_1 or above and below c_2.
3. Level 2: cost is at c_2 or above and below c_3.
4. Level 3: cost is at c_3 or above and below c_4.
5. Level 4: cost is at c_4 or above and below c_5.
6. Level 5: cost is at or above c_5.

At each level, the following decisions seem appropriate based on the properties of the tangent ICER interval: (1) accepted (simple dominance), (2) preferred to be accepted (extended dominance), (3) less preferred to be accepted, (4) barely accepted, (5) not accepted in principle but may be accepted through negotiation, and (6) not accepted.

Table 7.3 shows the decisions based on a hypothetical case. Assume that P_0 (6.09 QALYs, USD 50K) and P_1 (7.68 QALYs, USD 100K) are given, based on which the cost-effectiveness function is formulated as QALY $= -2.83 + 2.28 \log (\text{cost})$. The

Table 7.3 Example of multiple decisions for an ICER

Decision level	Range of cost (USD)	Range of ICER (USD/QALY)	Recommendation
Level 0 (under C_1)	Under 100,000	Under 0	Accepted
Level 1 (C_S–C_2)	100,000–129,248	0–31,638	Preferred
Level 2 (C_2–C_3)	129,248–140,547	31,638–43,860	Less preferred
Level 3 (C_3–C_4)	140,547–150,000	43,860–54,086	Minimally preferred
Level 4 (C_4–C_5)	150,000–160,820	54,086–65,789	Not preferred, but negotiable
Level 5 (over C_S)	Over 160,820	Over 65,789	Not accepted

values of the six levels are calculated as per Table 7.3, assuming that the effectiveness of a new technology is known to be 8.59 QALYs. Here, the six levels of decision are quantitatively identified. According to Table 7.3, we can recognize the threshold level where the technology is not accepted (c_5 or higher) is USD65.789K/QALY. It is noted that this is a more flexible threshold compared to the generally recognized threshold of USD50K/QALY. In any case, this approach no longer requires a single threshold to be established prior to analysis.

7.5.3   Self-Check!

1. In the above example, given that the ICER of the new technology is estimated to be USD 60K/QALY, determine at what level of decision the cost-effectiveness of the new technology is evaluated.
2. Similarly, what would be the decision if the ICER of the new technology were estimated at USD 45K/QALY.

7.6   The Relationship Between ICER and Budget Impact

7.6.1   Key Points

- Valuation in terms of ICER and financial impact are two different issues.
- Government officials are greatly concerned with financial impact.
- Under a constant spending cap, ICER and incremental effect are inversely proportional (hyperbolic model).
- Whether to accept the ICER obtained in CEA can be determined from the budget impact perspective.

7.6.2   Essential Knowledge

ICER allows for the valuation of healthcare technology in terms of JPY/QALY, although the financial consequences of these valuations of individual technologies are unclear. Government officials' interest in total healthcare expenditure and budgets tend to be more concerned with the financial impact than the value assessment of individual technologies. Assuming that individual health technologies are calculated by ICER, let us consider the financial consequences of these value assessments. Such an approach is referred to as budget impact analysis (BIA).

BIA generally uses analytical models different from those used in a CEA. In addition, the BIA will consider CEA and the ICER estimated would differ case by case. Therefore, the association between ICER and BIA cannot necessarily be generalized. At the same time, it is useful to formulate this association under a specific budget and using a simple model in order to understand the fundamental connection between a technology value assessment and a budget impact.

Let us consider the simplest case, where total cost is obtained by multiplying ICER by the number of patients for indication N. Conceptually, the following equation holds true if we let B_{max} be the upper limit of allowable increase in cost associated with the adoption of the technology of interest:

$$ICER \times N = B_{max}.$$

Since B_{max} is constant, ICER and N are inversely proportional. That is, to keep B_{max} constant, N has to be kept small when ICER is large and vice-versa. This approach is consistent with the underlying assumption that a drug with a small number of patients for the indication, such as an orphan drug, is allowed to have an ICER above the standard level. At the same time, it also leads to the argument that ICER needs to be maintained below the standard level (GBP 20K/QALY, for instance) for chronic conditions such as diabetes and hypertension where there are a large number of patients for the indication (see Sect. 5.2.12, Fig. 5.16).

The above equation should more accurately be written as follows:

$$\Delta C \times N = B_{max}.$$

By substituting ΔC using $ICER = \Delta C/\Delta E$, the equation can now be rewritten as:

$$ICER = (B_{max}/N)/\Delta E.$$

This indicates that, where B_{max}/N (i.e., the increase in cost per patient) is constant, ICER and ΔE (the incremental effect) are inversely proportional. This relationship is illustrated in Fig. 7.12 by a hyperbolic graph and the two resulting areas.

Figure 7.13 illustrates the relationship between the hyperbola and the single ICER threshold, λ_0. The single threshold λ_0 is represented by a horizontal line

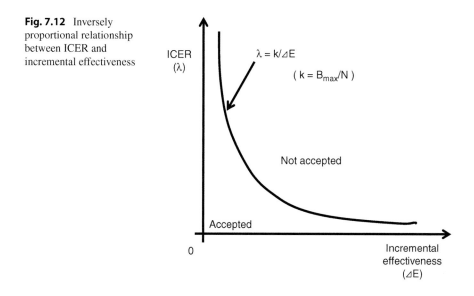

Fig. 7.12 Inversely proportional relationship between ICER and incremental effectiveness

Fig. 7.13 Difference between single-threshold decision and budget consideration

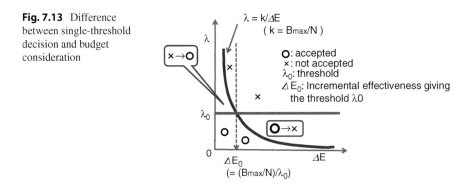

Table 7.4 Different assessment considering budget impact

λ_0	λ_{max}	
	$\lambda^* \leqq \lambda_{max}$	$\lambda^* > \lambda_{max}$
$\lambda^* > \lambda_0$	Accepted	Not accepted
$\lambda^* < \lambda_0$	Accepted	Not accepted

λ^*: ICER gained in CEA
λ_{max}: ICER gained in the formula $\lambda = k/\Delta E$
λ_0: a certain threshold

Table 7.5 Steps of judgement considering budget impact

Step 1. Calculate λ^*(=incremental cost ΔC^*/incremental effectiveness ΔE^*).
Step 2. Calculate λ_{max} by plugging in the maximum budget B_{max}, target patient population N, and incremental effectiveness ΔE^* for following equation.
$\lambda_{max} = (B_{max}/N)/\Delta E^*$.
Step 3. Compare λ^* and λ_{max}.
If $\lambda^* \leqq \lambda_{max}$, accepted.
$\lambda^* > \lambda_{max}$, not accepted.

parallel to the x-axis, where a technology is accepted in the area under the line and not accepted if in the area above the line. However, in a budget impact analysis, a technology is accepted in the area under the hyperbola and not accepted in the area above, which leads to differences in decisions for two of the six segmented areas (areas × → ○ and ○ → ×) shown in Fig. 7.13. Such a formulation of ICER and a spending cap using a hyperbolic model would allow for more flexible decisions as to whether to accept a given ICER depending on budget, unlike the classical single threshold approach adopted by UK NICE.

As per Fig. 7.13, when budget impact is considered, the allowable ICER level varies, depending on the incremental effect. Consequently, a different set of rules from the one used for the single threshold evaluation is required, based on the area under which ICER λ^* (=$\Delta C^*/\Delta E^*$) obtained from the cost-effectiveness analysis falls (Table 7.4). That is, as indicated in Table 7.4, the relationship in magnitude between λ^* and λ_{max} (=$(B_{max}/N)/\Delta C$) obtained by a given ΔE^* determines whether ICER is accepted. With UK NICE's single threshold approach, any λ^* above λ_0 is not accepted, whereas with these rules, such an λ^* is accepted as long as it is below λ_{max}. At the same time, any λ^* below λ_0 has traditionally been accepted, whereas such an λ^* will not be accepted under the rules in Table 7.4 if it is above λ_{max}. Table 7.5 summarizes the rules in Table 7.4 in three steps. Here, we first determine the hyperbola the ICER λ_{max} associated with the incremental effect ΔE^* obtained in CEA. We then compare λ^* with λ_{max}, whose relationship determines on what side of the hyperbola point $(\Delta E^*, \lambda^*)$ falls, thereby deciding whether λ^* is accepted.

Let us consider an example. Assume $\Delta C^* =$ USD 2K and $\Delta E^* = 0.02$ QALYs were obtained as a result of a CEA. Here, $\lambda^* = 2K/0.02 =$ USD 100K/QALY, which is absolutely not accepted if a single threshold of USD 50K/QALY is adopted. However, given 20,000 patients for the indication and the maximum budget B_{max} of USD 44M, λ_{max} is determined as follows:

$$
\begin{aligned}
\lambda_{max} &= \left(B_{max}/N \right)/\Delta E^* \\
&= \left(44{,}000{,}000/20{,}000 \right)/0.02 \\
&= 110{,}000 > 100{,}000 \, \text{USD/QALY} \left(= \lambda^* \right).
\end{aligned}
$$

Here, λ_{max} is above λ^*, and although the ICER of USD 100K/QALY is significantly higher than the standard threshold of USD 50K/QALY, it is still allowable from the perspective of budget impact (Fig. 7.14).

7.6.3   Self-Check!

1. In the above example, what would the λ_{max} be if the number of patients for the indication were 200,000?
2. What would be the decision in the case above?
3. In what case does a hyperbolic graph shift upward?

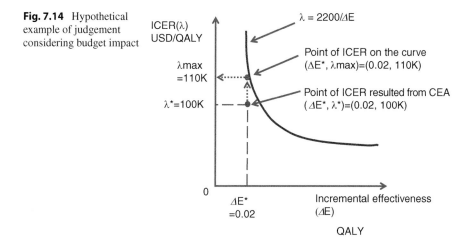

Fig. 7.14 Hypothetical example of judgement considering budget impact

7.7   ICER Formula and Japan's Value-Based Pricing

7.7.1   Key Points

- The two approaches to drug pricing are threshold and direct calculation (the ICER formula).
- The "premium" is characteristic for the Japanese quasi-VBP.
- The direct calculation approach allows for the calculation of a premium rate.

7.7.2   Essential Knowledge

Japan's pricing system is a well-known brand across the world and aligns well with the value-based pricing (VBP) concept: it is something in which we should take great pride. There is an additional advantage in that there is an affinity between our pricing system and current pharmaceutical economic methodologies.

ICER, an important pharmacoeconomic measure, can be formulated as follows:

1. Price for new drug = price of comparator + ICER × ΔE (where ΔE is the incremental effect) while the formula used for pricing in Japan is as follows:
2. Price for new drug = baseline price + premium.

Therefore, assuming that the two equations are equal, the "premium" of the second term can be considered equal to the product of ICER and the incremental effect in pharmacoeconomics. However, this compatibility does not allow for the direct translation of ICER into "premium" in the Japanese pricing scheme, as there is no fee schedule available that associates the second part of the two equations. Additionally, the "price" in the first equation technically represents the "cost," which is broader than the "price" used in a more restricted sense. Therefore, the apparent equivalence between the two equations only implies the theoretical compatibility of the methodologies. Nevertheless, it suggests a potential association, in which the "premium," as a feature unique to the Japanese pricing system, may evolve as an approach of direct pricing, which is different from the threshold approach of UK's NICE. In that respect there is the possibility to develop a Japanese version of VBP that differs from the UK system [1].

Currently, NICE has an established "threshold method" by which they quantify the society's willingness to pay using cost-effectiveness as the basis of that threshold. The threshold method determines a cost-effectiveness value that, if exceeded, will result in that new drug's rejection as a medical innovation. If the new drug does not exceed the threshold, it would be an accepted medical innovation. However, the Japanese VBP has the potential to evolve in a different direction from the UK's threshold approach by building on this base. Of course, if we were to utilize Japan's premium system as it stands today, it lacks a scientific basis for the assessments, and is, rather, based on subjective or political criteria with the aim of cost reductions; under these conditions, there is no way to develop a systematic or replicable approach to drug pricing. Overcoming these limitations is a future task of the

Japanese type of VBP. Toward that end, it is particularly important to consider the following two points.

1. **Formulation of the Premium Rate (Amount of Premium) Based on ICER**

   The similarity of second term for the above two equations indicates that the premium and product ICER $\times \Delta E$ are proportional, expressed as follows:

   $$\text{Premium} \propto \text{ICER} \times \Delta E.$$

   Based on this assumption, the premium rate can be formulated as $(w \times \text{ICER} \times \Delta E)$/baseline price (where w is the weight constant). Here, we assume that the ΔE of the new technology being evaluated is obtained from a clinical trial and that an appropriate default value is assigned to ICER. By comparing the amount of premium given under the current system and the estimate of ICER $\times \Delta E$, an appropriate adjustment constant w can be established. The advantage of this approach is that ΔE need not be measured in terms of QALY, and condition-specific clinical endpoints (e.g., HbA1c for diabetes) may be used instead.

2. **Upper and Lower Limits of Drug Price Estimated from ICER**

   The government wishes to set drug prices at an appropriate minimum, while the industry wishes to set prices at an appropriate maximum. Therefore, the question is: What are the appropriate upper and lower limits for drug pricing, and how can they be calculated from ICER? If we consider the formulation:

   $$\text{Price for new drug} = \text{baseline price} + \left(w \times \text{ICER} \times \Delta E \right)$$

   from the above point (1), the baseline price, w, and ΔE are known and take constant values, which indicates that the appropriate upper and lower limits of ICER, which are variable, determine the appropriate upper and lower limits of drug pricing. That is, the question is how to determine the appropriate range of ICER. To answer this question, we can apply interval estimations using the tangent ICER (see Sect. 7.2).

Let us consider a hypothetical case, in which we wish to determine the premium rate using the simplest ICER formula:

$$\text{Price for new drug} = \text{baseline price} + \left(\text{ICER} \times \Delta E \right),$$

obtained by letting $w = 1$. Assume that the baseline price for a new drug is USD 20/day, the incremental effect (ΔE) associated with treatment with the new drug for a period of 300 days is 0.01 QALY, and ICER is estimated to be USD 60K/QALY. Here, the total cost for treatment with the new drug for 300 days is calculated based on the ICER formula as follows:

$$\text{Total cost of new drug} = (20 \times 300) + (60,000 \times 0.01).$$
$$= \text{USD}\,6.6\text{K}$$

This gives the daily cost of 6600/300 = USD 22. If we compare this figure to the baseline price of USD 20, the premium rate is determined as follows:

$$\text{Premium rate} : (22 - 20) / 20 = 10\%.$$

Table 7.6 shows the calculations by varying the incremental effect. If we assume this new drug is administered with a frequency of three tablets daily, the price for

Table 7.6 Hypothetical example of estimating premium rates according to ICER principle

X New price per day	d_0 Old price per day	ICER Cost for 300 days (USD)	ΔE QALY gained in 300 days	Premium rate %	Price for a tablet
20	20	60,000	0	0	6.67
21	20	60,000	0.005	5	7.00
22	20	60,000	0.01	10	7.33
24	20	60,000	0.02	20	8.00
26	20	60,000	0.03	30	8.67

where $X = d_0 + (ICER \cdot \Delta E)$
Treatment by a new drug: Three times a day for 300 days
Kamae I, Kobayashi M: Value-Based Pricing and the Principle of the Incremental Cost-Effectiveness Ratio: The Case and Potential in Japan. ISPOR CONNECTIONS, 16 (4): 9-10, 2010

one tablet can also be obtained as shown in Table 7.6. Similarly, varying estimates of ICER such as USD 80K or 50K/QALY may also be used. For instance, if we assume a tangent ICER interval of (50K, 80K), we can easily determine the changes in premium rate within this interval.

7.7.3 Self-Check!

1. In the above hypothetical case, calculate the premium rate given an ICER of USD 80K/QALY and an ΔE of 0.01.
2. Similarly, what would be the premium rate if the ICER were estimated to be USD 50K/QALY?

7.8 Repricing by Bayesian Statistics in Japan

7.8.1 Key Points

- The Japanese drug repricing system can be thought of as a Bayesian approach.
- The Bayesian approach allows for a more quantitative and transparent scheme, based on the existing system.
- The R zone can be associated with the Bayesian degree of belief.
- The degree of belief may be arguable due to its subjectivity.

7.8.2 Essential Knowledge

This section considers drug repricing based on Bayesian statistics. As discussed in the previous section, the "premium" is one of the characteristics of the Japanese pricing system. If this "premium" can be quantitatively specified based on Bayesian statistics, it will be useful in establishing more quantitative and transparent rules.

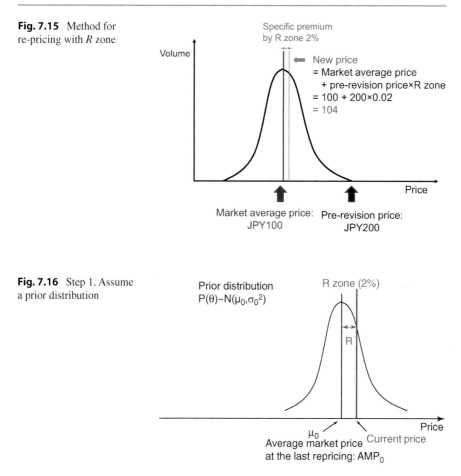

Fig. 7.15 Method for re-pricing with *R* zone

Fig. 7.16 Step 1. Assume a prior distribution

First, Fig. 7.15 outlines the current approach to repricing. Assume the pre-revision price is JPY 200, and the average price of JPY 100 is obtained from market research on the considered drug. The revised price is determined by adding a "specific premium" to the market average price. This "specific premium" indicates the amount of premium obtained by multiplying the pre-revision price by a 2% margin (the *R* zone). Therefore, the premium will be JPY 4 as shown in Fig. 7.15, and the price is revised to JPY 104.

Bayesian statistics assumes a prior probability distribution and considers newly acquired evidence to estimate a posterior (i.e., after the acquisition of evidence) probability distribution. The process of this inference is compatible with the repricing approach in Japan, with the respective elements corresponding as follows:

1. Price before revision: prior distribution
2. Market research: new evidence
3. Revision of price based on the *R* zone: posterior distribution

Fig. 7.17 Step 2. Obtain
new evidence for price
revision

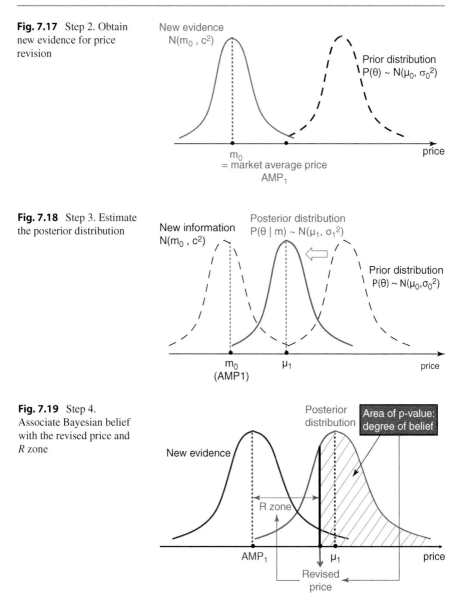

Fig. 7.18 Step 3. Estimate
the posterior distribution

Fig. 7.19 Step 4.
Associate Bayesian belief
with the revised price and
R zone

Accordingly, Figs. 7.16, 7.17, 7.18, and 7.19 illustrate in four steps how the Bayesian approach can be applied to the Japanese repricing system.

Step 1: Assume that the prior distribution $P(\theta)$ can be expressed by the normal distribution $N(\mu_0, \sigma_0^2)$ (where μ_0 is the mean and σ_0^2 the variance), and let μ_0 represent the average price AMP_0 obtained from a market research conducted 2 years ago, at the time of previous price revision.

Table 7.7 Posterior distribution: Bayesian estimates

Mean	$\mu_1 = \dfrac{\dfrac{n \cdot m_0}{c^2} + \dfrac{\mu_0}{\sigma_0^{\,2}}}{\dfrac{n}{c^2} + \dfrac{1}{\sigma_0^{\,2}}}$
Variance	$\sigma_1^{\,2} = \dfrac{1}{\dfrac{n}{c^2} + \dfrac{1}{\sigma_0^{\,2}}}$

n: sample size of target products in market research

Table 7.8 Posterior distribution: in the context of Japanese re-pricing

Mean	$\mu_1 = \dfrac{\dfrac{n \cdot \mathrm{AMP}_1}{c^2} + \dfrac{\mathrm{AMP}_0}{\sigma_0^{\,2}}}{\dfrac{n}{c^2} + \dfrac{1}{\sigma_0^{\,2}}}$
Variance	$\sigma_1^{\,2} = \dfrac{1}{\dfrac{n}{c^2} + \dfrac{1}{\sigma_0^{\,2}}}$

Step 2: New evidence is similarly obtained as the normal distribution $N(m_0, c^2)$. Let mean m_0 represent the average price AMP_1, obtained from market research conducted for this revision.

Step 3: Estimate the posterior probability $P(\theta \mid m)$, which is the normal distribution $N(\mu_1, \sigma_1^{\,2})$, according to Bayes' theorem.

Generally, as shown in Table 7.7, the posterior distribution is determined by Bayesian inference by the mean and variance of the two normal distributions representing the prior distribution and new evidence, as well as the sample size being studied [2]. Since we assumed $m_0 = \mathrm{AMP}_1$ and $\mu_0 = \mathrm{AMP}_0$, the mean and variance of the posterior distribution are obtained using the formula in Table 7.8.

Step 4: Once the posterior distribution is obtained, the degree of belief (corresponds to the p-value) for the posterior distribution is assigned to determine the revised price. Once this revised price is decided, it can be compared to AMP_1 to identify the R zone (%).

As shown above, the concept and theory of Bayesian statistics fit with the current repricing system in Japan and help establish a more quantitative and transparent scheme based on the existing system. This gives a statistical basis for the arbitrarily assigned R zone. At the same time, it also allows the government to adjust the revised prices by making appropriate changes to the degree of belief. On the other hand, the Bayesian approach may be challenging to use as it is less straightforward.

As shown in Fig. 7.20, a high degree of belief results in a narrow R zone, while a low degree of belief results in a wide R zone. The assignment of belief is subjective, and it is both an advantage and a disadvantage of the Bayesian approach.

Fig. 7.20 Relation
between the degree of
belief and the width of R
zone

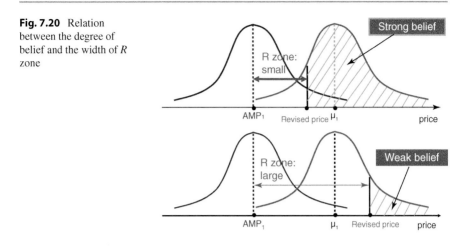

7.8.3 Self-Check!

1. What is the R zone?
2. Which element of the Japanese repricing system does the new evidence in Bayesian statistics correspond to?
3. How is the R zone formulated when the Bayesian degree of belief is 50%?

References

1. Kamae I (2014) A Japanese-style approach to value-based pricing: scientific basis and theoretical potential. In: Culyer AJ, Kobelt G (eds) Portrait of a health economist: Essays by Colleagues and Friends of Bengt Jonsson. Swedish Institute for Health Economics, Sweden, pp 73–80
2. Watanabe H (1999) Introduction to Bayesian statistics. Fukumura Shuppan, Tokyo

Correction to: MHLW Guidelines for Cost-Effectiveness Analysis

Correction to:
I. Kamae, *Health Technology Assessment in Japan*,
https://doi.org/10.1007/978-981-13-5793-0_3

This book was inadvertently published without updating the following corrections:
Table 3.1 of Chapter 3 was initially published with errors. The correct table is given here.

Table 3.1 The table of contents in the analysis guideline of the Ministry of Health, Labour and Welfare

1. Objectives	2. Analysis perspective	3. Target population
4. Comparator(s)	5. Additional benefit	6. Methods of analysis
7. Time horizon	8. Choice of outcome measure	9. Sources of clinical data (except costs)
10. Calculation of healthcare costs	11. Public long-term care costs and productivity loss	12. Discounting
13. Modeling	14. Uncertainty	

On page 79, in Figure 3.3 caption the below sentence has been removed:

"The utility values of health states S1, 2, 3, 4, and 5 are, respectively, 1, 0.9, 0.6, 0.2, and 0. The treatment effect is the same for both A and B for the first 8 years; however, B can survive for 4 years longer"

On page 97, in Figure 3.10 caption the word 'ellipsoid' has been changed to 'ellipse'.

On page 105, a question mark has been inserted at the end of point 10.

On page 105, for the equation under Step 3 parenthesis have been added for the nominator and denominator.

The updated version of the chapter can be found at
https://doi.org/10.1007/978-981-13-5793-0_3

On page 229, in the title 'C0RE2' has been changed to 'CORE2'.

On Page 229, 'Suggested Answers to "Self-Check" Questions' has been deleted from the contents list.

On page 257, Section 3.9, the word 'evaluaded' has been changed to 'evaluated'.

CORE2 HEALTH

Guideline for Preparing Cost-Effectiveness Evaluation to the Central Social Insurance Medical Council

Version 2.0 approved by CSIMC on 20th February, 2019

Prepared by: Research team (Team Leader: Takashi Fukuda) on cost-effectiveness evaluation supported by Health and Labour Science Research Grants (Strategic Integrated Scientific Research Project)

The English version is a translation of the original version in Japanese. The Japanese version is preferentially applied in cases of discrepancy between the two versions.

Contents

© Springer Nature Singapore Pte Ltd. 2019
I. Kamae, *Health Technology Assessment in Japan*,
https://doi.org/10.1007/978-981-13-5793-0

1 Objectives

1.1 This guideline presents standard methods to perform cost-effectiveness evaluations of medicines and medical devices selected by the Central Social Insurance Medical Council ("selected technologies").

1.2 This guideline is applied to manufacturers' submissions and academic analysis (review and reanalysis).

2 Analysis Perspective

2.1 The perspective of the analysis should be specified. In particular, the analysis should consider the range of costs corresponding to this perspective.

2.2 "Public healthcare payer's perspective" is a standard perspective that pertains to factors such as costs, comparator(s), and target populations within the range of the public healthcare insurance in Japan.

    2.2.1 Even when an analysis is conducted from a perspective other than the "public healthcare payer's perspective," an analysis from the "public healthcare payer's perspective" should also be submitted.

    2.2.2 There are some healthcare technologies that are not covered by the public healthcare insurance but are publicly funded, such as some prophylactic procedures (e.g., health checkups, vaccinations). Analyses including these technologies should be submitted from the "public healthcare payer's perspective."

2.3 If the effect on public long-term care costs is important with regard to the selected technology, it is acceptable to perform an analysis from the "public healthcare and long-term care payer's perspective."

2.4 If the introduction of a selected technology has a direct influence on productivity, it is acceptable to perform an analysis that considers the broader costs and counts productivity loss as a cost.

3 Target Population

3.1 Patient populations that meet the indications for the selected technology when the manufacturer's analysis is performed should be considered the target population of the cost-effectiveness evaluation.

    3.1.1 In the case that a new indication (or addition of a new dose and administration) is approved between the time of the selection of target technology and the manufacturer's submission of analysis, the new indication (or dose and administration) is also included in the target population.

3.2 If the technology has multiple indications or even in single-indication subpopulations which differ in outcome, application method/dose, and administration or comparator of cost-effectiveness evaluation, an analysis should be conducted for each population in principal.

3.2.1 However, if item "3.2" is difficult to achieve, it is acceptable to perform analyses of limited population(s) considering factors such as the number of patients or features of the illness. The exemption is determined based on agreement between the manufacturer and the National Institute of Public Health/public academic group in consultation.

4 Comparator(s)

4.1 The comparator(s) should be principally selected from among technologies which are expected to be replaced by the selected technology at the time when the technology was introduced to treat the target population. Among them, technologies which are widely used in clinical practice and which result in a better outcome should be selected.

4.1.1 Nontreatment or watchful waiting can also be used as comparators.

4.1.2 Except for the cases described in item "4.1.1," comparator(s) should be selected from among technologies reimbursed by public healthcare insurance.

4.1.3 If single comparator cannot be determined based on item "4.1," the comparator(s) should be selected considering the comparators in randomized controlled trials (RCTs), referred technology when determining the official price, cost-effectiveness, and other factors, based on agreement in consultation.

4.2 Sufficient explanation of the reasons underlying the selection of the comparator(s) is needed.

5 Additional Benefit

5.1 When a cost-effectiveness evaluation is conducted, the additional benefit of the selected technology to the comparator(s) should first be evaluated.

5.2 Evaluations of the additional benefit should be conducted on the basis of a systematic review (SR) of RCTs. The RCTs should be directly compared with the technology selected in Section "4." The results of unpublished clinical studies/trials may also be included in the SR if they are deemed appropriate.

5.2.1 When an SR is conducted, clinical questions (CQs) should be clearly presented. For example, a definition of structured CQs according to PICO (P, patient; I, intervention; C, comparator; O, outcome) may be provided.

5.2.2 There may be technologies with similar action mechanism or function category to the selected technologies or comparator(s) determined in Section "4," which will be expected to show equivalent outcomes to them. These technologies can be included as an intervention (I) or comparator (C) in the SR if they are deemed appropriate in consultation.

5.2.3 As outcome (O) in item "5.2.1," the most appropriate clinical outcomes (e.g., a "true outcome") should be used to evaluate selected technology from the viewpoint of clinical effectiveness, safety, and health-related quality of life (HRQOL).

5.2.4 A description of the inclusion/exclusion criteria, databases used, search algorithm, and research selection process (inclusion flow of information) is required in accordance with the PRISMA (Preferred Reporting Items for Systematic Reviews and Meta-Analyses) statement.

5.2.5 It is acceptable to utilize any existing reliable SR. In such cases, the existing review will be used directly or in combination with a new additional study. In this case, it should confirm the consistency of the existing review by considering the CQs and coverage of the most recent literature.

5.2.6 If deemed appropriate, pooled results by meta-analysis should be presented. In such cases, the required reporting factors include the employed statistical method, assessment of heterogeneity, forest plot, pooled results, and confidence interval, among others.

5.2.7 When it is obvious that no RCTs have been performed, the process described in item "5.2" can be skipped upon agreement in consultation.

5.2.8 A time point between determining the framework of analysis and manufacturer's submission can be used as a cutoff date for the literature search in the SR.

5.2.9 There may be cases in which the results of new clinical trials are published after the cutoff date defined in item "5.2.8" but are regarded as important information for cost-effectiveness evaluation (e.g., clinical trials with large sample size or reliable results different from current knowledge). Inclusion of these trials in the SR should be considered. In that case, additional SR is not necessarily required.

5.3 When no studies or only insufficient studies are available based on the result of SR described in item "5.2," additional benefit is evaluated by SR of comparative non-RCT (e.g., observational) studies based on item "5.2," if agreed upon in consultation. In that case, sufficient explanation on research quality is needed (e.g., study design, differences in background factors between groups, methods of statistical analysis, sample size, and number of institutions).

5.4 When more reliable results are obtained, additional benefit can be evaluated by reanalysis of existing observational study and/or registry data, if agreed upon in consultation. In that case, sufficient explanation on research quality is needed (e.g., study design, differences in background factors between groups, methods of statistical analysis, sample size, and number of institutions).

5.5 When there are no RCT studies using the same comparator selected in Section "4," but there are RCT studies of the selected technology compared to others, additional benefit is evaluated by indirect comparison using SR results, if agreed upon in consultation.

    5.5.1 The applicability of item "5.5" depends on the quality of study on the indirect comparison. If an indirect comparison is conducted, sufficient explanation on the prerequisites for the indirect comparison (e.g., heterogeneity of illness, severity, and patient background or similarity of the studies) is also needed.

5.6 When there are only single-arm clinical studies of selected technologies, SR results of the selected technologies (and comparator(s) if needed) should be shown.

    5.6.1 In such cases, the evaluation of additional benefit has to consider a number of factors such as the characteristics of the technology and/or disease, background of the participants, and the quality of the studies. Therefore, whether an additional benefit is shown is judged by agreement in consultation.

5.7 There may be cases in which the results obtained by the methods in items "5.3" to "5.6" have serious problems regarding the quality of the studies, and it is expected that the selected technology is not inferior to the comparator. In such cases, the analysis described in Section "6" can be performed, assuming the outcome of selected technology is equivalent to that of the comparator(s).

5.8 When there are not any available clinical data on the selected technology in humans, the analysis described in Section "6" can be performed, assuming the outcome of the selected technology is equivalent to that of the comparator(s) and considering the approval of the Pharmaceuticals and Medical Devices Agency (PMDA), if agreed upon in consultation.

5.9 When results obtained by the methods in items "5.2" to "5.6" show that outcomes of the selected technology are inferior to that of the comparator(s), no cost-effectiveness analysis is performed.

6 Methods of Analysis

6.1 A cost-effectiveness analysis should be used. In this guideline, cost-effectiveness analysis is defined as an analysis that calculates cost and effectiveness separately without converting effectiveness into monetary units.

6.2 If the analysis described in Section "5" allows a judgment that reveals additional benefit, the incremental cost-effectiveness ratio (ICER) should be calculated from the expected cost and effectiveness in each treatment group.

6.3 In the following cases, only the expected cost and effectiveness in each group need to be presented and the ICER should not be calculated.

    6.3.1 In cases where the technology is equivalent or superior in terms of effectiveness (nonnegative incremental effectiveness) and lower in terms of cost, relative to the comparator, the technology is considered "dominant" without a calculation of ICER.

6.3.2 A cost comparison with the comparator (so-called "cost minimization analysis" [CMA]) should be performed if the analysis described in Section "5" does not demonstrate an additional benefit compared to the comparator, but the outcome of the selected technology appears equivalent to that of the comparator.

6.4 If the selected technology has multiple indications or subpopulations defined in item "3.2" and/or "3.2.1," ICER should be calculated for each indication or subpopulation.

6.5 If a cost-effectiveness analysis for a selected technology published in an academic journal or an evaluation from a major public health technology assessment (HTA) agency is available, these results should also be presented.

7 Time Horizon

7.1 The time horizon should be sufficiently long to evaluate the influence of the technology on cost and effectiveness.

7.2 The same time horizon should be applied for both cost and effectiveness.

7.3 The reason for setting this time horizon should be specified.

8 Choice of Outcome Measure

8.1 Quality-adjusted life years (QALY) should be used in principle.

    8.1.1 When it is difficult to calculate QALY and CMA is applied, other outcome measures can be used, upon agreement in consultation.

8.2 When QALY is calculated, the QOL score should be reflective of the value in a general population (using preference-based measure [PBM] or direct methods such as the standard gamble [SG] and the time trade-off [TTO]). However, systematic difference may exist between QOL scores measured by SG and by TTO.

    8.2.1 If Japanese QOL scores are newly collected for a cost-effectiveness analysis, the use of PBMs with a value set developed in Japan using TTO (or mapped onto a TTO score) is recommended as the first choice.

    8.2.2 If data corresponding to item "8.2" are unavailable, it is acceptable to use mapping of other appropriate HRQOL data. When using a QOL score obtained from mapping, the conversion into a QOL score via an appropriate method should be explained.

8.3 When the QOL score is assessed by PBM, the subjects' own QOL responses should be used.

    8.3.1 In the case of using PBMs, responses from a proxy (e.g., family member or caregiver) may be used only when the subject cannot respond.

8.3.2 In the case of using PBMs by proxy responses from a healthcare professional, possible discrepancies from subjects' own responses should be explained.

8.3.3 If it is difficult to directly collect QOL scores from subjects, it is acceptable for general people to evaluate the presented health scenario by direct methods. It is better for the validity of the presented scenario to be confirmed by clinicians. In this case, use of the TTO method is recommended.

8.4 As long as a QOL score that satisfies items "8.2" and "8.3" is available, the use of Japanese results is preferentially recommended.

8.4.1 If Japanese research is absent or insufficient but high-quality research is available overseas, it is acceptable to use the data collected overseas.

9 Sources of Clinical Data (Except Costs)

9.1 Calculations of the ICER should preferentially use effectiveness, safety, and QOL data (inclusion of parameters such as transition probability for model analysis) derived from high-quality research, with a high evidence level reflective of practical clinical results in Japan.

9.1.1 The selection of effectiveness, safety, and QOL data on the basis of an SR of Japanese and overseas clinical research is recommended. This review may also include unpublished clinical study/trial data if deemed appropriate.

9.1.2 Data with a high evidence level should be used preferentially. The use of data deemed appropriate from the viewpoints of research quality, target population, and external validity is recommended (e.g., it is possible that the results of an RCT may differ markedly from practical clinical results).

9.1.3 Data by reanalysis of existing study and/or registry data can be used if deemed appropriate. In that case, detailed information on patient background, statistical methods, etc. must be provided.

9.2 Japanese data should be used preferentially if there is evident heterogeneity between Japanese and overseas data.

9.3 If the data do not differ statistically significantly between the selected technology and the comparator(s), pooled data of both groups should be applied. Otherwise, the rationale that additional benefit is shown by the process described in Section "5," etc. must be explained.

9.4 Regarding evaluation of medical devices, if there are reliable and quantitative data, analysis reflecting "learning effect" (i.e., improvement of treatment effect by the accumulation of clinicians' experience) or "product improvement effect" can be submitted in addition to analysis not considering the effects, upon agreement in consultation.

10 Calculation of Healthcare Costs

10.1 Only public healthcare costs should be included in the case of analysis from the public healthcare payers' perspective.

10.2 Healthcare costs of each health state include only related costs that are directly affected by the selected technology and do not include unrelated costs.

10.3 Healthcare costs of each health state should reflect the average resource consumption and standard clinical practices in Japan.

10.4 It is recommended that claims databases established in Japan, which reflect actual clinical practice from the viewpoint of item "10.3," should be used to estimate the costs of each health state, if deemed appropriate. However, this recommendation does not apply to cases in which it is difficult to define health states using only information from claims data, insufficient data have been accumulated in the database, and so on.

    10.4.1 Definition of each health state and its rationale is required when claims data are used for cost estimation.

    10.4.2 The methods and rationale for handling outliers and unrelated costs should be shown.

10.5 Micro-costing (by medical fee schedule, etc.) based on the definitions of the standard clinical process can be used, if it is difficult to estimate the costs of each health state by claims database or if micro-costing is more appropriate.

    10.5.1 In the case of the application of micro-costing, the rationale for costing should be shown from the viewpoint of item "10.3." It may be better to identify relevant items and/or estimate the amount of medical resource consumption in the claims database.

    10.5.2 When micro-costing is used, the medical resource consumption and unit costs should be reported separately.

    10.5.3 In principle, for the estimation of resource consumption in item "10.5.2," the amount of injection products consumed should be defined by the number of vials rather than by patient dosages.

10.6 The estimation should include not only the costs of the selected technology and the comparator(s) but also the costs of factors such as adverse events and related future events.

10.7 An analysis of the public healthcare costs should include not only the portion of costs paid by the insurer but also those paid by the government and patients as copayment (i.e., the total public healthcare expenses).

    10.7.1 Based on the principal in item "2.2.2," the analysis should include the costs of health checkups, vaccinations, or similar procedures that are funded publicly and not reimbursed by Japan's public healthcare insurance.

10.8 Unit costs should be derived from the latest medical fee schedule, drug price lists, or similar resources. It is particularly essential to use the latest unit costs for the selected technology or comparator(s).

10.8.1 Even if existing cost-of-illness studies or analyses of claims data are used, unit costs at the time of evaluation, not at the time that the medical resources consumed, should be applied. It is acceptable to make adjustments such as multiplication by the medical payment system revision rate.

10.8.2 Such adjustments may be omitted if the influence on results is minimal.

10.9 If generics of the comparator(s) are already on the market, analysis using these costs should be also submitted.

10.10 If the costs of selected technology and/or comparator(s) are included in bundled payment, the estimation should be based on fee-for-service payment.

10.11 Future costs should also be estimated on the basis of current medical resource consumption and unit costs.

10.12 Calculations of medical resource consumption based on overseas data will require attention regarding possible differences in healthcare technology use between Japan and overseas countries. The unit costs in Japan should be applied in the analysis.

11 Public Long-Term Care Costs and Productivity Loss

11.1 Public long-term care costs and productivity losses arising from an inability to perform work should not be included in the base-case analysis.

11.1.1 It is acceptable to include public long-term care costs and productivity losses in additional analyses only if they can be estimated by Japanese data. However, judgments regarding the appropriateness of including productivity losses should consider the possibility of working in the context of the illness characteristics.

11.2 When public long-term care costs are included in the analysis, it is recommended that these costs should be calculated based on the care level.

11.3 The amount utilized under public long-term care insurance should be based on the actual quantity of resources consumed. If this quantity is difficult to determine, it is acceptable to use the average amount utilized per beneficiary or similar data.

11.4 Decreases in productivity losses may be classified as follows:

(A) Decreases arising directly from healthcare technology (e.g., treatment-related shortening of hospital stay)

(B) Decreases arising indirectly from outcome improvements (e.g., alleviation of illness, survival period extension)

When productivity loss is included in an analysis, only (A) should be included in the calculation of costs.

11.5 Productivity losses should be estimated using the human capital method. This method was designed to generate estimations based on the expected earned wage in the absence of illness.

    11.5.1 The unit wage used for estimations of productivity loss should be the average wage across all industries, all ages, and both genders or the average wage for each age group in all industries and both genders derived from the latest "Basic Survey on Wage Structure" (Wage Census) and not discriminate by income.

    11.5.2 Estimations of productivity loss require an actual investigation of the employment status in the target population (i.e., a measure of the days or hours of work missed). The actual measured number of days or hours should then be multiplied by the average wage across all industries, all ages, and both genders to estimate the productivity loss.

    11.5.3 If the item described in item "11.5.2" is difficult to perform, productivity loss should be calculated by multiplying the expected number of days (excluding holidays) or hours of work missed in the target population by the average wage across all industries, all ages, and both genders. A 100% employment rate should be assumed for those aged 18 years and older. However, note that this method may overestimate productivity losses.

11.6 If other individuals (e.g., family members) experience productivity losses due to the provision of nursing or informal patient care, it is acceptable to count these productivity losses as costs under the same conditions and using the same methods as those used to calculate the patient's productivity loss.

11.7 Time costs that are unrelated to a decrease in work should not be included in the cost estimations.

12 Discounting

12.1 Future costs and effectiveness must be discounted and converted into present values.

    12.1.1 Discounting is not needed if the time horizon is 1 year or less or is otherwise sufficiently short to ignore the influence of discounting.

12.2 Both cost and effectiveness should be discounted at a rate of 2% per year.

12.3 The discount rate should be subjected to sensitivity analysis and should be changed at the same rate of 0–4% per year for both costs and effectiveness.

13 Modeling

13.1 To predict prognosis and future expenses, it is acceptable to conduct a model analysis using a decision analytic model, Markov model, and/or other models in accordance with the principle described in Section "7."

13.2 Model analysis should present the validity of the model. For example:

(A) Internal validity: This addresses why a model with a given structure has been created, whether or not the natural course of illness has been sufficiently evaluated, whether or not the parameters used are appropriate, and other factors.

(B) External validity: This addresses whether the estimation yielded from the model is appropriate in comparison to existing other clinical data and other factors.

13.3 The assumption used to create the model should be described clearly.

13.4 All parameters and data sources used for model creation should be shown.

13.5 The model used and the calculation processes should be submitted in the form of electronic files. The model must be easily understood by third-party experts and all main parameters (transition probability, QOL score, and healthcare costs) must be able to be changed.

    13.5.1 It is better that not only total costs but also the breakdown (in the case of micro-costing, the medical resource consumption and unit costs of each item) can be changed. Especially, the unit costs of the selected technology and comparator(s) must be able to be changed by academic analysis group in the model.

13.6 Half-cycle correction should be used in the Markov model if the length of the Markov cycle is long and its influence on the results is not negligible.

14 Uncertainty

14.1 If the patterns of clinical practice or other factors are not uniform and this discrepancy could affect the results, analyses based on multiple scenarios should be conducted.

14.2 For situations in which the uncertainty is large because of a long time horizon, a shorter-term analysis is necessary, such as an analysis of the period for which clinical study data are available.

14.3 If no available studies involve a comparison with the comparator according to Section "5," particularly when a comparison has been made concerning results between single-arm studies, a sensitivity analysis with a sufficiently wide range is required because of the large uncertainty.

14.4 Sensitivity analyses are needed for parameters with large variances, those based on assumptions rather than actual data, those with possible heterogeneity between overseas and domestic data, and others.

14.5 When the variance of the estimator should be considered (parametric uncertainty), the range moving parameter in the sensitivity analysis can refer to the 95% confidence interval of the estimator.

14.6 A probabilistic sensitivity analysis (PSA) is also desirable. In such cases, the distribution used for analysis, scatter plots of the cost-effectiveness plane, and cost-effectiveness acceptability curves (CEAC) must be presented.

Terminology

Additional Benefit

In a cost-effectiveness analysis, the additional benefit relative to the comparator should be demonstrated before calculating the ICER. The endpoint of effectiveness used to demonstrate the additional benefit does not always need to be equal to the outcome used for the cost-effectiveness analysis but should be clinically significant. If additional benefit is judged to be shown, cost-effectiveness analysis should be performed. On the other hand, if no additional benefit is shown, cost of both treatments should be compared by so-called CMA.

Cost-Effectiveness Analysis

Economic evaluations of healthcare technologies are often divided into the following patterns: (a) cost-minimization analysis (CMA), in which the outcome is deemed equivalent and only cost is analyzed; (b) cost-effectiveness analysis (CEA), which uses outcome units other than QALY (LY, event avoidance, etc.); (c) cost-utility analysis (CUA), which uses QALY; and (d) cost-benefit analysis (CBA), which involves an evaluation of outcomes after conversion into monetary units.

However, CMA, CEA, and CUA can all be considered analogous in situations where the cost and outcome are estimated in different units. For this reason, these types of analysis are collectively termed "cost-effectiveness analyses" in this guideline.

Discounting

In a cost-effectiveness analysis, a discount at a constant rate is usually made to convert future costs and arising (or obtained) outcomes to current values. Costs converted to the current value after applying yearly discounts (C_p) can be calculated from the cost at i years later (C_i) and the discount rate (d) using the following equation:

© Springer Nature Singapore Pte Ltd. 2019
I. Kamae, *Health Technology Assessment in Japan*,
https://doi.org/10.1007/978-981-13-5793-0

$$C_P = \frac{C_i}{(1+d)^{i-1}}$$

The same calculation can be used for effectiveness.

Dominant/Dominated

If a technology is lower in cost and equivalent or higher in effectiveness than the comparator, the technology is called "dominant." If the technology is higher in cost but equivalent or lower in effectiveness relative to the comparator, the technology is called "dominated."

Evidence Level

Diverse classification methods for evidence levels are available. MINDS (Medical Information Network Distribution Service) set forth the following classifications:

I	Systematic review/meta-analysis of RCTs
II	From one or more RCTs
III	From a non-randomized controlled study
IVa	Analytical epidemiological study (cohort study)
IVb	Analytical epidemiological study (case-control or cross-sectional studies)
V	Descriptive study (case reports or series)
VI	Views of an expert committee or individual experts that are not based on patient data

However, it has been often noted that the results of experimental studies such as randomized controlled trials (RCTs) can differ from real-world clinical data. Economic evaluations of healthcare technologies should primarily use data with a high level of evidence, although consideration should be given to appropriate clinical data.

Human Capital Method

The "human capital method" is used to estimate productivity loss based on the wages originally expected to be earned. However, when viewed from a long-term standpoints, the inability of an individual to work does not always lead to a productivity loss because in a situation with an employment rate less than 100%, as other individuals are likely to work in place of the affected individual who is unable to work. For this reason, one view suggests that productivity losses should include only friction costs (e.g., based on the period needed to restore the initial production level). Wages should be originally estimated through an investigation of the period for which an individual was actually unable to work because of illness. If this estimation is difficult due to lack of data including housework, it is acceptable to set the employment rate at 100%. From the viewpoint of fairness, the mean wage across all industries, all ages, and both genders should be used as the unit wage, regardless of the actual unit wage for individuals.

Incremental Cost-Effectiveness Ratio

The incremental cost-effectiveness ratio (ICER) is the incremental cost divided by the incremental effectiveness. ICER of treatment A compared with B is calculated using the following equation:

$$ICER = \frac{IC}{IE} = \frac{C_A - C_B}{E_A - E_B}$$

IC: incremental cost
IE: incremental effectiveness
C_A: expected cost of treatment A
C_B: expected cost of treatment B
E_A: expected effectiveness of treatment A
E_B: expected effectiveness of treatment B

ICER is an indicator of the cost to acquire one unit of effectiveness. A lower ICER indicates higher cost-effectiveness.

Indirect Comparison

When clinical studies yield results for "A vs. B" and "A vs. C," an estimation of the results for "B vs. C" in which no direct comparison is available from the head-to-head results is called an "indirect comparison." If no head-to-head study involving an appropriate comparator is available, an indirect comparison may occasionally be used.

The following conditions must be satisfied to enable indirect comparison: the results for "A vs. B" must also be applicable to the population "A vs. C," and the results for "A vs. C" must also be applicable to the population "A vs. B." This is called an "assumption of similarity." When an indirect comparison is performed, it is necessary to test this assumption and to use appropriate statistical methods (e.g., adjusted indirect comparison rather than naïve indirect comparison). This approach also enables analyses based on more advanced methods such as network meta-analyses (or multiple treatment comparisons; MTCs).

Mapping

When preference-based measure-determined QOL scores are unavailable, it is sometimes advantageous to use PRO data to calculate the QOL score used for cost-effectiveness analysis. The conversion of scores between measures is called "mapping." Mapping is acceptable as a second-best method when no other data are available but should be performed only after sufficient assessment of the statistical validity.

Meta-analysis

Meta-analysis is a method by which the results from a systematic review are integrated statistically to yield integrated values or their confidence intervals. If the heterogeneity is small, a fixed-effect model is usually used. If the heterogeneity is large, random effect or Bayesian models are usually employed. The results are often depicted as forest plots. If a comparison is made among multiple treatments rather than between two treatments (pairwise comparison), a "network meta-analysis" is used, employing different methods (ref. "Indirect comparison").

Probabilistic Sensitivity Analysis

Probabilistic sensitivity analysis (PSA) is a technique used to determine the distributions of incremental cost, incremental effectiveness, and ICER by applying model parameters to the distribution. The results of a PSA are usually shown as a scatter plot on the cost-effectiveness plane and as a cost-effectiveness acceptability curve (CEAC), defined as $f(\gamma) = \Pr(\gamma \cdot IE - IC > 0)$ (IC, incremental cost; IE, incremental effectiveness; γ, willingness to pay).

Productivity Loss

Depending on the perspective, a loss resulting from the inability to perform work/housework because of illness (or benefit from early recovery) may be counted as a cost (i.e., productivity loss) but is not included in the base-case analysis. It is acceptable to consider not only the loss experienced directly by the patient but also losses experienced by family members or others arising from the need to provide nursing or informal care. According to this guideline, however, an indirect productivity loss resulting from an improvement in the patient's health states (e.g., survival period extension) is not included in productivity loss to avoid double counting (i.e., counting a factor as both effectiveness and costs). Only a productivity loss directly attributable to the healthcare technology (e.g., shortened hospital stay) is permitted for inclusion.

Quality-Adjusted Life Year

A quality-adjusted life year (QALY) value is calculated by multiplying the life years (LYs) by the QOL score. A QOL score of 1 indicates full health, whereas 0 indicates death. If an individual has survived for 2 years under a health state with a QOL = 0.6, the LY is 2 years and the QALY is $0.6 \times 2 = 1.2$ (equivalent to 1.2 years survival under full health). If the QOL score changes over time, the QALY is represented by the area under the curve of the QOL score over time, as illustrated in the figure below.

Quality of Life (QOL) Score

The health state (i.e., value obtained from the health states) is scored using a one-dimensional scale ranging from 0 (death) to 1 (full health). Negative scores, reflective of a health state "worse than death," are also possible.

QOL scoring methods can be categorized as follows: (1) direct methods that evaluate health states under a hypothetical situation (or about himself/herself), including the standard gamble (SG) and time trade-off (TTO) methods, and (2) indirect methods that calculate QOL scores from patients' responses to QOL questionnaires using a scoring algorithm.

The QOL score used for cost-effectiveness analysis cannot always be calculated from any patient-reported outcome (PRO) or QOL data. Cost-effectiveness analysis can utilize only QOL scores determined using a preference-based measure developed for QALY calculation, as described below.

The EQ-5D (EuroQol-5 dimension) is one currently available measure for which a scoring algorithm has been developed in Japan.

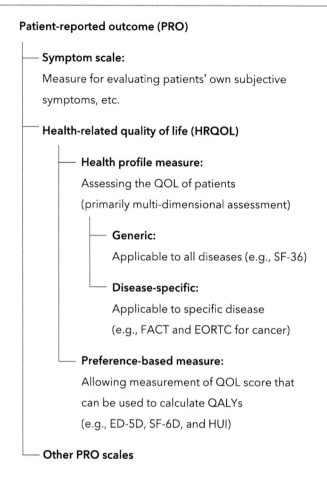

Patient-reported outcome (PRO)

— **Symptom scale:**
Measure for evaluating patients' own subjective
symptoms, etc.

— **Health-related quality of life (HRQOL)**

— **Health profile measure:**
Assessing the QOL of patients
(primarily multi-dimensional assessment)

— **Generic:**
Applicable to all diseases (e.g., SF-36)

— **Disease-specific:**
Applicable to specific disease
(e.g., FACT and EORTC for cancer)

— **Preference-based measure:**
Allowing measurement of QOL score that
can be used to calculate QALYs
(e.g., ED-5D, SF-6D, and HUI)

— **Other PRO scales**

Sensitivity Analysis

When uncertainty is present, its influence on the results can be evaluated by changing the parameter in a "sensitivity analysis." Sensitivity analyses can be further classified as a one- (only one parameter is changed) and two-dimensional (two parameters are simultaneously changed) sensitivity analyses, as well as PSA (simultaneous uncertainty in multiple parameters; see "Probabilistic Sensitivity Analysis").

Systematic Review

A systematic review is a method by which the literature is comprehensively searched regarding a specific topic and the results are evaluated/reported without bias if at all possible. This method was defined by MINDS as follows: "When defined from the aspects of practical actions, systematic review means 'searching studies on a given clinical question comprehensively, grouping studies of identical quality on each research design and analyzing/integrating them being accompanied by evaluation of biases'."

A systematic review is often confused with meta-analysis. The results of a systematic review do not always require statistical integration; this type of systematic review is also known as a "qualitative systematic review." In cases where the integration of results is deemed appropriate, a meta-analysis of the systematic review results is needed.

Regarding the reporting style for a systematic review (meta-analysis), the style presented in the PRISMA (Preferred Reporting Items for Systematic Reviews and Meta-Analyses) statement has been used as a standard and can be used as a reference.

Uncertainty

Various types of uncertainty accompany cost-effectiveness analyses.

Broadly, heterogeneity is a type of uncertainty that indicates a situation lacking uniformity in terms of the comparator, healthcare patterns, targeted patients, and other factors. This differs from the uncertainty in the narrow sense, as explained below. This is not a technical problem related to statistics or health economics but rather arises from real-world variety. If such heterogeneity is present, a sensitivity analysis based on multiple scenarios is recommended.

Uncertainty in the narrow sense can be divided into (a) model and (b) parameter uncertainties. Model uncertainty can result from (a)-1 methodological uncertainty and (a)-2 model structure/assumptions.

Methodological uncertainty, mentioned in (a)-1, arises from the theoretical impossibility of setting uniform methods for the estimation of the discount rate and productivity loss, measuring the QOL score, and other parameters. To avoid this type of uncertainty, it is important to conduct an analysis in accordance with common and standard procedures. If results such as the discount rate are markedly affected, uncertainty should be evaluated through one-way sensitivity analysis.

Uncertainty arising from the model structure/assumption, as mentioned in (a)-2, is caused by the method used to model the health states and treatment processes, selection of parameters for incorporation into the model, assumptions regarding predictions of long-term prognosis beyond the observation period, and other factors. This uncertainty should be evaluated in a sensitivity analysis.

Parameter uncertainty, as mentioned in (b), arises from uncertainty inherent in the parameter estimation. For example, if 10 of 100 subjects develop events during a clinical study, the true incidence rate might not be $10/100 = 0.1$ in the whole population. To deal with this type of uncertainty, which is attributable to statistical inference, it is useful to conduct a PSA in addition to a deterministic sensitivity analysis.

Unrelated Medical Costs

Medical costs can be divided into related (i.e., those directly affected by the selected technology) and unrelated (i.e., those affected indirectly through survival extension or those not related to the illness). For example, a hypertension treatment that reduces the incidence of cardiovascular disease and stroke will extend life expectancy, possibly leading to an increase in unrelated medical costs (e.g., costs related to dementia, diabetes, and hemodialysis). These unrelated costs are not included in the cost.

Abbreviations

CBA	Cost-benefit analysis
CEA	Cost-effectiveness analysis
CEAC	Cost-effectiveness acceptability curve
CMA	Cost-minimization analysis
CSIMC	Central Social Insurance Medical Council (Chuikyo)
CUA	Cost-utility analysis
CQ	Clinical question
EQ-5D	EuroQol-5 dimension
HRQOL	Health-related quality of life
ICER	Incremental cost-effectiveness ratio
MTC	Multiple treatment comparison
PBM	Preference-based measure
PRO	Patient-reported outcome
PRISMA	Preferred Reporting Items for Systematic Reviews and Meta-Analyses
PSA	Probabilistic sensitivity analysis
QALY	Quality-adjusted life year
RCT	Randomized controlled trial
SG	Standard
SR	Systematic review
TTO	Time trade-off

© Springer Nature Singapore Pte Ltd. 2019   249
I. Kamae, *Health Technology Assessment in Japan*,
https://doi.org/10.1007/978-981-13-5793-0

Suggested Answers to "Self-Check" Questions

Section 1.1

1. Health technology assessment
2. Micro and macro levels
3. NICE (National Institute for Health and Care Excellence)
4. Policy and system, guideline, and HTA assessment bodies
5. April 2016
6. INAHTA (International Network of Agencies for Health Technology Assessment)
7. No. They oppose to use cost/QALY as a threshold.
8. Yes. They have the PRO guidance for industry.
9. South Korea, Taiwan, and Thailand
10. Special Committee on Cost-Effectiveness Evaluation

Section 1.2

1. Value-based medicine
2. Pharmacoeconomics
3. Incremental cost-effectiveness ratio (ICER)

Section 1.3

1. Incremental cost ÷ incremental effectiveness = 203/2.73 = 74.36
2. The operation takes additional cost of JPY 743.6K per 1 year saved, compared to non-operation.
3. Non-operation yields 6-year life expectancy with 4M of JPY. Therefore, the operation is dominant to non-operation with increased benefit and decreased cost. In this case, the estimate of ICER is not necessary.

© Springer Nature Singapore Pte Ltd. 2019
I. Kamae, *Health Technology Assessment in Japan*,
https://doi.org/10.1007/978-981-13-5793-0

Section 1.4

1. It is not clear whether the estimate, JPY 2M/QALY, is the average cost or ICER. If it is ICER, the comparator should be noted as "compared to ...."
2. The nominal GDP is JPY 4M per capita in 2015. If the threshold is one GDP, it is judged as "not cost-effective", but if two GDP, it becomes "cost-effective."
3. $(x - 350)/(1.37 - 1.25) = 600$

Hence, $x = 422$ ($\times$10K JPY)

Section 1.5

1. 14,319 Euros/QALY
2. Cost-effective compared to a threshold about 40K–50K Euros/QALY
3. As the estimate of 57,219 is over the threshold of 50,000, the cost-effectiveness is an open question to recommend it.
4. Although the ICER estimates "over the age 65" are all lower than the threshold of 40K Euros/QALY, they are not cost-effective in five of the eight countries in the case of "over the age 85." Therefore, it is not necessarily recommended without considering any subclass analysis. In principle, the subject population for analysis should be targeted as small as possible.
5. There is no information on uncertainty of each estimate of ICER (e.g., confidence interval, sensitivity analysis). No information on comparator(s) also makes it hard to interpret the ICER estimates properly. No description about comparators usually suggests that the vaccination group is compared to "non-vaccination."

Section 1.6

1. The words "based on effectiveness" should be "based on the cost-effectiveness."
2. Misunderstanding. The CEA would rather be favorable for "humanistic medicine."
3. (1) Most of new technologies bring additional benefit with additional costs. (2) The cost differs, not only depending on the ICER of a single technology but also on the priority among multiple technologies. (3) The ICER of a technology is not necessarily proportional to the budget impact.
4. (1) The clinical benefit can be bidimensionally measured with quantity (life years) and quality (utility values). (2) A unique outcome measure with which clinical benefit can be compared between different diseases.
5. Not comparable due to inconsistency caused by different methods for measurement

Section 1.7

1. CEA studies are excluded in the USA but commonly included in Europe.
2. VBM represents a process of decision-making based on the value in medicine and healthcare including wider social benefit as well as the benefit for patients. The evidence referred by EBM can include the effectiveness as "value" in a broad sense, while it is commonly limited to the efficacy proven by clinical trials.

Section 2.1

1. HTA with the standards in Western countries does not exist, but a Japanese-style HTA has been established and organized.
2. Innovation in healthcare
3. August, 1992
4. The submission rate has been generally decreased since 2000.
5. No benefit return was expected for the industry by submitting economic evidence.
6. From Table 2.4, cost analyses and cost-minimization analyses
7. Yes (especially, quasi-VBP at the micro level of official pricing).
8. Type I at new listing after approval and type II at repricing conducted biennially
9. The multiplication of ICER and the incremental effectiveness

Section 2.2

1. The listing of outpatient smoking cessation treatment (the Nicotine Dependence Management Fee) in 2006
2. Beyond the policy in MHLW, the new approach on cost-effectiveness evaluation has been integrated into a part of the healthcare and medical strategy proposed by the Abe administration.

Section 2.3

1. It was initially announced that a threshold approach would be not used in the pilot period of 2016–2017, but in late 2017, they changed such a policy and proposed a method for pricing based on multiple thresholds.
2. (1) Verification of the scientific validity of the results, (2) consideration of ethical and social impacts

3. In the pilot program, the cost-effectiveness evidence is used as a reference to reprice the subject products in the market (not applied for new products).
4. Yes.
5. Central Social Insurance Medical Council (known as Chuikyo)
6. Allowed if a company is willing to submit the cost-effectiveness evidence
7. Yes ($\Longrightarrow$Chap. 3).
8. An official, independent experts group (reanalysis group)
9. During the appraisal process, if the Special Organization for Cost-Effectiveness Evaluation (tentative name) deems it necessary, companies that have submitted their data may present themselves at the Special Organization and express their views.
10. Initially planned to evaluate a dichotomous judgment, "good" or "not good," but in late 2017, three categories, "good," "intermediate," and "not good," were proposed using two thresholds of JPY 5M/QALY and JPY 10M/QALY.
11. It was not announced in the early phase of the pilot program, but in late 2017, a repricing method using two thresholds of JPY 5M/QALY and JPY 10M/QALY was proposed.
12. The Special Organization for Cost-Effectiveness Evaluation (tentative name)
13. Not applied in the pilot program

Section 2.5

1. Threshold-stair (or step) method.
2. Premium portion.
3. The ICER thresholds are shifted upward to JPY7.5M, 11.25M and 15M/QALY.
4. ICER-based pricing.

Section 2.6

1. HTAi Annual Meeting 2016 and ISPOR Asia-Pacific Conference 2018.
2. (1) scientific evaluation and (2) deliberation.
3. Refer to Table 2.7.

Section 3.1

1. (1) The standard format for decision-making by the government, (2) a guide for designing and conducting patient outcome studies and informing of treatment recommendations, (3) a template for evaluating publications and reports on economic evaluations
2. Most of them.

Section 3.2

1. (1) Patients and families, (2) service provider institutions such as hospitals, (3) insurers (in Japan, the public health insurance system), and (4) society
2. Society

Section 3.3

1. If the item 3.2 in the MHLW guidelines is difficult to achieve
2. The target population for analyses must be clearly defined based on objective criteria. No qualitative approach is recommended.

Section 3.4

1. A technology expected to be replaced by the target technology at the time when it was introduced to treat the target population. As a rule, the comparator(s) should be those that are reimbursed from public health insurance.
2. It is not always appropriate because no treatment does not necessarily mean no cost and no effect ("do nothing" problem).

Section 3.5

1. It is not mandatory but may be conducted.
2. The results of unpublished clinical studies/trials may also be included if they are deemed appropriate.
3. P, patient; I, intervention; C, comparator; O, outcome. In epidemiology, it is sometimes referred as PECO regarding P: Population and E: Exposure.
4. Endpoint finally relevant to death such as mortality and life years. The word "true" is used in contrast with "intermediate" (surrogate) outcomes such as blood pressure, level of glucose, white cell account, etc.
5. Yes. In such cases, the existing review will be used directly or in combination with a new additional study. The consistency of the existing review should be confirmed by considering the CQs and coverage of the most recent literature.
6. (1) The employed statistical method, (2) assessment of heterogeneity, (3) forest plot, (4) integrated results, and (5) confidence interval
7. Preferred Reporting Items for Systematic Reviews and Meta-Analyses
8. (1) illness, (2) severity, (3) patient background
9. (Item 5.5) When there are no RCT studies using the same comparator selected), but there are RCT studies of the selected technology compared to others,

additional benefit is evaluated by indirect comparison using SR results, if agreed upon in consultation.

10. (Item 5.6) When there are only single-arm clinical studies of selected technologies, SR results of the selected technologies (and comparator(s) if needed) should be shown.

Section 3.6

1. N/A
2. $(26,760,804 - 23,296,564) \div (6.28 - 4.35) = 3,464,240 \div 1.93 = 1,794,943$
3. Cost-effective analysis should not be conducted unless the additional health benefit is statistically "not significant." The reasons of being "statistically not significant" include (1) truly no difference in terms of health benefit between two groups compared, and (2) power is insufficient (i.e., β error is large). In the first case, consider non-inferiority/equivalence test. If it is statistically confirmed, cost-minimization analysis may be conducted. In the second case, calculate the minimal sample size for testing statistical difference. If the sample size of the trial conducted is smaller than the minimal sample size calculated, conduct the trial with increased sample size, and test the statistical difference again. Then if the difference is statistically significant, we can conduct CEA.
4. (1) Dominant (more effective and less costly). (2) Additional benefit is not demonstrated despite the same outcomes.

Section 3.7

1. Analysis by modeling
2. Validity of modeling (including parameters validity), validity of results, transparency of the analysis, etc.

Section 3.8

1. $77.6 \times 0.832 = 64.6$
2. $76.5 \times (0.72 - 0.67) = 3.8$
3. QALE A: $4 \times 1 + (8 - 4) \times 0.9 + (12 - 8) \times 0.6 + (16 - 12) \times 0.2 = 10.8$
   B: $4 \times 1 + (16 - 4) \times 0.9 + (20 - 16) \times 0.6 = 17.2$
   QALY $= 17.2 - 10.8 = 6.4$
4. DALY $= (20 \times 1 - \text{QALY of A}) - (20 \times 1 - \text{QALY of B})$
   $= (20 - 10.8) - (20 - 17.2)$
   $= 9.2 - 2.8 = 6.4$

Section 3.9

1. Domestic data should be the first.
2. Accepted, but need to present the detailed information on patient background, statistical methods, etc.
3. Accepted, but if and only if medical devices are evaluated.

Section 3.10

1. An economics term that refers to the value of what you have to give up in order to choose something else
2. Productivity loss: perspective to consider a wider range of costs
3. Include the costs which the insurer, patients, and the government pays and the public costs relevant to health checkups, vaccinations, etc.
4. Consumption of medical resources and unit cost
5. No, Fee for service should be used, not flat payment of DPC.

Section 3.11

1. Public healthcare payer's perspective
2. It is recommended that the costs should be calculated based on the care level.
3. The unit wage used for estimations of productivity loss should be the average wage across all industries, all ages, and both genders or the average wage for each age group in all industries and both genders derived from the latest "Basic Survey on Wage Structure" (Wage Census), not to discriminate by income.

Section 3.12

1. The present value decreases as the denominator increases in the discount formula.
2. $CP = C_1 + C_2/(1 + d) + C_3/(1 + d)^2$

Section 3.13

1. A certain time interval to make a state transition
2. (1) Markov property cannot be applied in the real world, (2) State transition does not depend on the past history (memory-less), (3) validity of state setup
3. (1) Increase the number of states, (2) change the state-transition probability depending on time (time-dependent Markov model). However, the more com-

plex the analytic model is, the more difficult the modeling validity or data availability is.
4. No theory to investigate the validity. Need to have comprehensive evaluation by experts and clinicians

Section 3.14

1. Two approaches: statistical analysis and sensitivity analysis
2. Confidence interval (confidence area (ellipse) on 2D-plane of cost and effectiveness)
3. Deterministic and probabilistic sensitivity analysis
4. Parameters with large variances, those based on assumptions rather than actual data, those with possible heterogeneity between overseas and domestic data.
5. A sensitivity analysis with a sufficiently wide range is required because of the large uncertainty.
6. A probabilistic sensitivity analysis is not required, but desirable. In such a case, it is necessary to present the distribution used for analysis, scatter plots on the cost-effectiveness plane and cost-effectiveness acceptability curves.
7. Monte Carlo simulation and bootstrapping
8. First order: trace each Markov state transition of an individual patient (micro-simulation).
    Second order: consider probability distribution function based on micro-simulation.
9. The Y-axis of CEAC provides a proportion of the number of dots in the area under the threshold line in a scatted plot diagram (e.g., 53% for JPY 600M/QALY at Fig. 3.15).
10. It is applicable beyond clinical trial. In the case of clinical trials, a pair of data of cost and benefit for each patient is required to conduct bootstrapping.

Section 4.1

1. (1) Data submission, (2) reanalysis, (3) appraisal, and (4) decision-making based on the results
2. When the Task Force for Cost-Effectiveness Evaluation deems necessary, companies may attend the meeting and express their views.
3. The assessment of cost-effectiveness is not possible without any objective standard for evaluating ICER. However, in the Japanese pilot program for cost-effectiveness evaluation since 2016, it was initially announced that the Appraisal Committee determines whether the cost-effectiveness of the product is qualitatively "good" or "not good" without any objective cost-per-QALY threshold.

This initial policy of the Chuikyo intended to avoid conflict with the following policies: (1) Appraisal Committee leaves certain room for judgment on cost-effectiveness by not only ICER but also the other factors and (2) the policy without any objective cost-per-QALY threshold allows the committee members to judge the cost-effectiveness in a subjective way of their own thinking. Those policies, however, return the Appraisal Committee to the same subjective discussions as before the pilot program, and so they were confronted with a dilemma between subjective and objective decisions, utilizing ICER as a scientific evidence.

The best way to avoid this dilemma is to determine a price directly based on ICER using a method such as MCDA (Multi-Criteria Decision Analysis) which can consider multiple factors in a scientific way. However, the Chuikyo eventually changed the policy of "not using a cost-per-QALY" into "using JPY5M (about USD 50K) per QALY" as the primary threshold for price discounting. This change was announced in 2018 in the late phase of the pilot program.

Section 4.2

1. A selection of comparator of "Doing Nothing" such as no treatment or observation without a new treatment does not necessarily mean no benefit or cost for the comparator regimen. So, the ICER estimation depends on how much benefit or cost is measured for the comparator. Setting no benefit or cost for "Doing Nothing" is not always correct ($\Longrightarrow$Sect. 3.4, Self-Check).
2. Not considered.
3. It is not correct in theory, because the ICER estimate can be made arbitrarily decreased by discount of cost only, not with discount of benefit ($\Longrightarrow$Sect. 3.12).

Section 4.3

1. KP5
2. For example, multiple stakeholders, including industry representatives and patients, are engaged with the decision processes in the Appraisal Committee. Especially, the patient engagement is one of the important issues with respect to a range of commitment and representativeness of patient opinions.
3. KP2 and KP15

Section 6.1

1. $100 - 85 = 15\%$
2. At 2×2 table in Fig. 6.1, A = 48 persons (=60×0.8), B = 4 (=$40 \times (1 - 0.9)$). Hence, the true positive rate among test positives is $48 \div (48 + 4) = 0.92$ (92%).

3. {(1 − pretest probability) × specificity}/{pretest probability × (1 − sensitivity) + (1 − pretest probability) × specificity}

Section 6.2

1. Even though the estimate of ICER is identical, the amount of original cost and benefit for each drug can be different (e.g., X, USD 100K/2 QALY; while Y, USD 1000/0.02 QALY). Hence, we cannot regard drug X as being equivalent to drug Y.
2. A: 4 × 0.43 = 1.72, B: 5 × 0.38 = 1.90. So, the QALY for B is larger. Therefore, the conclusion is the same as the case of EQ-5D but different from the case of time trade-off.

Section 6.3

1. NMB と NHB
2. As shown in Fig. 6.6, NMB is a linear function of threshold.
3. Cost-effectiveness acceptability frontier
4. The advantage of CEAF is that it shows the best treatment alternative for a given range of the threshold, along with the probability that the alternative is cost-effective.

Section 6.4

1. ICER (strictly, the reciprocal of ICER)
2. Type A

Section 6.5

1. The sum for A and B is 65 and 51, respectively. So, the sum for A is larger, while the sum of the larger number for A and B is 69. Hence, EVPI = 69 − 65 = 4 years.

Section 6.6

1. (1) To estimate the probability that the event being studied occurs (e.g., prevalence of a disease), (2) to provide with a systematic approach to performing a stratified analysis with classical two-by-two tables using a mathematical model.

2. We cannot say that it is absolutely incorrect, but it is difficult to interpret correctly as case-control study is retrospective (the same as the incidence cannot be retrospectively estimated based on case-control study.) In principle, logistic regression based on case-control data does not provide an appropriate estimate of probability (for more details, refer to propensity score (Sect. 6.9)).
3. Odds ratio estimated in consideration of the influence of confounding factors

Section 6.7

1. Prefix which means transcending/higher/comprehensive
2. The presence or absence of bias can be determined by assessing whether or not the distribution of studies is funnel-shaped.
3. (1) Preparations, (2) data collection, (3) evaluation and analysis, (4) report
4. To weigh the study estimates by the inverse of the estimates' variance (inverse variance-weighted method).
5. Since the pooled summary odds ratio of 1.54 is included within the 95% confidence interval, (0.83–1.96), it is not statistically significant with 5% risk (or alpha error).
6. (1) A: $(10^2 + 12^2)/61 = 4$, B: $(8^2 + 10^2)/82 = 2$, C: $(12^2 + 8^2)/52 = 4$, (2) A: 1/4, B: 1/2, C: 1/4, (3) $D_{meta} = \{30 \times (1/4) + 40 \times (1/2) + 44 \times (1/4)\}/\{(1/4) + (1/2) + (1/4)\} = 38.5$, (4) 38.5 ± 1.96 root $(1/(1/4 + 1/2 + 1/4)) = (36.5, 40.5)$. It shows statistical significance as the confidence interval does not include zero.
7. The synthesis must be terminated and reasons for heterogeneity investigated.
8. Not required but one of options. (MHLW Guideline Ver. 2.0 Item 5.5).
9. Mixed (or multiple) treatment comparison.

Section 6.8

1. $S(t) = e^{-\lambda t}$. When $t = 0$, $S(t) = e^0 = 1$. That is, the time of "$t = 0$" means the beginning of the observation at which all the patients are alive.
2. Log-rank test. Null hypothesis: $S_A(t) = S_B(t)$, or $h_A(t) = h_B(t)$
3. $h(t|x_1, x_2) = h_0(t)e^{\beta 1x1 + \beta 2x2}$

Section 6.9

1. Prospective, retrospective model
2. Refer to Sect. 6.6.
3. The overlapping region on the X axis between the two groups, A and B
4. Matching and stratification

Section 6.10

1. Frequentist and Bayesian
2. Probability revisions
3. In Fig. 6.27, $a_0 = 12$, $b_0 = 8$, $a = 70$, $b = 30$. Then, $a_1 = a_0 + a = 12 + 70 = 82$, $b_1 = b_0 + b = 8 + 30 = 38$. Hence, posterior distribution is Be(82, 38). Efficacy is calculated with the expression: $a_1/(a_1 + b_1) = 82/(82 + 38) = 0.68$.
4. Conditional probability table
5. An advantage of Bayesian statistics is that it allows one to insert in the analysis information newly acquired during the phases of a clinical trial in a more timely manner than is possible with Frequentist statistics, and to perform a phased meta-analysis when new findings from published reports become available. Also, the concept of pre- and posttest probability can be applied for medical diagnosis.

   Unlike in traditional Frequentist statistics, interpretation of clinical trial results is slightly more complex with the Bayesian approach. The assumption of prior distribution is unique to Bayesian inference, although this subjective assumption has been historically controversial. As the Bayesian model is more complex than Frequentist one, it may prevent the analysis from being completed within a realistic time frame, confronted with difficulty of data availability.

Section 7.1

1. $(150K - 100K)/(8.6 - 7.6) = $ USD 50K/QALY
2. According to the expressions for p and q in the first column of Table 7.1, we obtain $p = -20.794$, $q = 2.466$ for drug A. Then, the tangent ICER is estimated with USD 60,800/QALY by plugging in p, q and $E(=8.6)$ for the tangent-ICER formula in the second column of Table 7.1. As well, the tangent ICER for drug B is USD 40,600/QALY.
3. As well as Question 1, we estimate $q = 0.000324$, $E = 8.6$. Then, USD 53,100/QALY for drug A, and USD 46,900/QALY for drug B.

Section 7.2

1. The ICER of 50,000 (refer to Question 1 at Sect. 7.1) is included in both of the tangent ICER interval (46,900, 53,100) for quadratic model and (40,600, 60,800) for exponential model.
2. The width of tangent ICER interval $= 60,800 - 40,600 = 20,200$. Hence, the proportion of the interval width is $20,200/50,000 = 0.404$ (i.e., 40.4%).
3. The WTP threshold of 60,000 comes up to the area 2 (i.e., greater than 50,000, but smaller than 60,800) in Fig. 7.5. So, the ICER is almost accepted as a rule, although it may not be accepted since the upper limit, 60,800, of tangent ICER is a little over the WTP threshold of 60,000.

4. The WTP threshold of 60,000 comes up to the area 1 as it is over the tangent ICER interval (46,900, 53,100). The ICER of 50,000 can be accepted, considering the uncertainty in terms of tangent ICER interval.

Section 7.3

1. The average cost is 2200 ÷ 4.2 = JPY 5.24M/QALY for a new drug X, while 1200 ÷ 2.2 = JPY 5.45M/QALY for the comparator S. Hence, the new drug X is selected.
2. (2200 − 1200)/(4.2 − 2.2) = JPY 5.00M/QALY
3. The comparator S is selected because the ICER of X compared to S is higher than the threshold of JPY 3.00M/QALY. (However, further discussion will be necessary whether S can be accepted or not since the average cost of S is larger than the threshold of JPY 3.00M/QALY.)
4. Select X.

Section 7.4

1. In the case of Fig. 7.8 (not dominant)
2. In the case of Fig. 7.9 (extended dominance)

Section 7.5

1. Level 4
2. Level 3

Section 7.6

1. USD 11K/QALY
2. λ_{max} = 11K<100K. Hence, the ICER of 100K cannot be accepted.
3. In the case of larger k (i.e., B_{max} becomes larger or N smaller.)

Section 7.7

1. Drug price per day = (20 × 300 + 80,000 × 0.01)/300 = USD 22.67. Hence, the premium rate is (22.67 − 20)/20 = 0.13 (i.e. 13%).
2. Drug price per day = (20 × 300 + 50,000 × 0.01)/300 = USD 21.67. Hence, the premium rate is (21.67 − 20)/20 = 0.08 (i.e. 8%).

Section 7.8

1. The R zone means a certain margin (currently 2%) which determines the amount of premium to be added onto the average market price. The premium amount is obtained by multiplying pre-revision price by the R zone (currently 2%).
2. Data obtained from a market survey.
3. As Bayesian degree of belief is 50%, the revised price is given by the mean of posterior distribution, that is, μ_1. Hence, the following relation is satisfied:

Pre-revision price $\times R = \mu_1 - \mathrm{AMP}_1$

Consequently, the R zone is formulated as follows:

$R = (\mu_1 - \mathrm{AMP}_1)/$pre-revision price.

Index

© Springer Nature Singapore Pte Ltd. 2019
I. Kamae, *Health Technology Assessment in Japan*,
https://doi.org/10.1007/978-981-13-5793-0

Printed in the United States
By Bookmasters